A NATURALIST'S

REPTILES

OF

AUSTRALIA

Peter Rowland and Chris Farrell

JOHN BEAUFOY PUBLISHING

Reprinted in 2020, 2021

This edition published in the United Kingdom and Australia by John Beaufoy Publishing Ltd
11 Blenheim Court, 316 Woodstock Road, Oxford OX2 7NS, England
www.johnbeaufoy.com

10 9 8 7 6 5 4 3

Photo Credits
Front cover *main image* Water Dragon © Peter Rowland; *bottom left* Shingleback Lizard © Peter
Rowland; *bottom centre* Frilled Lizard © Jannico Kelk; bottom *right* Green Python © Chris Farrell
Back cover Kristin's Spiny-tailed Gecko © Peter Rowland
Title page Golden-crowned Snake © Ollie Neuman
Contents page Green Turtles © Valerie Taylor
Main descriptions Photos are denoted by a page number followed by t (top), b (bottom), l (left),
c (centre) or r (right).

Cameron Baker 8br, 15t&b, 35t, 68t, 104t, 121tl&br, 127t, 146t; **Casey Clews** 9tl, 118bl; **Chris
Dryburgh** 81tr, 90b, 100t&b; **Alex Dudley** 46b; **Scott Eipper (Nature 4 You)** 21b, 24b, 27t, 41b, 48b,
64b, 75t, 91t, 119br, 134t, 137b, 139b, 149t; **Tie Eipper (Nature 4 You)** 47b, 51b, 132t, 147b; **Adam
Elliott** 19t, 30b, 33rt, 30b, 33tr, 75b, 86t, 91b, 103b, 106b, 107t, 109t, 150t, 151t; **Damien Esquerre** 22t,
28b, 33tl, 65t, 122b; **Jules Farquhar** 8cr, 10bl, 11tl, 18t, 37b, 43t&b, 44t, 49b, 52t, 53b, 54t&b, 57b, 59t,
73t, 78t, 79t, 82b, 93t, 125t, 131t, 137t, 138b, 144tl&tr; **Chris Farrell** 5c, 6t, 7t, 27b, 114t, 154t, 155b;
Bradley Foy 131b; **Ryan Francis** 29b, 35br, 42b, 47t, 50t, 61b, 64t, 77b, 78b, 79b, 81bl, 83b, 86b, 87b,
90t, 92t, 93b, 94t, 96t, 97b, 101b, 102tl&tr, 104b, 112t, 115b, 117t, 133b, 135t, 141tr, 143b, 150b, 151b,
152b, 153; **Nicholas Gale** 32t, 84b, 102b; **Grant Husband** 36t, 42t, 123b; **Brett Jarrett** 5b; **Jannico Kelk**
11bl, 19c, 40t, 57t, 71t, 111b, 136c, 139t; **Damian Lettoof** 31t, 52b, 58t, 63t, 82t, 102tl&tr, 127b, 128t,
135b; **Stephen Mahony** 28t, 49t, 63b, 69bl, 69br, 77t, 95b, 101tl, 113b, 126t; **Angus McNab** 17b, 19b,
20t, 32b, 33b, 48t, 59b, 60t, 61t, 62t, 67b, 68b, 88b, 89t&b, 92b, 97t, 99t, 101tr, 105t, 108b; **Steve McNeil**
94b, 95t, 136b; **Jordan Mulder** 58b, 80t; **Joshua Prieto** 20b; **Peter Rowland** 5t, 6b, 7c&b, 8tl,tr&cl, 10br,
11tr, 23b, 26t, 29bl&br, 39t, 50b, 51tc, 56t, 81br, 83t, 85t&b, 108t, 109b, 110t&b, 115tr, 117b, 118t,
120t, 121bl, 136t, 141b, 145b, 152t, 155t; **Ross Sadlier** 35bl, 88t, 98t, 99b, 105b; **Aniket Sardana** 22b,
38b; **Doug Schurman** 17t; **Shawn Scott** 9br, 24t, 30t, 31b, 38t, 39b, 44b, 45t, 51tl&tr, 72t, 72b, 76b, 84t,
96b, 123t, 124b, 126b, 140t, 142t, 145t, 149b; **Peter Soltys** 23t, 53t, 74b, 106t, 130b; **Ruchira Somaweera**
9bl, 34t&b, 41t, 55b, 66t, 73b, 74t, 98b, 112b, 113tl&tr, 116t, 119t&bl, 121tr, 146bl&br, 147t, 148t,
154b; **Gary Stephenson** 9tr, 11br, 21t, 25t&b, 26b, 36b, 37t, 40b, 45b, 46t, 55t, 56b, 60b, 62b, 65bl&br,
66bl&br, 67t, 69tl&tr, 70t&b, 71b, 76t, 80b, 81tl, 107b, 111t, 114b, 116b, 119bc, 120bl&br, 124t, 125b,
128b, 129t&b, 130t&b, 132b, 133t, 134bl&br, 140b, 141tl, 143tl&tr, 144b; **Geoff Swan** 87t;
Gerry Swan 103t, 138t, 142b; **Valerie Taylor** 148bl&br; **Uncredited** 8bl, 16t,bl&br, 18b, 118br.

ISBN 978-1-912081-03-5

Edited by Krystyna Mayer

Designed by Gulmohur Press, New Delhi

Printed and bound in Malaysia by Times Offset (M) Sdn. Bhd.

·CONTENTS·

Introduction

There are more than 10,000 species of reptile in the world, and Australia is home to more than 1,000 of these. Australia has more reptile species than 95 per cent of other countries, and more than 95 per cent of Australia's reptiles are found nowhere else in the world (endemic). The number of Australian species described by scientists has grown quite markedly in recent years, doubling from the approximately 500 species known in 1975. This total will certainly continue to rise as people get better access to more remote areas of Australia, and as the result of the increasing availability of high-quality cameras, and advancements in DNA testing and analysis.

The aim of this book is to include the reptile species that are most commonly found, and more broadly distributed, in the eastern states and oceans of Australia, from the Gulf of Carpentaria and Cape York Peninsula, Queensland, in a broad arc through central and south-eastern central Queensland, central and eastern New South Wales, Victoria, Tasmania and to Adelaide in South Australia. Many species are localized in remote areas and others are deep-ocean dwellers, coming ashore either to breed or purely by accident. Although some locally common species within this range have been omitted, the authors have tried to include representatives from all groups. Some species outside this range have also been included, such as the Perentie, Australia's largest lizard, and the Fierce Snake, which possesses the most potent venom of any Australian land snake.

Reptiles and their Habitats

WHAT ARE REPTILES?

By definition, reptiles are vertebrate animals that are ectothermic (cold blooded), breathe air and have either scales or bony plates covering the body. Some reptiles lay eggs (oviparous), others give birth to live young (viviparous), and some do both. Some reptiles, such as the Tiger Snake and Red-bellied Black Snake *Pseudechis porphyriacus*, hold the fertilized membranous eggs within the body and, when ready, give birth to live young (ovoviviparous).

MAJOR THREATS AND IMPACTS

While only one Australian reptile species, the Christmas Island Forest Skink *Emoia nativitatis*, is considered to have become extinct since human settlement, many have declined significantly within their previously known ranges. As is the case with other native animals, reptile numbers and distribution ranges have been negatively impacted by factors such as habitat loss, fragmentation and degradation, due to land clearing for agricultural use and urban development; removal of reptile-shelter sites, including bush rock and logs, for use in gardens or as firewood; poor roadside management practices leading to roadkills; predation by feral animals such as foxes and cats, which feed on reptiles and their eggs; and from the introduction of other animals, including the poisonous

Cane Toad *Rhinella marina*, which has powerful toxins that kill reptile predators after being ingested, and the House Gecko, which outcompetes native geckos for food and shelter and also preys on other gecko species. Other non-native reptile and amphibian species are illegally brought into Australia as pets, and pose similar ongoing threats to native animals should they become established in the wild. Native reptiles are also illegally collected as pets or for use in traditional medicines.

Another major impact is climate change, which is causing extreme weather events and more frequent floods and bushfires than in the past. These kill animals, and destroy shelter and nest sites, and if a reptile cannot achieve a specific temperature range, it cannot digest its food properly, grow correctly or even breed successfully. Global warming may also impact on sex determination of some reptile species. The sex of the hatchlings of animals such as crocodiles and some dragon lizards is determined by temperature, with warmer temperatures leading to more female offspring. A significant change in the temperature of nests could result in just a single-sex hatching.

The introduced, and deadly, Cane Toad

In addition to the above, freshwater turtles are also under threat from loss of sand banks, changes to water flow, pollution and degradation of riverside vegetation zones and waterway substrates due to livestock. Marine turtles are also threatened by collisions with watercraft, entanglement with debris and discarded nets, and ingestion of plastic bags; at nesting colonies on beaches they are impacted by disturbance during laying and loss of nesting sites due to development.

Wildlife habitat cleared for farming

Legislation has been enacted to curb the illegal clearing of land, protect waterways from the impacts of livestock, outlaw the collection of bush rocks, control poor fishing practices that can impact on turtles and, more challengingly, to slow the rate of global climate change. Some Australian states have already eliminated or reduced the use of plastic shopping

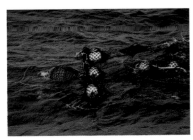

Two turtles entangled in discarded nets

bags, and biodegradable plastic bags are becoming increasingly common. Many private groups, the government and corporate organizations are actively working to control feral cat populations and the introduced Cane Toad, and trying to raise awareness of the importance of fallen timber, hollow logs and hollow-bearing trees to native reptiles and other animal species.

AUSTRALIA'S VEGETATION

At localized levels Australia is home to many thousands of vegetation types. The following broad groups are the ones most widely referred to throughout this guide and broader published material.

Rainforests
These include tropical, subtropical and cool temperate rainforests. They are found in the wetter climatic zones of Australia and are typically characterized by dense foliage and a high diversity of plant species. A large percentage of Australia's rainforests has been extensively cleared for timber, farming and agriculture, and although the rate has slowed since the early twentieth century, clearing still continues today.

Tropical rainforest

Open Forests
Tall, open forests Tall trees more than 30m in height.
Open forests Trees typically 10–30m in height and widespread in eastern (including Tasmania), northern and south-western Australia. They have a shrubby or grassy understorey.
Low, open forests Trees with an average height of 5–10m, generally found in areas that are cooler, drier, lower in nutrients, have rocky slopes or incur regular flooding.

Tall, open forest

Woodland/Open Woodland
Woodland can contain a diverse assemblage of mixed tree species, and many are restricted in total range. Others are dominated by a single plant genus. Open woodland has a wider spacing between trees than forests, allowing neighbouring grassland and shrubland to invade, and forming a valuable mosaic of these different vegetation communities. Dominant woodland types include:

Eucalypt woodland Generally forms a transitional zone between areas of higher rainfall and arid areas, and is typical of mountain ranges and plains. Contains a range of eucalypt species and, in uncleared areas, has either a shrubby or grassy understorey.

Acacia woodland Trees tend to be less than 10m in height, occasionally to 25m, and are dominated by acacias.

Callitris woodland Dominated by cypress pine (*Callitris* spp.) with a herbaceous understorey.

Casuarina woodland Dominated by she-oaks (*Casuarina* and *Allocasuarina* spp.) and mainly associated with littoral and riverine zones.

Melaleuca woodland Dominated by paperbarks (*Melaleuca* spp.) and found most extensively in the tropical north, but also in temperate coastal and montane wetlands.

Shrubland
This is typified by multi-stemmed shrubs, either monotypic or in a broad range of species. The dominant shrubland type in Australia is acacia, including Mulga and Gidgee, with other shrubland having a mix of grevilleas, samphires, saltbush, chenopods, banksias and emu bushes.

Heaths
These are typically a mixture of dense-canopied species, with many having a mature height of 1m or less. They are associated with low-nutrient soils, including in coastal montane, laterite and sandy areas, or areas subject to erosion or waterlogging.

Grassland
This is generally dominated by herbaceous (non-woody) species and occurs in a range of areas. Two main communities are found extensively in Australia:

Tussock grassland Characterized by broad range of perennial grasses growing in tufts (including Mitchell Grass and Blue Grass).

Hummock grassland Dominated by spinifex (*Triodia* and *Plechrachne* spp.) and typical

Eucalypt woodland

Chenopod shrubland

Montane heath

of the arid lands of Australia. Evergreen perennials form mounds up to 1m in height, with areas of open, exposed and usually bare soil in between hummocks. Soils in which hummock grassland appears are typically sandy or rocky (skeletal), and the areas are either hilly or flat.

Mangroves
These are found in the intertidal zone in coastal areas that are protected from high waves. Mangroves tend to form tall, closed forests in the north, and low, open forests or shrubland in the south.

Arid hummock grassland

Mangrove

Paperbark swamp

Gidgee Skink on bare rocky outcrop

Green Turtle on marine coral reef

Eastern Blue-tongue in an urban garden

Inland Waterways
These are a mixture of fresh and brackish aquatic areas, including rivers, creeks, billabongs, lakes, swamps and marshes. Fresh water in inland waterways has an average salinity of less than 5g of salts per kilogram of water, while brackish water can range from 5 to 29g per kilogram. Australia also has numerous inland salt lakes, which can have salinity levels as high as 300g per kilogram.

Bare Ground
Areas that are largely lacking in vegetation, or with some pioneer plant species present, fall into this category, and can be in the form of exposed rock, coastal sands and dunes, desert sands and claypans. The soils have low nutrient content and are prone to erosion.

Marine Waters
These consist of open water in oceans and estuaries bounded by the Australian continental shelf, with salinity levels of 30–35g per kilogram.

Urban Areas
These habitats are diverse and include remnants of bushland areas (as described above), but also contain wasteland, dwellings and gardens, which are homes to large numbers of invertebrate animals, and thus provide a habitat for native reptiles. Scrap heaps and wood piles have provided shelter sites, and some species have taken advantage of outdoor and sometimes indoor lights that attract flying insects to a convenient feeding site.

Using this Book

BODY PARTS AND SIZES

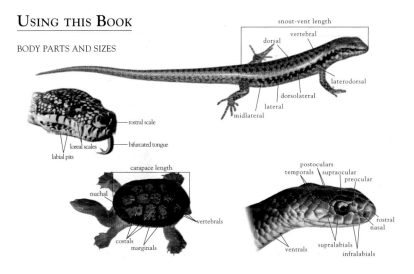

▪ Using this Book ▪

Due to variations in sizes within subspecies and geographically isolated populations, the sizes shown in the species accounts are approximates of the average maximum sizes for full-grown adults, unless otherwise indicated. As many reptiles have the ability to lose and regrow their tails (for many this is a successful defensive strategy), most measurements are given as Snout–Vent Length (SVL). For turtles a Carapace Length (CL) is given, and Total Length (TL) is also provided in species accounts, where relevant.

Alternative names of species are provided in parentheses under the main species headings.

DISTRIBUTION KEY

The following abbreviations for localities with the Australian geographic zone are used in this book:

ACT	Australian Capital Territory
NSW	New South Wales
NT	Northern Territory
Qld	Queensland
SA	South Australia
Tas	Tasmania
Vic	Victoria
WA	Western Australia

SNAKE OR SNAKE-LIZARD?

Some snake-lizards (legless lizards) have a distinct snake-like appearance, and some even have markings that mimic those of venomous snakes (see opposite). The Hooded Scaly-foot *Pygopus nigriceps* has very similar head markings to the juvenile Common Brown Snake, although it is not known whether this is due to direct mimicry, whether the pattern helps to regulate temperature, or if there are other reasons for it. Some scaly-foots, such as the Brigalow Scaly-foot, take this mimicry a step further to include the flattened neck threat posture used by some venomous snakes, flicker their tongue and even pretend to strike. These actions are more purposeful, and seem to indicate that the combination of similar markings and posture are intended to bluff potential predators and protect the non-venomous snake-lizard from harm.

Peninsula Brown Snake (juvenile)

Hooded Scaly-foot

It is important to be able to understand some key characteristics that differentiate the Hooded Scaly-foot and other snake-lizards, from similar-looking venomous snakes.

Key distinguishing characteristics in snake-lizards:
1. External ear openings usually present.
(Note that snake-lizard species without ear openings have movable eyelids.)
2. Hindlimbs reduced to small flaps.
3. Tongue broad (undivided) and fleshy.
4. Belly scales roughly the same size as those on sides and back.

Common Scaly-foot

Black Whipsnake

Key distinguishing characteristics in snakes:
1. External ear openings always absent.
2. Limbs absent.
3. Tongue bifurcated.
4. Belly scales either half or full width of body, and much larger than scales of sides and back.

SNAKE SAFETY AND FIRST AID

Many of the snakes found in Australia are capable of lethal bites to humans, but bites are quite rare and fatalities from them are even rarer, with fewer than three deaths (average) per year. This is due to the application of prompt and correct first-aid treatment, and the availability of antivenom for all venomous Australian snakes. Hospitals in Australia also have Snake Venom Detection Kits (SVDKs), so precise identification of the snake is not critical, as long as there is sufficient venom for testing.

Australia's venomous snakes are among the world's most toxic. They include taipans, brown snakes, tiger snakes and many sea snakes, with the young snakes – although having smaller fangs and less venom – having the same toxicity as the adults.

SNAKE VENOM DETECTION KITS

Snake Venom Detection Kits (SVDKs) are used in Australia to identify the correct antivenom required to treat suspected envenomation. SVDKs work by analyzing a sample of venom, normally obtained by taking a swab of the bite site (the victim's blood and urine may also be required).

SNAKE ENCOUNTERS

If you see a snake in an area where you are living or working:

- Avoid the area where the snake was seen until later in the day (often it is a one-off sighting). Most snakes (with the notable exception of ambush snakes such as death adders *Acanthophis* spp.) will not stay in the immediate vicinity.
- If possible, take a photo or two and get advice on the identification and risk of this species from a snake expert, wildlife office or natural history museum.
- *Do not antagonise the snake to get an action image.*
- Advise others using the area that a snake has been seen there and/or place a warning sign there.
- If the snake appears to be habitually using the same location and people frequently use the area, call a licensed snake catcher to relocate it. *Do not take matters into your own hands.*
- If it is a known area where snakes are frequently seen, wear protective clothing such as closed-in footwear, long trousers and thick socks, but remember that species with long fangs can easily bite through thick clothing.
- Whenever possible, avoid placing your body in places you cannot see (like long vegetation). If you must enter such an environment, additional safety equipment such as leg gaiters may be beneficial.

FIRST AID'

Snakes inject venom through a pair of fangs in the maxilla (upper jaw). The venom is produced in varying quantities in modified salivary glands and, when biting, the snake may inject none, some or all of this into a human victim. Most bites (about 85 per cent) do not result in significant envenoming.

The bite itself may not be felt, and may not leave any visible bite marks, but normally a pair of puncture wounds and some localized bruising are evident. Early symptoms of snake bite may include headache, nausea and vomiting, abdominal pain, blurred vision, confusion and difficulty breathing.

If someone is bitten, correct first aid and prompt medical attention are vital. The following steps are current for Australia at the time of publication:

- Confirm that the snake is not still in the immediate area and posing a threat to the first aider, the victim or other people in the area.
- Sit or lie the victim down with their head and shoulders raised, and instruct them against moving their limbs.

- Call 000 or 112 for emergency medical help and ask for ambulance.
- *Do not wash the area, cut the bite site or try and suck out the venom.*
- Remove clothing if it is easy to do so, or leave it in place.
- Apply a sterile pad over the bite and wind a wide (7.5–15cm) elasticated compression pressure bandage around the limb from extremity to the armpit or groin, leaving the fingers or toes exposed to check circulation (several bandages may be required to cover the entire limb).
- Bandages should be firm, but not tight (at least 40mmHg for arms and 55mmHg for legs). Check that a pulse can still be felt at the extremity of the limb, and that you can slide a finger underneath the bandage.
- If a first-aid kit is not available, use clothing or anything that is available to restrict the flow of the venom through the lymphatic system.
- *Do not apply a tourniquet.*
- Immobilize the limb with a splint on either side of the bite site, as any movement of the limb quickly speeds up venom absorption.
- If the bite is on the back, head or neck of the victim, apply firm localized pressure.
- *Do not try and catch or kill the snake for identification purposes.* Identification of the required antivenom can be made at the hospital from venom present on clothing or the skin using an SVDK.
- Keep the victim calm and reassure them. Monitor their breathing and apply emergency resuscitation if the victim goes into cardiac arrest.
- *Do not give the victim alcohol, tea, coffee or any stimulants.*

Glossary

aestivate (estivate) Torpor during extended periods of drought or heat (*see also* **brumate**).
albino With skin lacking in dark pigments.
anterior Front of the body.
aquatic Adapted to living in water.
arboreal Living in or climbing trees.
beak Rostral shields on snout of snake.
brackish water Water that is slightly salty or briny, at 5–29g of salt per kilogram of water or soil.
brumate Torpor induced by extended periods of low temperatures (see also **aestivate**).
carapace Hardened upper shell, such as that in turtles.
carnivorous Feeding only on animal matter (*see also* **herbivorous** and **omnivorous**).
caudal Pertaining to the tail.
clutch Number of eggs laid in a single reproductive cycle.
constriction Act of coiling tightly around an animal, causing suffocation.
crepuscular Active at dawn and dusk
crest Ridge of skin or spikes on neck, back or tail.
dewlap Flap of skin on throat.
diurnal Active during the day.

▪ GLOSSARY ▪

dorsal Upper surface, or back.
ecdysis (or sloughing) Process of shedding skin.
ectothermic Body temperature being influenced by temperature of an animal's surroundings.
fossorial Capable of burrowing.
gravid Having eggs or young inside body (pregnant).
herbivorous Feeding only on plant matter (*see also* **carnivorous** and **omnivorous**).
insectivorous Feeding solely on insects.
invertebrate Animal that lacks a backbone.
mandible Jaw (lower).
marine Living in or partly in aquatic environments where water salinity is greater than 30g of salt per kilogram of water.
maxilla Jaw (upper).
medial/median Centre (midline) of body.
melanism Darkening of tissues, primarily the skin, through increased production of the pigment melanin.
nocturnal Active at night.
nuchal In neck area.
omnivorous Feeding on both animal and plant matter (*see also* **carnivorous** and **herbivorous**).
oviparous Reproduces by laying eggs.
ovoviviparous Reproduces by forming unshelled egg sacs to house developing young, which are held inside the female until they are ready to hatch, then expelled either still within the egg sac or after they leave it.
parthenogenesis Asexual reproduction (without male involvement).
plastron Bottom part of a turtle's shell.
posterior Rear of body.
prehensile (tail) Adapted to grasp or attach to objects.
riparian Zone adjacent to a river.
saxicolous Living within rock crevices or caves.
scutes Thickened scales typically found on turtle shells and on upper part of tail of crocodiles.
semiaquatic Living on land but spending amounts of time in water.
setae Tiny, hair-like projections on toe-pads of some geckos.
sloughing See **ecdysis**.
terrestrial Living on or spending time on the ground.
tubercle Small, rounded nodule or projection.
vent Exterior opening of anus or cloaca.
ventral Undersurface or belly of an animal.
vertebral Along the line of the spine (vertebrae).
vertebrates Animals that have a backbone.
viviparous Reproduces by giving birth to live young.

> **TURTLES AND TORTOISES (TESTUDINES)**
> Globally about 346 turtle and tortoise species currently make up the Testudines order.
> Australia has 24 native side-neck turtles, six wider roaming sea-turtles (including the
> Leathery Turtle) and one introduced species of pond turtle.

Loggerhead Turtle ▪ *Caretta caretta* CL 1.2m; TL 1.5m

DESCRIPTION Dark reddish-brown above with some irregular darker speckling. Pale
yellowish-cream on underside. Head large in comparison to overall body size, particularly
on older adults, and triangular. Shell somewhat heart shaped, with 5 costal shields along
each side. **DISTRIBUTION** Tropical and warm temperate waters around the world.
In Australia most commonly seen in coastal waters of WA, NT, Qld and NSW, and
occasionally further south. **HABITAT**

AND HABITS Inhabits shallow
and deeper waters around beaches
and coral reefs, feeding mainly on
molluscs, crustaceans, sponges, sea
urchins, jellyfish and fish. Young
feed on algae and small molluscs.
Oviparous, laying around 125 small,
soft-shelled eggs in a clutch, with up
to 3 clutches laid in a year. Female digs
a hole for eggs in dry sand, well above
high-water.

Green Turtle ▪ *Chelonia mydas* CL 1.1m; TL 1.5m

DESCRIPTION Generally olive-green above, mottled with dark reddish-brown or black,
and pale cream below. Juveniles shiny black above and white on underside. Comparatively
small head for size of overall body. **DISTRIBUTION** Coastal, tropical and warm temperate
waters worldwide. In Australia most commonly seen in coastal waters of WA, NT, Qld and
NSW, and occasionally further south.

HABITAT AND HABITS Inhabits
seagrass beds and coral reefs. Juveniles
carnivorous, feeding on jellyfish, sponges,
snails, crustaceans and marine worms, but
adults herbivorous, feeding on seagrass,
algae and mangrove seeds. Oviparous, the
female excavating a hole high on beach,
using strong front flippers, and laying
about 110 soft-shelled eggs inside hole
before covering them with sand.

Hawksbill Turtle ■ *Eretmochelys imbricata* CL 875mm; TL 1.15m

DESCRIPTION Medium-sized turtle with narrow head and beak-like snout. Scales on head and flippers have dark centres with pale sutures. Remainder of upperparts predominantly olive-green to brown, mottled with dark reddish-brown and black. Underparts whitish. Young generally blackish above and below. Shell has 4 costal shields down either side, and scutes are overlapping. This latter attribute has made the species a target for the

tortoiseshell industry, a major cause of its global conservation status of Critically Endangered. **DISTRIBUTION** Found in tropical and warm temperate seas around the world. In Australia ranges from central-west Australian coast, along northern coastline to central-east coast, and occasionally further south. **HABITAT AND HABITS** Found in coral reefs, where it feeds mainly on sponges, but also on jellyfish, anemones, molluscs, fish, crustaceans, anemones and marine algae. Oviparous, laying up to 140 small, soft-shelled eggs in a clutch, with 2–4 clutches laid in a year.

Flatback Turtle ■ *Natator depressus* CL 900mm; TL 1.2m

DESCRIPTION Grey to olive-green above and without any distinguishable patterning; creamy-yellow below and on sides of neck. Broadly oval shell noticeably flattened with upturned edges; 4 costal shields on each side, and scutes do not overlap. In adults, shell covered with thin, fleshy skin. Young turtles predominantly olive-brown with black edges to scutes. **DISTRIBUTION** The only sea turtle restricted to waters bounded by Australian continental shelf. Most common in north, between Kimberley region of WA and east coast of Qld, but can venture further south. **HABITAT AND HABITS** Prefers soft-bottomed, inshore waters, and less likely to inhabit coral reefs than other sea-turtles seen in Australian waters. Carnivorous, feeding predominantly on soft-bodied animals, including

cuttlefish, jellyfish, sea cucumbers and soft corals. Oviparous, laying up to 80 large, round, soft-shelled eggs in hole dug in soft sand above high-water mark.

Adult

Hatchlings

Leathery Turtle ▪ *Dermochelys coriacea* CL 2m; TL 3m
(Leatherback; Leatherback Turtle; Luth; Trunkback Turtle; Trunk Turtle; Coffin-back)

DESCRIPTION Very large, with hard, leathery skin covering carapace and large, powerful front flippers. Dark grey-brown to black above, often with some paler marbling and pitting, and 5 distinct longitudinal ridges on carapace (in addition to outer lateral ridges). Whitish on underside with 4 ridges on plastron. Young turtles blue-black above with whitish edging, with numerous pale osteoderms giving a beaded appearance; whitish below. **DISTRIBUTION** The most widely distributed of all sea-turtles, occurring in temperate and tropical waters worldwide. In Australia can be seen in all coastal waters, including larger bays and estuaries. **HABITAT AND HABITS** In Australia appears to favour more temperate coastal waters and deeper ocean. Feeds predominantly on jellyfish and other soft-bodied invertebrates, as well as algae and seaweed. Oviparous, with up to 110 round, soft-shelled eggs laid in hole excavated in soft sand above high-water mark. Nesting was considered to occur every 2–3 years, although recent evidence suggests that it could occur annually, with 4–7 clutches laid in a season.

Cann's Long-necked Turtle ▪ *Chelodina canni* CL 270mm
(Cann's Snake-necked Turtle)

DESCRIPTION Distinguished from other similar turtles by distinctly oval-shaped shell, which is around 1.5 times longer than it is wide. Brown, with darker mottling, or black above and cream below, with variable darker edging to sutures, and reddish-pink tinge to head, neck and limbs. Long, slender neck and broad head are not able to be retracted into carapace, instead being curved around edge of shell. Hatchlings have extensive orange-red suffusion to underparts. **DISTRIBUTION** Drainage systems of north-eastern NT and northern Qld, including Roper River. **HABITAT AND HABITS** Prefers billabongs, lagoons, dams and swamps, where it is active during both night and day, feeding on aquatic vertebrates, principally amphibians and fish, and invertebrates, including insects and crustaceans. Will also feed on carrion. Oviparous, laying up to 24 hard-shelled eggs per clutch in excavated hole near water. When handled, releases a pungent, foul-smelling fluid.

Broad-shelled Turtle ▪ *Chelodina expansa* CL 490mm; TL 800mm
(Giant Snake-necked Turtle)

DESCRIPTION Australia's largest long-necked turtle. Brown to dark grey-brown above, with darker lines and flecks; pale grey or cream below. Very long, thick neck and broad, flat head. Carapace oval shaped, broad and flattened, and plastron long and narrow, roughly twice as long as it is wide. Second and third vertebrals of carapace longer than they are wide.
DISTRIBUTION Follows Murray Darling River systems, from south-eastern Qld, through

NSW, Vic and to south-western SA. Also on south-east coastal Qld drainages and Fraser Island. **HABITAT AND HABITS** Found in permanent waterways, including slow-moving rivers, streams and waterholes. Lies concealed under mud and other debris on bottom of waterway, with only head exposed, waiting for aquatic vertebrates and larger invertebrates to come past, and seizing them in its open mouth with a quick thrusting extension of its neck. Oviparous, laying about 12 hard-shelled eggs in excavated nest in bank of waterway. During long, dry winter, individuals dig themselves into mud and aestivate until the water returns. Rarely seen far from water.

Eastern Snake-necked Turtle ▪ *Chelodina longicollis* CL 250mm
(Snake-necked Turtle; Eastern Long-necked Turtle; Common Long-necked Turtle; Long-necked Tortoise; Stinker)

DESCRIPTION Shell rich light brown with black sutures outlining scutes, to dark blackish-brown above and whitish-cream below, again with black sutures. Anterior of plastron broadened laterally. Hatchlings often have dark orange-red instead of whitish-cream on plastron, giving a striking contrast with black sutures. Flesh parts generally brown-grey above and cream below. Neck long and slender, and head small and somewhat flattened. Males have thicker and longer tails than females. **DISTRIBUTION** Coastal

and inland waterways throughout eastern Australia, from Wilton River in central-eastern Qld, south-west through NSW, Vic to Adelaide SA. Introduced into north-eastern Tas. **HABITAT AND HABITS** Largely aquatic, favouring swamps, lagoons, wetland and slow-moving rivers, but often seen wandering overland as it moves from one waterway to another. Omnivorous, feeding on range of smaller vertebrates and aquatic invertebrates, including frogs, tadpoles, snails, insects and small fish, and aquatic vegetation. Will also feed on carrion. Oviparous, producing 8–24 brittle-shelled eggs in a clutch. Ejects a pungent fluid when handled.

Northern Snake-necked Turtle ■ *Chelodina oblonga* CL 350mm
(Narrow-breasted Snake-necked Turtle)

DESCRIPTION Generally dark brown with variable darker markings, to black above and whitish below. Carapace oval shaped, wider towards rear; plastron long and narrow, up to twice as long as it is wide. Neck long and slender, and flattened head only slightly wider than neck. **DISTRIBUTION** Widely distributed in north of Australia from Kimberley, WA, to Cape York Peninsula, Qld. **HABITAT AND HABITS** Largely aquatic, favouring permanent waterways, but can inhabit swamps, streams, billabongs and slow-flowing rivers. During extended dry periods individuals either bury themselves in mud and remain in a dormant state (aestivate) until the water returns, or travel overground to nearby waterways. Carnivorous, feeding on range of small vertebrates and aquatic invertebrates. Oviparous, laying up to 20 brittle-shelled eggs in burrow under waterline, which do not start to develop until water level drops below burrow.

Plastron is up to twice as long as it is wide

White-throated Snapping Turtle ■ *Elseya albagula* CL 410mm
(Southern Snapping Turtle)

DESCRIPTION Large freshwater turtle with numerous round tubercles covering neck. Brown with darker blotches, to black above and greyish below. Carapace generally broad and oval shaped, straighter across front, with tapered plastron. Rear of carapace deeply serrated in hatchlings and young individuals. Head and neck dark brown above and cream below, tending to be darker in males than females. Head shield prominently wrinkled. **DISTRIBUTION** South-eastern Qld, within rivers and drainage systems of Fitzroy, Mary and Burnett Rivers.

HABITAT AND HABITS Shows marked preference for clear, flowing and oxygen-rich waters, including rivers and associated billabongs. Cloacal respiration, used to extract oxygen from water, enables individuals to remain underwater for up to 3 hours while foraging. Adults largely herbivorous, feeding predominantly on aquatic vegetation and fallen fruits, although will take some aquatic invertebrates and small vertebrates. Oviparous, laying around 10–13 eggs in shallow nest excavated in riverbank.

Irwin's Snapping Turtle ■ *Elseya irwini* CL 350mm
(White-headed Snapping Turtle)

DESCRIPTION Carapace brown to blackish with upturned edges in mature individuals. Neck short and head large, with 2 barbels on chin, and raised, rounded tubercles on top of neck. Adults have pink noses, and female has white head with yellowish crown. Five claws on forelimbs. Plastron moderately narrow, whitish-grey to yellowish with black blotches. Carapace broadly oval, around two-thirds as wide as it is long. Juvenile has more olive-

brown carapace than adults, with serrated marginal shields. **DISTRIBUTION** Restricted to Burdekin and Johnstone River catchments, eastern and north-eastern Qld. **HABITAT AND HABITS** Occurs in rivers and billabongs, where it is active at night, feeding mainly on leaves, algae and other vegetable matter, supplemented with some invertebrates, crustaceans, mussels and carrion. Oviparous, laying up to 12 eggs in hole that female digs in a riverbank. Often seen basking on exposed rocks and logs.

Macquarie Turtle ■ *Emydura macquarii* CL 350mm (inland) 185mm (coastal);
(Murray River Turtle; Murray Turtle; Southern River Turtle)

DESCRIPTION Generally pale to dark olive-brown above and yellowish-white below, with obvious pale yellow stripe along jaw and down neck. Short neck and small head, although some individuals may have enlarged head. Iris colour variable between populations, but generally yellow, green or orange. Carapace broadly oval (serrated at rear in juveniles), and plastron elongated, being twice as long as it is wide. Morphological variations evident throughout 4 recognized subspecies of the species complex, including variations in size, shape of carapace and colouration of eye, shell and body. **DISTRIBUTION** As currently conceived, the species is broadly distributed in eastern Australia along extent of Murray and Darling River system of Qld, NSW, Vic and eastern SA, Cooper Creek drainage of

inland Queensland, eastern flowing drainages of central and north coast of NSW, and Queensland north to Cape York, with an isolated population on Fraser Island. **HABITAT AND HABITS** Occurs around large rivers, tributaries and billabongs, where it can often be seen basking on exposed logs. Omnivorous, feeding on both plants and animals, including algae, fungi, plant shoots and leaves, aquatic invertebrates, tadpoles and fish. Oviparous, laying 10–15 elongated, brittle-shelled eggs in a clutch, with up to 3 clutches per year.

Northern Yellow-faced Turtle ■ *Emydura tanybaraga* CL 270mm
(Red-bellied Short-necked Turtle)

DESCRIPTION Medium-sized, pale brown to brownish-grey turtle, with prominent bright yellow facial stripe extending from snout to ear. Second yellow to yellowish-pink stripe along jawline and down neck, often less obvious. Carapace spotted with darker brown and plastron has pink or yellow colouration. Eye has 2 small black spots on either side of pupil, giving appearance of an elongated horizontal pupil. This characteristic is shared with **Jardine River Turtle** *E. subglobosa* subglobosa, which has bright reddish stripe along lower jaw and neck, and **Worrell's Turtle** *E. s. worrelli*. Males smaller than females, but have larger tails.

DISTRIBUTION Two separated populations, one in northern NT and one in Cape York Peninsula, Qld. **HABITAT AND HABITS** Relatively common in deep tropical rivers and permanent lagoons, where it feeds on range of aquatic vegetation and fruits that hang near water. Oviparous, nesting at end of wet season and laying up to 11 eggs in a clutch.

Common Sawshell Turtle ■ *Wollumbinia latisternum* CL 240mm
(Saw-shelled Turtle)

DESCRIPTION Brown to dark olive-brown above and whitish-cream below, the two contrasting colours forming distinct line on sides of head and neck. Carapace broadly oval and, in young turtles, has raised central keel that flattens down with age. Rear of carapace has prominent, 'saw-like' serrations, which also reduce in size as a turtle ages. Plastron whitish and almost twice as long as it is wide. Neck short with numerous spiny tubercles, and small head. Young individuals and some adults have yellow stripe on sides of face.

DISTRIBUTION North-western NT and in broad coastal band from northern NSW to Cape York, Qld. **HABITAT AND HABITS** Usually found in rivers, streams, billabongs and, occasionally, farm dams. Omnivorous, feeding on vertebrates such as fish, frogs and tadpoles, aquatic invertebrates including molluscs, crustaceans and insects, and aquatic vegetation and fallen fruits. Potential predator of poisonous Cane Toad *Rhinella marina*. Oviparous, laying around 20 brittle-shelled eggs in a clutch, in September–January, in nest excavated in sand or other substrate on bank close to water.

LIZARDS (Sauria)

Lizards belong to the suborder Sauria, which – along with the snakes in the suborder Serpentes – forms the order Squamata that comprises more than 95 per cent of the world's reptile species. Australia's largest lizard family is the skinks (Scincidae), with about 440 currently described species, most of which are found nowhere else in the world.

Jacky Lizard ▪ *Amphibolurus muricatus* SVL 110mm, TL 350mm
(Jacky Dragon; Tree Dragon)

DESCRIPTION Pale grey to dark brown lizard with spiny scales on sides of neck and bright yellow lining inside mouth. Black patches along middle of back, with 2 paler stripes on either side. Particularly large and prominent scales along back in longitudinal rows from neck to base of tail. Males generally have larger heads than females. **DISTRIBUTION**

South-eastern Australian mainland, from south-eastern Qld, through eastern NSW and Vic, to far south-western SA. **HABITAT AND HABITS** Found on rocky ridges and in open areas in dry sclerophyll woodland and coastal heaths, where it is usually seen on fallen or standing timber. Feeds on small invertebrates, including grasshoppers, ants and worms, flowers, berries and small skinks. Oviparous, laying 3–12 soft-shelled eggs in shallow burrows, with 1–2 clutches produced during summer. Sex of young is influenced by temperature of nest.

Frilled Lizard ▪ *Chlamydosaurus kingii* SVL 275mm, TL 890mm
(Frill-necked Lizard; Frilled Neck Lizard; Frilled Dragon)

DESCRIPTION Unmistakable, with large, extendable, grey, red or orange frill that is folded along neck when at rest. Brown to orange-brown or blackish-grey above, with

darker brown markings on back and sides, and generally paler or blackish below. Tail long and whip-like, often with blackish tip. **DISTRIBUTION** Northern and eastern Australia, from Kimberley region WA, through northern NT, to northern and eastern Qld. **HABITAT AND HABITS** Occurs in wooded environments of tropical north, including dry forests, grassy woodland and monsoonal woodland, where it is mainly arboreal, perching on trunks and branches of trees. Feeds on invertebrates and their larvae, including ants, cicadas and spiders, as well as small lizards, mammals and some plant matter. Oviparous, laying 1–2 clutches of about 12 soft-shelled eggs each year. If startled, either runs away on its hindlegs, or expands its large frill and hisses with its mouth wide open.

Mallee Military Dragon ▪ *Ctenophorus fordi* SVL 55mm, TL 175mm
(Mallee Dragon; Mallee Sand-dragon)

DESCRIPTION Brown to reddish-brown above, with black and smaller whitish spots on back and tail. Edges of back have whitish longitudinal stripes from neck to base of tail. Sides of body and tail blackish, more so in males than females, with several small paler spots, and lower longitudinal stripe, bordered with blackish below. Front limbs have thin whitish bands in midlateral area. Belly, throat and chin black with rest of undersurface white. Females paler than males, with black spots on throat. **DISTRIBUTION** Arid to semi-arid southern Australian mainland, from south-eastern WA, through southern SA and far north-western Vic, to south-western NSW. **HABITAT AND HABITS** Found in sandy and stony deserts with areas of mallee and spinifex, where it forages in open areas for ants, retreating to dense tussocks for safety. Oviparous, with 2 or more eggs in a clutch, and high mortality rates in eggs laid in hot, dry summers. Bobs head when in presence of other dragon species, but not thought to be territorial.

Central Netted Dragon ▪ *Ctenophorus nuchalis* SVL 120mm, TL 265mm
(Central Netted Ground-dragon)

DESCRIPTION Small and stocky, with large, rounded head, short limbs and tapering tail. Spines scattered on sides of neck. Light orange-brown to reddish-brown above with white to creamish-yellow mid-vertebral stripe from nape to base of tail, and series of transversally aligned similarly coloured spots, forming reticulated (netted) pattern. Back of head and nape thin, spiny scales. Underparts whitish with grey marbling, and sexually active males flushed with orange. **DISTRIBUTION** Drier mainland Australia, from WA coast, east through NT and SA, to south-western Qld and north-western NSW. Absent from south, north and east. **HABITAT AND HABITS** Favours open, semi-arid to arid areas, where it is active throughout the day, and shelters at night in burrows at bases of shrubs and tree stumps. Feeds on invertebrates, including ants, termites and beetles, and fruits and flowers. Oviparous, laying up to 3 clutches in a year, each containing 2–6 soft-shelled eggs.

Painted Dragon ■ *Ctenophorus pictus* SVL 70mm, TL 190mm

DESCRIPTION Sexually active males are among the most colourful of Australia's lizards, being bluish-grey to reddish-brown above, often with bright blue sides and throat, and yellow-orange flush on head. Non-breeding males and females reddish-brown, with darker blotches and paler spots arranged in transverse rows on back and upper tail. Males

generally darker than females and often have small nuchal crest. Underparts whitish, with males having black patch on back of forearm and chest. **DISTRIBUTION** Drier areas of central-southern Australia, from south-western WA, through SA, western Vic and western NSW, to south-western Qld. **HABITAT AND HABITS** Most commonly seen at rest on low perches in arid to semi-arid shrubland and grassland, generally with sandy and saline soils. Digs short burrows at bases of shrubs for shelter. Feeds predominantly on invertebrates, including ants, and some plant matter, by foraging in open areas, but will also eat hatchling dragons. Oviparous, laying 2–6 soft-shelled eggs.

Tommy Roundhead ■ *Diporiphora australis* SVL 70mm, TL 190mm

DESCRIPTION Moderately sized dragon with keeled dorsal scales, short nuchal crest in males and long, slender tail that is about 2–3 times length of body (SVL). Greyish-brown or yellowish-brown above, with series of dark brown transverse bars and pair of thin grey or creamish longitudinal stripes from nape to base of tail. Sides have pale flecks,

with or without light midlateral stripe. Underparts yellowish-white with darker peppering. **DISTRIBUTION** Coast and eastern interior, from north-east NSW to southern Cape York Peninsula, Qld. **HABITAT AND HABITS** Found in variety of timbered habitats, including arid woodland, mallee, hummock grassland, swampland and shores of salt lakes, where it is semiarboreal. Forages for insects, which are pounced on from an elevated perch. Oviparous, laying up to 6 soft-shelled eggs in clutch.

Two-lined Dragon ▪ *Diporiphora bilineata* SVL 60mm, TL 300mm
(Northern Two-lined Dragon)

DESCRIPTION Variably coloured and patterned. Grey or yellowish-brown to reddish-brown above, with enlarged keeled scales on sides. Back with narrow grey vertebral stripe and cream or yellowish lateral stripes, and with large, pale brown spots from nape to tail. Black throat on some males in eastern populations. Belly whitish to yellowish, with keeled scales and fine lines from throat to vent. **DISTRIBUTION** Northern Australia,

from east of WA to Cape York Peninsula, Qld. **HABITAT AND HABITS** Found in variety of habitats including forests, open, grassy woodland and sandy coastal dunes, where it is active during the day, foraging mainly on the ground, but also on low branches, for small invertebrates, including moths and grasshoppers. Oviparous, laying up to 8 eggs in a clutch and up to 2 clutches in a year.

Nobbi Dragon ▪ *Diporiphora nobbi* SVL 80mm, TL 270mm

DESCRIPTION Similar to Jacky Lizard (see p. 22), but generally lighter greyish- or yellowish-brown, and with distinctive pale longitudinal dorsal stripes, with or without series of roughly triangular darker blotches along length and down tail. Both sexes may be

tinged with pink or red on rump and tail, and yellowish on body. Inside of mouth is pink. **DISTRIBUTION** Eastern and south-eastern mainland, from north-western Vic, through central NSW, to inland and north-eastern Qld. **HABITAT AND HABITS** Occurs in variety of timbered habitats throughout its range, including forests, woodland and mallee scrub, generally in more arid areas than Jacky Lizard. Often seen basking on logs, fence posts and rocks. Semiarboreal, feeding within trees or on the ground on insects. Oviparous, laying eggs in burrow that female digs in the ground.

Water Dragon ▪ *Intellagama lesueurii* SVL 200mm, TL 900mm
(Eastern Water Dragon; Gippsland Water Dragon)

DESCRIPTION Large, very distinctive dragon, with angular head, enlarged nuchal crest, raised, 'saw-like' vertebral crest running length of body, and laterally depressed, long tail. Colour variable between subspecies. *I. l. lesueurii* grey to brownish-grey above with black transverse dorsal stripes, and broad blackish facial stripe. Yellowish-brown underneath, but males often flushed with bright red on chest and throat. Gippsland Water Dragon *I. l. howittii* has smaller spinose scales and no stripe between eye and ear. Yellow and blue on neck and throat, and dark blue-green on chest. **DISTRIBUTION** Eastern Australia. *I. l. lesueurii* from northern Qld to southern NSW. *I. l. howittii* from southern NSW to eastern Vic. Introduced to other areas, including Mount Lofty Ranges near Adelaide SA.

HABITAT AND HABITS Varied, from alpine streams to rainforests, but always in association with water, where it is omnivorous, feeding on flowers, fruits, invertebrates and small vertebrates. Often seen basking on branches overhanging water or on banks of waterways, and dives into the water when approached. Strong swimmer and can stay submerged for long periods. Oviparous, laying up to 2 clutches of 18 soft-shelled eggs in hole that female digs in sandy soil.

Burns' Dragon ▪ *Lophognathus burnsi* SVL 130mm, TL 450
(Burns' Lashtail)

DESCRIPTION Medium-sized, rough-scaled dragon with long, thin tail that is around 3 times length of body (SVL), and with longitudinal rows of spiny scales along length of body. Generally pale grey to brown or blackish, with longitudinal white stripes or series of large white blotches on back. Cheeks have enlarged spiny scales and underparts whitish. **DISTRIBUTION** Adjacent waterways of inland northern NSW and southern Qld, west

of Great Dividing Range. **HABITAT AND HABITS** Occupies dry, open forests and woodland along margins of rivers, where it is active during the day, feeding on small invertebrates. Fast moving, and on being disturbed runs to safety on its hindlegs. Oviparous, laying about 4–5 soft-shelled eggs in hole that female digs in the ground. Habit of waving its foreleg has given rise to the alternative common name of Ta-ta Lizard, which is shared with other related lizards.

Gilbert's Dragon ■ *Lophognathus gilberti* SVL 110mm, TL 420mm
(Ta-ta Lizard)

DESCRIPTION Medium-sized, rough-scaled dragon with long, thin tail that is around 3 times length of body (SVL). Small nuchal crest that meets single longitudinal vertebral row of spiny scales. Pale greyish-brown to reddish-brown or blackish above, with broad whitish or creamish-yellow stripe along jaw that roughly meets similarly coloured line extending from shoulder to rump, with adult males more distinctly patterned and generally darker than females. Whitish, yellowish or black (mature males) below, with females having dark flecks on throat. Colour and patterning varies at different times within the same individual. **DISTRIBUTION** Northern Australia, from north-western WA, through NT, to western Qld. **HABITAT AND HABITS** Found in dry, open forests and woodland along margins of rivers, where it is active during the day, feeding on small invertebrates. Fast moving, and upon being disturbed runs to safety on its hindlegs. Habit of waving its foreleg has given rise to alternative common name of Ta-ta Lizard, which is shared with other related lizards. Oviparous, laying up to 8 soft-shelled eggs.

Boyd's Forest Dragon ■ *Lophosaurus boydii* SVL 150mm, TL 500mm

DESCRIPTION Laterally compressed, angular head and body, with large, spiny nuchal crest, enlarged white scales on cheeks, 'saw-like', keeled vertebral scales, long, slender tail and long limbs. Greyish-blue to olive-brown above, with obscure light and dark transverse barring, and blackish patch on sides of neck, bordered above and below by short white horizontal bars. Large, extendable, yellowish-orange throat-patch, with remaining underparts whitish to pale brown. **DISTRIBUTION** Base of Cape York Peninsula, north-eastern Qld. **HABITAT AND HABITS** Found in rainforests and margins, where it is active during the day, feeding on invertebrates that are pounced on from perch in tree, as well as on some fruits and small vertebrates. Although largely arboreal, more commonly seen foraging on the ground. Oviparous, laying up to 4 clutches of 4–6 soft-shelled eggs in a year.

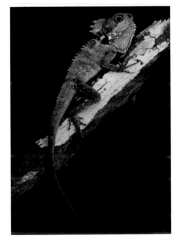

Southern Angle-headed Dragon ▪ *Lophosaurus spinipes*
SVL 105mm, TL 370mm
(Rainforest Dragon)

DESCRIPTION Large dragon with long tail that is about twice as long as body (SVL), large, angular head, enlarged nuchal crest and raised, 'saw-like' vertebral crest. Grey to greenish or rich brown above, with numerous raised spinose scales, arranged in transverse rows along body. Dark band from ear to eye and dark bars on jaw. Back and tail have

yellow flecks or spots, and belly is whitish to pale brown. **DISTRIBUTION** Wetter forests of south-eastern Qld and north-eastern NSW. **HABITAT AND HABITS** Occurs in rainforests and wet forests, where it is active during the day, feeding mostly on invertebrates that are pounced on from perch in tree. Although largely arboreal, more commonly seen foraging on the ground in clearings, often freezing and relying on camouflage for protection if disturbed. Oviparous, laying up to 8 soft-shelled eggs in shallow nests, with evidence suggesting communal laying.

Bearded Dragon ▪ *Pogona barbata* SVL 250mm, TL 600mm
(Common Bearded Dragon; Eastern Bearded Dragon)

DESCRIPTION Robust, flattened body, triangular head and long, tapering tail. Upperparts covered in raised tubercles, longer under expandable beard (throat). Pale grey, yellowish-brown or blackish above, with series of pale blotches arranged longitudinally on both sides of spine, either circular, oval or merging together to form broad line. Tail normally banded, becoming darker grey or blackish towards tip. Underparts whitish-grey, with round markings. Inside of mouth pale to bright yellow. **DISTRIBUTION** Eastern and southern mainland, from south of Cape York Peninsula, through eastern NSW, to central Vic, and

in south-eastern SA. **HABITAT AND HABITS** Found in forests, woodland and adjacent areas, where it is semiarboreal. Often seen basking on tree branches, timber posts and sides of roads. Feeds on invertebrates, small lizards and plant material, especially flowers. Relies on camouflage to avoid detection, clinging to trees and flattening body. Oviparous, laying up to 30 (average 16) soft-shelled eggs in burrow that female digs, then backfills to conceal the eggs. If threatened, expands spiny beard and opens mouth to show bright yellow lining.

Downs Bearded Dragon ■ *Pogona henrylawsoni* SVL 140mm, TL 280mm
(Blacksoil Bearded Dragon)

DESCRIPTION Large, flattened body, with bulbous head and medium-length, rounded, lightly banded tail. Beard (gular pouch) poorly developed, and covered in spiny scales, which extend around sides of head. Yellowish-brown to greyish-brown above, with irregular spiny scales and series of longitudinally arranged, paler oblong blotches on either side of spine. Underparts generally whitish, sometimes darker brownish on throat and with series of rounded markings. **DISTRIBUTION** Black soil plains of central Qld. **HABITAT AND HABITS** Occupies dry grassland and shrubland, where it is terrestrial, sheltering in soil cracks and emerging to feed on invertebrates during daylight. Oviparous, laying up to 20 soft-shelled eggs. If threatened, expands spiny beard and opens mouth to show bright yellow lining.

Central Bearded Dragon ■ *Pogona vitticeps* SVL 250mm, TL 550mm
(Inland Bearded Dragon)

DESCRIPTION Robust, flattened body, broad, triangular head and short, rounded, tapering tail. Upperparts covered in raised tubercles, longer under expandable beard (gular pouch) and sides of body. Grey, yellowish, reddish-brown or blackish, with series of paler elongated, longitudinally arranged blotches on either side of back. Pale-edged dark streaks from eye through ear to edge of head. Undersurface grey, blackish on throat, with longitudinal, oval-shaped rings. **DISTRIBUTION** Semi-arid interior of eastern Australia, including western NSW, south-western Qld, south-eastern NT, eastern SA and north-western Vic. **HABITAT AND HABITS** Occurs in dry grassland, shrubland and woodland, where it is active during the day, foraging on the ground for plant matter and invertebrates. Good climber, and normally seen basking on rocks, trees and fence posts. When alarmed extends beard and opens mouth. Oviparous, laying up to 15 soft-shelled eggs in a clutch.

Adult male showing black throat

Mountain Dragon ■ *Rankinia diemensis*
SVL 80mm, TL 190mm (larger in south than in north)
(Mountain Heath Dragon)

DESCRIPTION Small, laterally depressed agamid with triangular-shaped head and numerous spiny scales along sides of head, body and obscurely banded tail. Light grey to dark brown above, with darker patches arranged in 4 longitudinal lines on back. Underparts whitish-cream, heavily flecked with brown, and with keeled scales on

head, throat and belly. Blue mouth lining distinguishes it from Jacky Lizard (see p. 22). **DISTRIBUTION** Ranges and uplands of temperate south-eastern Australia, from north-eastern NSW, through Vic and into eastern Tas. **HABITAT AND HABITS** Occurs in dry forests, woodland, heaths and fringes of wet forests, where it forages on the ground around fallen timber and low rocks for ants and other small insects. Shelters at night within ground litter and in low vegetation. Oviparous, laying up to 7 soft-shelled eggs, with generally only a single clutch laid in a year.

Lined Earless Dragon ■ *Tympanocryptis lineata* SVL 55mm, TL 140mm
DESCRIPTION Moderately robust body with medium-length, slender tail that is around one and a half times longer than body (SVL). Light greyish-brown to reddish-brown above, with numerous keeled scales and larger spinose scales, and broad pale vertebral line from nape to base of tail, intersected by obscure transverse dark brown bars. Tail

banded and underparts whitish, peppered with brown or black. **DISTRIBUTION** South-eastern mainland, including eastern SA, north-western Vic, central and western NSW and southern Qld. **HABITAT AND HABITS** Favours variety of drier areas, including open woodland and grassland, where it is active during the day, foraging for small invertebrates. Shelters in spider holes, soil cracks and grassy tussocks. Oviparous, laying up to 12 eggs in a clutch.

Grassland Earless Dragon ■ *Tympanocryptis pinguicolla*
SVL 70mm, TL 150mm

DESCRIPTION Stout-bodied, small dragon, with large number of scattered spiny scales on dorsal surface and lacking external ear opening. Pale grey-brown to reddish-brown above, with thin pale longitudinal lines from nape to tail, and darker transverse blotches on back. Underparts whitish with some yellow (females and juveniles) or orange (breeding adult males) flushing, at times confined to throat. **DISTRIBUTION** South-eastern mainland Australia, including southern NSW and eastern Vic. **HABITAT AND HABITS** Found in temperate native grassland with embedded rocks and grassy tussocks, where it shelters in grass tussocks, under rocks and in burrows of crickets and wolf spiders, foraging during the day for small invertebrates, including spiders, beetles, grasshoppers and crickets. Little known about its breeding, but in captivity has a lifespan of up to 5 yrs, and only lays viable eggs for 3 of those years. Listed as vulnerable on the IUCN Red List and Endangered in Australia, with loss of suitable groundcover and modification of habitat for agriculture being key threats.

Eyrean Earless Dragon ■ *Tympanocryptis tetraporophora* SVL 75mm, TL 190mm

DESCRIPTION Moderately robust body with medium-length, slender tail that is around one and a half times longer than body (SVL). Light greyish-brown to reddish-brown above, with numerous keeled scales and larger spinose scales. Thin pale vertebral stripe from nape to base of tail and 2 longitudinal dorsolateral lines, intersected by dark brown transverse bars. Tail banded and underparts whitish, occasionally peppered with brown or black, and throat with pale yellow flush. **DISTRIBUTION** Broad inland band from north-western to eastern mainland Australia, including north-western WA, central and southern NT, northern and eastern SA, central and south-western Qld, and western NSW. **HABITAT AND HABITS** Found in dry, open habitats, including grassland and shrubland, where it is active during the day, foraging on the ground for small invertebrates, including spiders, beetles, grasshoppers and crickets. Often seen basking on the ground on large clods of earth, or sheltering in low shrubs up to 2m off the ground. Oviparous, laying up to 14 (average 8) eggs in a clutch, with clutch size related to size of female.

Marbled Gecko ■ *Christinus marmoratus* SVL 70mm

DESCRIPTION Slender, slightly flattened body with moderately long tail. Variable; generally grey or brownish above with intense darker marbling that surrounds irregular paler blotches or fine, jagged blackish lines, and occasionally with orange specks on tail. Belly whitish. Fingers and toes long, with large pads and retractable claws. **DISTRIBUTION** Southern mainland and islands, from south-western WA, through southern SA (including Kangaroo Island) and central Vic, to central NSW. **HABITAT**

AND HABITS Occurs in dry forests, woodland and rocky outcrops, also entering adjacent suburban gardens, in moist coastal and semi-arid areas. Arboreal and nocturnal, sheltering under logs or loose tree bark during the day, and emerging at night to feed on small invertebrates. Oviparous, laying 2 brittle-shelled eggs in a single clutch.

Ring-tailed Gecko ■ *Cyrtodactylus tuberculatus* SVL 120mm
(Coastal Ring-tailed Gecko; Cooktown Ring-tailed Gecko)

DESCRIPTION Large gecko with large head, slightly flattened body, and long, thin tail conspicuously banded with white and blackish-brown. Body cream to pale brown above

with broad, brownish transverse bands, each edged darker, and numerous large, rounded tubercles on back. Broad band extends around nape, from one eye to the other, and top of head is mottled olive-brown. Belly whitish. Digits lacking expanded pads and have strong claws. **DISTRIBUTION** Stanley Island and coastal north-eastern Qld, from Cape Melville to around Mt Leswell. **HABITAT AND HABITS** Found in wet and dry forests (including lowland tropical rainforests) and woodland, where it is associated heavily with rocky outcrops, caves and dense creek-line vegetation; also enters buildings in adjacent human settlements. Largely arboreal and nocturnal, actively foraging on tree trunks and within leaf litter for invertebrates such as arthropods, and vertebrate species including frogs and smaller geckoes. Oviparous, laying 1–2 brittle-shelled eggs.

Dubious Dtella ▪ *Gehyra dubia* SVL 80mm
(Dtella)

DESCRIPTION Pale greyish-cream to grey-brown above, with irregular darker blotches, streaks and dashes, and paler whitish spots. Whitish to yellowish below. Appears generally paler and with less patterning at night. Each digit is expanded, forming large, circular pad, with large claw coming from centre of each, except inner digits. **DISTRIBUTION** North-eastern Australia, from Cape York Peninsula through coastal and inland Qld, to northern NSW. **HABITAT AND HABITS** Common inhabitant of dry forests, open, grassy woodland and rocky areas, and readily enters buildings in rural and suburban areas. Generally arboreal, sheltering during the day under loose bark of dead trees, and emerging at night to feed on invertebrates such as cockroaches and spiders, which are supplemented to a degree with plant material, including fruit and sap. Oviparous, laying 2 round, brittle-shelled eggs in a clutch, with northern populations producing more than 1 clutch in a year.

 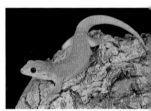

Southern Rock Dtella ▪ *Gehyra lazelli* SVL 50mm
(Lazell's Dtella)

DESCRIPTION Moderately built and somewhat dorsally flattened, with long, slender tail and small, smooth scales. Pale grey above, with darker markings forming reticulated pattern on head, body and original tail, and with small white spots arranged in obscure transverse pattern. Belly whitish. Digits expanded and pad-like, with no webbing between third and fourth toes. **DISTRIBUTION** From central NSW to southern SA. **HABITAT AND HABITS** Strongly associated with rocky areas, including outcrops and stony hills, where it shelters during the day beneath exfoliating rock, within rock crevices or under loose tree bark. Forages on rock surfaces and in cracks for invertebrates. Oviparous, laying a single egg in a clutch.

Northern Spotted Rock Dtella ■ *Gehyra nana* SVL 50mm

DESCRIPTION Smooth, small-scaled, somewhat slender gecko, with slightly flattened body and medium-length, slender tail. Greyish-brown or reddish-brown above, with alternating irregular transverse rows of paler pinkish and blackish-brown spots. Belly

whitish. Digits expanded and pad-like, lamellae divided and with no webbing between third and fourth toes. **DISTRIBUTION** Northern Australia (including coastal islands), from Kimberley region NT, through northern NT, to Cape York Peninsula Qld. **HABITAT AND HABITS** Found in rocky outcrops within open woodland and rocky hills, where it shelters during the day beneath exfoliating rock, within rock crevices or in caves. Forages on rock surfaces and in cracks for invertebrates. Oviparous, laying 2 eggs in a clutch.

Eastern Tree Dtella ■ *Gehyra versicolor* SVL 50mm

DESCRIPTION Robust and somewhat dorsally flattened, with small, smooth scales and moderately long, slender tail. Pale brownish-grey above, with whitish spots and obscure darker variegations forming obscure transverse and longitudinal bars. Belly whitish. Digits expanded and pad-like, and with no webbing between third and fourth toes. **DISTRIBUTION** Central and eastern interior, including south-western NT, central and

south-western Qld, central and western NSW, northern-western Vic and eastern SA. **HABITAT AND HABITS** Found in woodland, shrubland, rocky outcrops and nearby houses. Arboreal and largely nocturnal, sheltering during the day under ground litter or loose bark, or within crevices in trees. Emerges at night to forage on open surfaces of trees or rocks in the understorey. Prey comprises invertebrates, including spiders, moths, cockroaches and termites, supplemented by the sap of wattles *Acacia* spp. Oviparous, laying a single brittle-shelled egg in a clutch, with older females laying up to 2 clutches in a year.

House Gecko ▪ *Hemidactylus frenatus* SVL 65mm
(Asian House Gecko; Common House Gecko; Pacific House Gecko)

DESCRIPTION Whitish, pinkish-brown or dark grey above, with series of tubercles along back and edges of tail, and either unpatterned or variably mottled with blackish flecks and lines. Underparts whitish. Appearance changeable depending on activity levels and exposure to light, with individuals being paler at night. All toes have claws. **DISTRIBUTION** Introduced, and successfully spreading throughout northern and eastern Australia, in association with human habitation. **HABITAT AND HABITS** Introduced in Australia. Natively arboreal, but now mostly in human buildings, with populations firmly established in woodland areas of the NT. Nocturnal, gathering in numbers near artificial light sources and feeding on insects, spiders and other small lizards. Oviparous, usually laying 2 brittle-shelled eggs in a clutch, with females capable of laying eggs every 3–4 weeks, although laying probably coincides with suitable conditions. Emits distinctive barking *chuck-chuck-chuck* sound.

Bynoe's Gecko ▪ *Heteronotia binoei* SVL 50mm
(Bynoe's Prickly Gecko)

DESCRIPTION Scales granular with scattered low dorsal tubercles, roughly aligned in longitudinal rows. Variable in dorsal colour and pattern, from pale grey to reddish-brown to blackish-brown, with lighter and darker speckling or spotting forming irregular transverse pattern. Belly whitish with fine darker mottling. Tail medium length and slender, with alternating light and dark cross-bands. **DISTRIBUTION** Throughout mainland Australia, with the exception of far south-west and south-east. **HABITAT AND HABITS** Found in dry, open forests, woodland, shrubland and disturbed areas. Nocturnal and mostly terrestrial, although it can forage arboreally under loose bark on dead trees, close to the ground, for various invertebrates. Shelters during the day under leaf litter, logs and other ground material, and in burrows of other animals. Oviparous, laying 2 brittle-shelled eggs in a clutch.

Examples of variable dorsal colouration and patterning between different individuals

Chevert's Gecko ▪ *Nactus cheverti* SVL 55mm
(Chevert Gecko; Southern Cape York Nactus)

DESCRIPTION Small, slender, rough-scaled gecko, with long, tapering tail. Typically brown to blackish above, with small paler spots and blotches on head and sides, and dark and light-edged transverse bands on back and tail. Lips paler and usually barred. Distinguished from Bynoe's Gecko (see p. 35), and **Eboric Island Gecko**

N. eboricensis, which is found further north, by small morphological characteristics. **DISTRIBUTION** South-eastern Cape York Peninsula and nearby islands, Qld. **HABITAT AND HABITS** Found in seasonally dry forests and woodland, where it is most numerous in rocky areas. Primarily terrestrial, although may climb the bases of trees and shrubs, and nocturnal, sheltering during the day under rocks, fallen logs and other ground debris. Forages for invertebrates among plants and leaf litter. Oviparous, laying 2 eggs in a clutch in late July and August. Secretive, quickly dashing for cover of foliage if disturbed.

Prickly Knob-tailed Gecko ▪ *Nephrurus asper* SVL 110mm
(Rough Knob-tail Gecko; Rough Knob-tail; Spiny Knob-tail Gecko)

DESCRIPTION Grey-brown to reddish-brown, with series of alternating rows across body made up of darker spots and more conspicuous paler spots, with each spot located on

cluster of rounded tubercles. These extend to large head, limbs and tail, which is very short and ends in an enlarged knob. **DISTRIBUTION** North-eastern and central Qld. **HABITAT AND HABITS** Occupies drier open woodland, forests and sandy heaths where rocky outcrops occur. Individuals shelter in crevices or in sandy soil under large rocks. Carnivorous, feeding primarily on invertebrates, including beetles, spiders and scorpions, but will also feed on smaller lizards and geckoes. Oviparous, laying up to 5 clutches in a year, each containing 1–2 parchment-shelled eggs.

Smooth Knob-tailed Gecko ■ *Nephrurus levis* SVL 100mm
(Three-lined Knob-tail; Common Knob-tailed Gecko)

DESCRIPTION Purplish-brown to orange-brown above, with series of dark and pale bars on rear of head and upper back, and varying numbers of whitish tubercles extending along sides of back and onto heart-shaped tail. Underparts white. Three subspecies, differing in intensity of colouration, size and number of tubercles. **DISTRIBUTION** Throughout arid and semi-arid Australia in broad band from WA central coast, through NT and SA, to western Qld and NSW.

HABITAT AND HABITS Occurs in range of habitats, including open woodland, scrubland, deserts and spinifex-covered sand plains. Nocturnal, sheltering in burrows during the day and emerging at night to forage. Carnivorous, feeding largely on invertebrates such as beetles, spiders, scorpions and centipedes, but will also take smaller reptiles. Water is obtained from food. Oviparous, laying 2 parchment-shelled eggs.

Broad-tailed Gecko ■ *Phyllurus platurus* SVL 90mm
(Southern Leaf-tailed Gecko)

DESCRIPTION Brown or grey above with cryptic darker brown and black speckling; original tail darker and occasionally with number of bands towards tip. White below. Head, body and tail flattened, and covered with numerous small, raised tubercles. Tail wide and either heart- or leaf-shaped. **DISTRIBUTION** Confined to Sydney Hawkesbury sandstone along central coast and ranges of NSW. **HABITAT AND HABITS** Found in sandstone caves and crevices, and nearby houses, within forests and heaths. Shelters,

often communally, in rock crevices during the day and emerges at night to forage. Insectivorous, feeding on small insects and spiders; extra fat reserves are stored in tail. The tail keeps moving when dropped, distracting potential predators while the gecko makes its escape; it is then regrown. Oviparous, laying 2 eggs per clutch.

Rough-throated Leaf-tail Gecko ▪ *Saltuarius salebrosus* SVL 150mm

DESCRIPTION Flattened wide body and cryptic pattern that gives excellent camouflage against a similarly coloured background. Olive-grey or brown above, with numerous darker flecks and 3–5 paler patches along back. Whitish below. Tail broad, with original

tail ending with short, slender tip. Common name is derived from prominent tubercles on throat. **DISTRIBUTION** Ranges in near coastal and inland areas of mid-eastern Qld. **HABITAT AND HABITS** Principally an inhabitant of rocky outcrops and escarpments within rainforests and scrubland, where it shelters within caves, crevices or tree hollows. Insectivorous, feeding mostly on small insects, with hunting taking place at night. Oviparous, laying 2 oval-shaped, soft-shelled eggs in a clutch. Eggs are buried in moist soil and hatch after about 100 days.

Southern Leaf-tailed Gecko ▪ *Saltuarius swaini* SVL 130mm

DESCRIPTION Brown or olive-grey above, with 3–5 paler cream-grey blotches along back and similarly coloured bands on broad, flat tail; narrower on regrown tails. Flat, triangular head, with several conspicuous large scales on snout, and series of transverse zigzag lines

between eyes and on rear of head and neck. Whitish below with varying amounts of brown speckling. Wide, flattened body and lichen-style patterning provides excellent camouflage. **DISTRIBUTION** Coastal ranges that run either side of Qld and NSW border. **HABITAT AND HABITS** Arboreal; often seen on trunks of trees, but will come to the ground to feed. Carnivorous, feeding primarily on invertebrates, but also preys on young of other gecko species. Forages at night. Oviparous, producing 1 or more clutches in a year, with 2 soft-shelled eggs per clutch.

Barking Gecko ▪ *Underwoodisaurus milii* SVL 90mm
(Thick-tailed Gecko)

DESCRIPTION Pink to purplish-brown above and white below, often with purplish wash. Upperparts decorated with numerous large, yellowish-white spots, covering tubercles, and original tail has several black-and-white bands; lacking, or greatly reduced, on regenerated tail. Tail narrow at base, then broadens out before tapering away to form carrot shape. Fingers and toes lack pads. **DISTRIBUTION** Wide ranging but not common.

From southern WA through SA and southern NT, into NSW, Vic and Qld. **HABITAT AND HABITS** Terrestrial. Found in rocky outcrops in wide variety of habitats, both wet and dry, including sclerophyll forests, woodland, heaths and shrubland, where it shelters in burrows or conceals itself under rocks during the day, emerging at night to hunt. Carnivorous, feeding on range of small invertebrates, including spiders, scorpions and beetles, and also on smaller lizards. Oviparous, laying 1 or more clutches of 2 soft-shelled eggs per clutch. When threatened, rises up and barks at an attacker.

Border Thick-tailed Gecko ▪ *Uvidicolus sphyrurus* SVL 70mm
(New England Thick-tailed Gecko; Granite Belt Thick-tailed Gecko)

DESCRIPTION Grey-brown, with numerous white spots and black speckling above, the spots forming loose transverse bands. Whitish below, occasionally with fine brown speckling. Original tail fat with long, tapering tip; blackish, with 4 conspicuous cream bands and numerous raised tubercles within paler rings. Regenerated tail mottled grey-brown and rounded.

DISTRIBUTION Granite highlands of northern NSW and southern Qld. **HABITAT AND HABITS** Found in undisturbed rocky areas within woodland. Nocturnal, sheltering during the day among rocks and under fallen timber, and emerging shortly after dusk to feed. Insectivorous, feeding primarily on insects and spiders. Oviparous, laying 2 eggs in a clutch. Appears to be largely solitary and generally uncommon; listed as Near Threatened on IUCN Red List.

Clouded Gecko ▪ *Amalosia jacovae* SVL 60mm
(Clouded Velvet Gecko)

DESCRIPTION Slender. Pale grey-brown above with darker narrow zigzag pattern along sides of back and down original tail, enclosing broad, pale zone that is fragmented by narrow bars. Cylindrical tail moderately long, tapered and slightly flattened. Whitish below, with noticeably larger scales than on back. Flanks and limbs have several indistinct

pale spots; webbing between third and fourth toes. **DISTRIBUTION** South-eastern Qld. Originally discovered on Mt Coot-tha, Brisbane. North to around Gladstone and Fraser Island, west to Toowoomba. **HABITAT AND HABITS** Occupies both wet and dry, open eucalypt forests, woodland, coastal heaths, rocky outcrops and houses in adjacent urban areas. Mainly arboreal, using enlarged pads on toes to assist in climbing. Insectivorous, feeding on insects and other invertebrates. Oviparous, with 2 eggs laid in clutch.

Lesueur's Velvet Gecko ▪ *Amalosia lesueurii* SVL 80mm
(Lesueur's Gecko)

DESCRIPTION Moderately large. Grey-brown above with broad, zigzag, diamond-shaped band running along length of back and original tail, occasionally visible only as series of dark-edged blotches; regrown tail mottled grey-brown. Tail moderately long and flattened. Sides and legs darker and mottled with numerous paler blotches and finer flecking.

Whitish below, with finer scales. **DISTRIBUTION** Coast and ranges of far south-eastern Qld and eastern NSW, south to Kiama. **HABITAT AND HABITS** Often found in caves and rock crevices in dry sclerophyll forests and rocky outcrops, favouring sandstone and granite, and in adjacent human structures. Shelters during the day in tight spaces, emerging at night to forage. Insectivorous, hunting on open rock faces and in adjacent leaf litter for range of invertebrates, including crickets, spiders and cockroaches. Oviparous, laying 2 soft-shelled eggs in a clutch.

Zigzag Velvet Gecko ■ *Amalosia rhombifer* SVL 75mm
(Zig-zag Gecko)

DESCRIPTION Grey-brown above, with broad paler band on tail and back, edged darker in notched zigzag pattern, and dividing at neck into 2 stripes that pass over each eye. Original tail long, slender and mostly cylindrical. Sides and limbs have numerous dark brown spots, and head has distinct dark brown stripe running from tip of snout and through each eye. Toes lack webbing between third and fourth toes. **DISTRIBUTION** Northern Australia, including north-east WA, northern NT and northern Qld, and an isolated introduced population in Alice Springs NT. **HABITAT AND HABITS** Found in most wooded habitats throughout tropical Australia, and frequently seen in buildings. Nocturnal and largely arboreal. Shelters during the day in tree hollows or leaf litter, or under loose bark. Forages in trees for variety of invertebrates. Oviparous, laying 2 eggs per clutch.

Fat-tailed Diplodactylus ■ *Diplodactylus conspicillatus* SVL 65mm
(Fat-tailed Gecko; Variable Fat-tailed Gecko; Burrow-plug Gecko)

DESCRIPTION Stout, with short, bulbous tail and pale stripe running from tip of snout to front of eye. Pale sandy-brown to reddish above, with varied darker brown spots and streaks; whitish below. Paler spots along sides and on legs, and short toes tipped with white. Original tail has large scales and tubercles forming rings. **DISTRIBUTION** Central coast and inland WA, NT, northern SA, western Qld and north-western NSW. **HABITAT AND HABITS** Found in wide variety of arid to semi-arid habitats across its range, including shrubland, woodland, stony ranges and sandy spinifex grassland. Terrestrial and nocturnal, sheltering during the day in small burrow and using its enlarged tail, which stores fat, to seal the hole in the burrow against intruders and keep in moisture. Feeds almost exclusively on termites. Oviparous, laying 2 parchment-shelled eggs in a clutch.

Eastern Fat-tailed Gecko ■ *Diplodactylus platyurus* SVL 60mm

DESCRIPTION Largely similar to Fat-tailed Diplodactylus (see p. 41), with which it was considered to be synonymous until 2014, but can be distinguished by absence of dark stripe from snout to front of eye. Generally pale to reddish-brown above, the sides heavily spotted with darker brown, and pale stripe, or series of blotches, along length of back and tail. **DISTRIBUTION** Arid to semi-arid regions of north-eastern SA, north-western NSW and Qld. **HABITAT AND HABITS** Found in wooded habitats, including riverine

vegetation, and arid stony and sandy areas. Terrestrial and nocturnal, occupying disused burrow of large spider during the day, and using its enlarged tail to seal the hole in the burrow. Also shelters in cracks in the ground. Feeds primarily on termites, but will take other small invertebrates. Oviparous, laying 2 parchment-shelled eggs in a clutch.

Tessellated Gecko ■ *Diplodactylus tessellatus* SVL 50mm

DESCRIPTION Highly variable pattern. Light grey to rich reddish-brown above, with variety of pale spots, blotches and transverse stripes. Spots on midline of back and tail often in pairs. Tail short, plump and slightly flattened. Underparts whitish with a number

of darker patches. **DISTRIBUTION** Arid and semi-arid regions of north-eastern SA, south-eastern NT, south-eastern Qld, western NSW and north-western Vic. **HABITAT AND HABITS** Occurs in variety of wooded and open habitats, including floodplains of inland waterways, cracking claypans and black soil plains. Terrestrial and nocturnal, sheltering on the ground in soil crevices or disused spider holes, or under logs. Forages at night for insects and other small invertebrates, including grasshoppers, spiders and high numbers of termites. Oviparous, laying 2 parchment-shelled eggs in a clutch, with 1 or 2 clutches in a year.

Eastern Stone Gecko ■ *Diplodactylus vittatus* SVL 55mm
(Wood Gecko; Stone Gecko)

DESCRIPTION Grey to dark brown above with paler, dark-edged, zigzagging or straight stripe from neck to tip of original tail; absent on regrown part. Top of head pale, often with darker centre. Sides often with series of pale spots, usually with no darker edging. Tail moderately short, just over half of SVL, and plump. Paler underneath.

DISTRIBUTION In broad coastal and inland band from central Qld, through NSW, Vic and into eastern SA; absent from southern coastline. **HABITAT AND HABITS** Occupies arid, sandy bushland, open scrub, tall, open forests and cooler wet forests, where it shelters in disused spider burrows, or under rocks or fallen timber. Carnivorous, feeding on invertebrates, including spiders, cockroaches, beetles and other small arthropods. Oviparous, laying 1–2 parchment-shelled eggs.

Gibber Gecko ■ *Lucasium byrnei* SVL 55mm
(Byrne's Gecko)

DESCRIPTION Pale brown to dark reddish-brown above with 4–5 large dorsal blotches, and numerous smaller pale spots and darker tubercles. Whitish below. Tail tapering and somewhat cylindrical, measuring about three-quarters of length of body when fully grown. **DISTRIBUTION** Interior of south-eastern Australian mainland, including far south-western NT, eastern SA, western NSW and far south-western Qld.

HABITAT AND HABITS Occurs in open woodland, chenopod shrubland and gibber plains (note that 'gibber' is an Aboriginal word for stone from the Dharuk language spoken around Sydney). Nocturnal and terrestrial, sheltering during heat of the day in deep soil crevices, small burrows or leaf litter, and emerging at night to forage for small invertebrates, including spiders, crickets, ants and termites. Oviparous, laying 2 parchment-shelled eggs per clutch.

Beaded Gecko ■ *Lucasium damaeum* SVL 55mm

DESCRIPTION Reddish-brown above with either pale brown, ragged vertebral stripe, or series of large blotches along back, and numerous paler spots, becoming whitish on sides. Tail long and tapering, with several larger paler blotches. Head slightly paler and with dark

line passing through each eye from snout. Whitish below. **DISTRIBUTION** Inland regions of southern Australian mainland, including far south-western WA, southern NT, SA, north-western Vic, central and western NSW, and south-western Qld. **HABITAT AND HABITS** Found in drier woodland, shrubland or grassland on sandy or clay soils. Largely nocturnal, sheltering during the day in small disused burrows and emerging at dusk to forage for small invertebrates, including termites, spders, crickets and beetles. Oviparous, laying 1–2 parchment-shelled eggs in a clutch.

Box-patterned Gecko ■ *Lucasium steindachneri* SVL 55mm
(Steindachner's Ground Gecko)

DESCRIPTION Slender, with relatively large head and moderately long tail that measures around two-thirds of length of body. Pale brown to reddish-brown above with pale stripes above each eye, which meet at nape and form broad vertebral stripe that ends at base of tail, and encloses 3 elongated oval darker patches along back and rump. Sides have

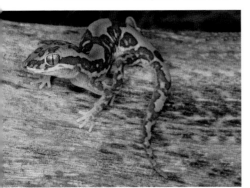

paler spots and tail has irregular pale blotches. Underparts whitish. **DISTRIBUTION** Arid to semi-arid eastern Australia, from northern Qld to western NSW and north-eastern SA. **HABITAT AND HABITS** Occupies drier forests, mallee and grassy woodland with cracking soils. Terrestrial and nocturnal, sheltering during the day in small, disused burrows, and emerging at dusk to forage for small invertebrates, including termites, spiders, crickets and beetles. Oviparous, laying 1–2 parchment-shelled eggs in a clutch.

Robust Velvet Gecko ■ *Nebulifera robusta* SVL 85mm

DESCRIPTION Grey with large, dark-edged, rectangular pale blotches extending from head onto flattened plump tail. Toes expanded to form pads; underside covered with 2 rows of large plates, including large circular pair under tip. **DISTRIBUTION** Central-eastern Australian coastline and associated areas inland, from central Qld to north-western NSW. **HABITAT AND HABITS** Found in dry forests and woodland, and adjacent buildings. Arboreal and nocturnal, sheltering during the day in tree hollows or exfoliating bark. Emerges at night to feed on small invertebrates, including insects and spiders, on branches and trunk of tree that it lives on. Oviparous, with 2 parchment-shelled eggs in a clutch, and up to 3 clutches per year.

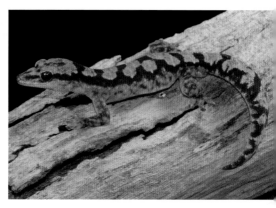

Northern Velvet Gecko ■ *Oedura castelnaui* SVL 90mm

DESCRIPTION Orange to yellowish-brown or purplish-brown above, with contrasting whitish, cream or yellowish, broad transverse bands from nape to tip of original tail. This varies in thickness, but is normally fat and slightly flattened, and is used as a fat-storage organ. Whitish below. **DISTRIBUTION** Cape York Peninsula, Qld. **HABITAT AND HABITS** Found in dry forests and woodland, and rocky outcrops. Mostly arboreal, sheltering under loose bark or ground litter. Emerges at night to feed on small invertebrates, including spiders and insects, as well as smaller geckoes. Oviparous, with 2 parchment-shelled eggs in a clutch, and occasionally 6 or more clutches per year.

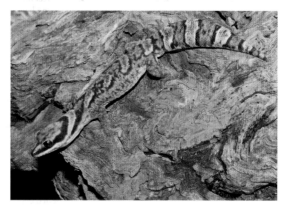

Northern Spotted Velvet Gecko ■ *Oedura coggeri* SVL 70mm

DESCRIPTION Smooth-scaled, dorsally depressed body, with broad, moderately flattened tail that tapers sharply towards tip. Yellowish-brown above with dark-edged cream to olive-grey blotches that form irregular transverse pattern. Head has some darker streaks and mottling, and broad dark stripe passing through base of eye, edged paler on lower, and occasionally upper, edge. Limbs have large, dark-edged spots. Underparts whitish. Young

darker than adults, and more purplish-brown with yellow spots. **DISTRIBUTION** North-eastern Qld. **HABITAT AND HABITS** Occurs in rocky outcrops in drier woodland. Nocturnal, sheltering during the day under exfoliating rock, in rock crevices or under bark of fallen trees, and emerging at night to forage on open rock faces for small invertebrates. Oviparous, laying 2 eggs in a clutch.

Marbled Velvet Gecko ■ *Oedura marmorata* SVL 100mm
(Inland Marbled Velvet Gecko)

DESCRIPTION Highly variable in colour, pattern and body shape. Generally purplish-brown above, with 5 or 6 narrow yellowish transverse bands between nape and base of tail, or with numerous pale blotches and spots. Head can be largely uniform or with paler stripes or blotches. Tail similarly patterned to body, but can be either slender or plump and

moderately flattened. Underparts whitish. **DISTRIBUTION** Broad range throughout Australian mainland, excluding far east, south-east, north-west, and southern parts of SA and WA. **HABITAT AND HABITS** Favours grassy woodland in more humid regions, and rocky outcrops among spinifex grassland in arid areas of central Australia. Nocturnal and largely arboreal, sheltering during the day under exfoliating rock, in rock crevices or caves, or under loose bark, emerging at night to forage on open rock faces for small invertebrates. Oviparous, laying 2 eggs in a clutch.

Ocellated Velvet Gecko ■ *Oedura monilis* SVL 85mm

DESCRIPTION Moderately robust with long, slightly flattened tail. Yellowish-brown above with darker purplish-brown mottling and dark-edged pale spots, in 5 or 6 pairs, or with individual pairs pooling together in centre of back, from nape to base of tail. Head has some darker streaks and mottling. Broad dark stripe passes through base of eye, from snout to nape. Original tail has similar patterning, but regenerated tail mottled. Whitish below. **DISTRIBUTION** Great Dividing Range of eastern Australia from central NSW to northern Qld. **HABITAT AND HABITS** Found in dry forests and woodland. Arboreal and nocturnal, sheltering during the day under loose bark or in crevices in trees, and emerging at night to forage for small invertebrates, which are supplemented to a degree with plant materials, including sap. Oviparous, laying 2 parchment-shelled eggs in a clutch.

Southern Spotted Velvet Gecko ■ *Oedura tryoni* SVL 85mm
(Tryon's Velvet Gecko)

DESCRIPTION Slender, with slightly flattened body, long, slender tail and strongly spotted pattern. Yellowish-brown to dull purplish-brown or reddish-brown above, with small, dark-edged pale spots on body, limbs and original tail. Underparts whitish. **DISTRIBUTION** Coast and adjacent ranges of eastern Australia, from south-eastern Qld to north-eastern NSW. **HABITAT AND HABITS** Occupies rocky habitats, including granite outcrops, and dry forests, and tolerant of cooler climates at higher altitudes. Nocturnal, sheltering during the day under exfoliating rock slabs or in crevices, and emerging at night to forage on open rock faces, using retractable claws that allow pads on digits to expand for better grip, for small invertebrates, including crickets and moths. Oviparous, laying 2 parchment-shelled eggs in a clutch, occasionally with several clutches laid in a year.

Giant Tree Gecko ■ *Pseudothecadactylus australis* SVL 130mm

DESCRIPTION Large, robust gecko with long, slender tail, which has modified hair-covered scales on underside of tip that provide extra grip when climbing. Brown or dull greenish-grey above with fine darker mottling and larger pale, dark-edged patches, forming

obscure transverse bands, on nape, back and original tail. Toes have large pads. Underparts whitish. **DISTRIBUTION** Far north-eastern Qld. **HABITAT AND HABITS** Occupies rainforests and tropical woodland, through to adjoining habitats such as mangroves and creek lines. Arboreal and nocturnal, sheltering during the day in tree hollows, and emerging at night to forage on trunks and tree branches for invertebrates, which are supplemented to a degree with plant materials, including sap. Oviparous, laying average of 2 eggs in a clutch. If disturbed, often emits a call from its hiding spot.

Brigalow Beaked Gecko ■ *Rhynchoedura mentalis* SVL 50mm

DESCRIPTION Small gecko with long, slender, rounded body and short, pointed, 'beak-like' snout. Reddish-brown with darker mottling above, and numerous whitish or yellow spots along back, sides and original tail. Head paler with greyish mottling and obscure pale

streak from front of eye to rear of mouth. Underparts white and feet have narrow, tapering digits. **DISTRIBUTION** Arid to semi-arid regions of central south-eastern Qld. **HABITAT AND HABITS** Found in open, grassy woodland, Mulga shrubland and grassland. Nocturnal and terrestrial, sheltering in small, disused burrows or soil cracks, or under leaf litter, feeding at night on small invertebrates, including mainly termites, spiders and ants. Oviparous, laying 2 parchment-shelled eggs in a clutch.

Eastern Beaked Gecko ■ *Rhynchoedura ormsbyi* SVL 50mm

DESCRIPTION Small gecko with long, slender body and short, pointed, 'beak-like' snout. Reddish-brown with darker mottling above, and numerous whitish or yellow spots along back, sides and original tail. Head paler with greyish mottling and obscure pale streak from front of eye to rear of mouth, and white upper eyelid. Underparts white and feet have narrow, tapering digits. **DISTRIBUTION** Arid to semi-arid regions of central inland eastern Australia, from southern NSW to south-eastern Qld. **HABITAT AND**

HABITS Occurs in open, grassy woodland, shrubland and grassland. Nocturnal and terrestrial, sheltering in small, disused burrows or soil cracks, or under leaf litter, and feeding at night on small invertebrates, including mainly termites, spiders and ants. Oviparous, laying 2 parchment-shelled eggs in a clutch.

Southern Spiny-tailed Gecko ■ *Strophurus intermedius* SVL 65mm
(Spiny-tailed Gecko)

DESCRIPTION Pale grey to dark brownish-grey above, cryptically patterned with small black blotches, flecks and broader wavy lines on body, head, limbs and tail. Back and tail have raised orange-brown tubercles, more loosely arranged on back but forming 2 more structured longitudinal rows down tail. Small spines above eye. Fingers and toes have enlarged pads and small, retractile claws. Underparts pale grey with darker speckling. **DISTRIBUTION** Southern and central Australian mainland, from central NSW, through

north-western Vic, north-eastern SA and southern NT to south-eastern WA. **HABITAT AND HABITS** Found in dry forests, woodland and grassland. Generally arboreal in wooded areas, becoming more terrestrial and occupying tussocks in arid grassland. Nocturnal, sheltering during the day under flaking bark or in spinifex tussocks, and emerging at night to feed on small invertebrates. Oviparous, laying 2 eggs in a clutch. If threatened, capable of squirting a thick, sticky, repellent fluid from its tail.

Kristin's Spiny-tailed Gecko ■ *Strophurus krisalys* SVL 70mm

DESCRIPTION Pale to dark grey above, with 4 longitudinal rows of raised orange-brown tubercles, and occasionally with darker grey wavy vertebral pattern that extends down original tail. Tail medium in length and slender, with 2 rows of larger spiny tubercles; similar spiny tubercles above eyes. Fingers and toes have enlarged pads and small, retractile

claws. Underparts whitish with darker speckling. Distinguished from **Northern Spiny-tailed Gecko** S. *ciliaris* by its dark blue mouth lining. **DISTRIBUTION** Gulf country of western Qld. **HABITAT AND HABITS** Found in dry woodland, grassland (including spinifex) and shrubland. Semiarboreal and nocturnal, preferring to perch in foliage of small trees and shrubs, and occasionally spinifex, where it feeds on invertebrates. Oviparous, laying 2 leathery-shelled eggs in a clutch. If threatened, capable of squirting a thick, sticky, repellent fluid from its tail.

Phasmid Striped Gecko ■ *Strophurus taeniatus* SVL 50mm
(White-striped Gecko)

DESCRIPTION Small, slender-bodied gecko, with gradually tapering, cylindrical tail

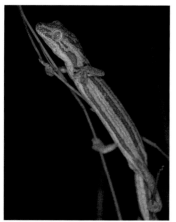

and thin limbs. Pale grey to brown above, with whitish, brown and yellow alternating longitudinal stripes from head to tip of tail. Back and side pattern continued on belly. Tail about 80 per cent as long as SVL, and prehensile. **DISTRIBUTION** Northern Australia from north-western Qld, through the inland of northern NT, to coast of north-western WA. **HABITAT AND HABITS** Found in seasonally dry woodland, spinifex grassland and shrubland. Largely terrestrial and nocturnal; believed to shelter during the day under spinifex clumps, emerging at night to feed on small invertebrates. Also feeds in early morning and late afternoon (crepuscular), and moves with slow, jerky steps. Oviparous, laying 2 leathery-shelled eggs in a clutch. If threatened, capable of squirting a thick, sticky, repellent fluid from tail.

Golden-tailed Gecko ■ *Strophurus taenicauda* SVL 70mm
(Golden Spiny-tailed Gecko)

DESCRIPTION Very attractive gecko with large, bright red, orange or greyish eyes, and long tail, often with golden-yellow longitudinal stripe. White to pale grey above, cryptically patterned with small black blotches and flecks on body, head and limbs. Eyes have vertically elliptical pupils, and inside of mouth has dark blue lining. Fingers and toes have enlarged pads and small retractile claws. Underparts pale grey with darker speckling. **DISTRIBUTION** The Brigalow Belt of South-eastern Qld. **HABITAT AND HABITS** Occurs in dry, open forests and woodland, particularly those dominated by ironbark, cypress, brigalow or ribbon gums. Arboreal and nocturnal, sheltering during the day under loose bark and in hollow branches, or among foliage, and emerging at night to forage for small invertebrates. Oviparous, laying 2 parchment-shelled eggs in a clutch. If threatened, secretes sticky fluid from pores on tail, which can irritate the eyes. Classified as Near Threatened by the IUCN, due to habitat loss and fragmentation.

Eye colour is variable, being greyish, orange or bright red

Eastern Spiny-tailed Gecko ■ *Strophurus williamsi* SVL 60mm

DESCRIPTION Pale to dark grey above, cryptically patterned with small black blotches and flecks, and with numerous pale brown raised tubercles. Tail moderately long, slender and with 4 rows of larger spiny tubercles. Fingers and toes have enlarged pads and small, retractile claws. Underparts whitish with darker speckling. **DISTRIBUTION** Coast and inland of eastern Australia, from northern Qld, through central and eastern NSW, to south-eastern SA. Absent from Cape York Peninsula and south-east. **HABITAT AND HABITS** Found in dry ironbark forests, woodland and shrubland, where it resides among foliage and smaller branches. Nocturnal, spending the day on a small branch, relying on its cryptic patterning for camouflage, and emerging at night to forage among the foliage or on the ground for small invertebrates. Oviparous, laying 2 parchment-shelled eggs in a clutch. If threatened, secretes a sticky fluid from pores on tail, which can irritate the eyes.

Mallee Worm-lizard ■ *Aprasia inaurita* SVL 135mm
(Red-tailed Worm-lizard; Pink-nosed Worm-lizard)

DESCRIPTION Slender, 'snake-like', smooth-scaled lizard, with no front limbs, and short, blunt tail that is shorter than body length (SVL). Pale yellowish-brown to grey-brown above and whitish below, with reddish-brown head and neck, and reddish-orange tail.

Snout rounded when viewed from above, and external ear openings absent. Hindlimbs reduced to small flaps. **DISTRIBUTION** Central southern mainland Australia, from south-eastern WA, through southern SA, to north-western Vic and south-western NSW. **HABITAT AND HABITS** Semi-arid to arid woodland (including mallee), where it burrows through sandy soils, feeding mainly on eggs of ants, but also on larvae and adults of black ants, as well as some termites. Diurnal, sheltering underground during the day, in dense leaf litter or ants' nests. Oviparous, laying 2 elongated parchment-shelled eggs in a clutch.

Pink-tailed Legless Lizard ■ *Aprasia parapulchella* SVL 150mm
(Pink-tailed Worm-lizard)

DESCRIPTION Slender, 'snake-like', smooth-scaled lizard, with no front limbs and moderately long tail that is almost same length as body length (SVL). Pale grey to greyish-brown above, with small blackish markings on each scale forming longitudinal lines, dark brown head and pinkish-red tail. Snout rounded when viewed from above and side, external ear openings absent and hindlimbs reduced to small flaps. Underparts whitish.

DISTRIBUTION Ranges of south-eastern mainland Australia, from central-eastern NSW to central Vic. **HABITAT AND HABITS** Found in native grassland with little or no leaf litter, on soils with numerous semi-exposed rocks, where it burrows under rocks, feeding mainly on eggs of ants, but also on larvae and adults of black ants, as well as some termites. Diurnal, sheltering during the day typically within ants' nests under rocks. Oviparous, laying 2 elongated parchment-shelled eggs in a clutch.

Marble-faced Delma ■ *Delma australis* SVL 90mm
(Marble-faced Worm-lizard; Southern Legless Lizard)

DESCRIPTION Slender, 'snake-like' lizard with blunt, rounded snout and tail around twice as long as body (SVL). Brown to rich reddish-brown above and greyish-white below, with variegated blackish markings on top of head and along underparts. Sides of head and neck have series of distinct vertical blackish bars. Forelimbs absent and hindlimbs reduced to flaps. **DISTRIBUTION** Southern and south-western mainland, from western WA coastline, through SA and southern NT, to western Vic and NSW. **HABITAT AND HABITS** Occurs in various semi-arid to arid habitats, including woodland, mallee, chenopod shrubland, heaths and spinifex grassland, where it shelters at night under rocks and fallen timber, and within grass tussocks. Largely terrestrial, but can climb within spinifex tussocks, foraging in sandy soil, soil cracks and leaf litter, and perhaps within tussocks, for invertebrates including spiders. Oviparous, laying 2 elongated parchment-shelled eggs in a clutch.

Unbanded Delma ■ *Delma butleri* SVL 100mm
(Butler's Legless Lizard; Spinifex Snake-lizard)

DESCRIPTION Slender, 'snake-like' lizard with long tail that is around 3 times as long as body (SVL). Uniformly grey-brown to dark greenish-brown above, with each scale having blackish rear edge, giving faint reticulated pattern. Sides of head and neck generally have paler blotches. Underparts usually white or pale yellow, but can rapidly change to bright yellow, perhaps in response to stress. Forelimbs absent and hindlimbs reduced to flaps.

DISTRIBUTION Southern and western Australia, from central western WA coast, through central SA, to western NSW and north-western Vic. **HABITAT AND HABITS** Found in variety of arid to semi-arid habitats across its range, but restricted to mallee woodland with Triodia grassland in south-east of distribution. Active at any time of the day or night, foraging in and around tussocks or on the ground for small invertebrates, including spiders, crickets and grasshoppers. When not active, shelters in spinifex tussocks. Oviparous, laying 2 elongated parchment-shelled eggs in a clutch.

Many-lined Delma ■ *Delma impar* SVL 95mm
(Striped Legless Lizard)

DESCRIPTION Slender, 'snake-like' lizard with conspicuous external ear openings and long tail that is about 3 times as long as body (SVL). Pale grey-brown above, darker on head, usually with longitudinal blackish-brown and whitish stripes, and lines of spots on sides of body, starting above ear and ending on tail. Underparts whitish. Forelimbs absent and hindlimbs reduced to flaps.

DISTRIBUTION Inland south-eastern Australian mainland from central eastern NSW, through southern and central Vic, to far south-western SA. **HABITAT AND HABITS** Occurs in open, grassy woodland and grassland, generally dominated by native grassy tussocks, but also in disturbed grassland, where it feeds mainly on moth larvae, but also on other small invertebrates, including spiders, crickets and grasshoppers. Shelters underground or under rocks and fallen timber. Oviparous, laying 2 elongated parchment-shelled eggs in a clutch.

Patternless Delma ■ *Delma inornata* SVL 135mm
(Common Delma; Plain Delma; Olive Legless Lizard)

DESCRIPTION Slender, rough-scaled body with large external ear openings, and tail around 3 times length of body (SVL). Conspicuous yellowish wash to face and throat. Body uniformly greyish to olive-brown above, darker on head, with dark margins on scales giving reticulated appearance. Belly whitish. Forelimbs absent and hindlimbs reduced to moderately sized flaps. **DISTRIBUTION** South-eastern mainland Australia, from inland south-eastern Qld, through central NSW, to southern Vic and south-western

SA coastlines. **HABITAT AND HABITS** Occurs in variety of habitats, including wet and dry forests, woodland, mallee, shrubland and open grass plains, but generally associated with grassy areas. Active from dawn to dusk, foraging on the ground and within grassy tussocks for small invertebrates, including spiders, cockroaches, grasshoppers and moths. When inactive, burrows deep underground, but shelters at night under logs, rocks or other ground debris. Oviparous, laying 2 elongated parchment-shelled eggs in a clutch.

Leaden Delma ■ *Delma plebeia* SVL 120 mm
(Basalt Delma; Common Delma [Qld])

DESCRIPTION Slender, rough-scaled body with large external ear openings, tail around 3 times length of body (SVL), and often with conspicuous darker barring on lips. Uniform grey-brown, or brown above and white below, occasionally with reddish-brown wash or faint stripes on neck and anterior sides, generally brighter in younger individuals. Forelimbs absent and hindlimbs reduced to flaps. **DISTRIBUTION** Central-eastern mainland, from coastal south-eastern Qld, to inland north-eastern NSW.

HABITAT AND HABITS Found in dry forests, grassy woodland, heaths and spinifex sandplains, and adjacent suburban gardens, where it shelters under leaf litter, fallen timber or other ground debris. Nocturnal, foraging on the ground and in low vegetation for small invertebrates. Oviparous, laying 2 elongated parchment-shelled eggs in a clutch.

Excitable Delma ■ *Delma tincta* SVL 85mm (females larger than males)

DESCRIPTION Slender, smooth-scaled lizard, with tail around 3 times length of body (SVL). Grey-brown to reddish-brown above, sometimes with glossy black on top of head and normally 3 distinct, narrow, cream-yellow transverse bands, more distinct in younger individuals and fading with age. Underparts white. Forelimbs absent and hindlimbs reduced to moderately sized flaps. **DISTRIBUTION** Arid to semi-arid regions of northern and western NSW, central SA and southern-central WA, northwards to coast of northern Australia. **HABITAT AND HABITS** Found in variety of habitats, including wet coastal

forests, dry forests, tree-lined watercourses, shrubland, sandy spinifex deserts and rocky outcrops, where it can be active at any time of the day or night, foraging on the ground in open areas for small invertebrates, including spiders. When not foraging, shelters under rocks or fallen timber, or in vegetation. Oviparous, laying 2 elongated parchment-shelled eggs in a clutch.

Burton's Snake-lizard ■ *Lialis burtonis* SVL 270mm
(Burton's Legless Lizard)

DESCRIPTION Robust, smooth-scaled, 'snake-like' lizard. Elongated head with long, pointed, wedge-shaped snout, and short tail. Highly variable in colour, including grey, yellow, reddish-brown or blackish above, with or without longitudinal stripes or broken lines on body, and conspicuous white or cream stripe on sides of head and neck. Underparts covered with variable amounts of small dark and pale flecks. Forelimbs absent and hindlimbs reduced to tiny flaps. Eyes have vertical pupils. **DISTRIBUTION** Throughout mainland Australia and islands of Torres Strait. Absent from far south-west and far south-east. **HABITAT AND HABITS** Occupies wide range of habitats, including forests,

woodland, heaths, shrubland and spinifex deserts. Active by day and night, foraging on the ground almost exclusively for smaller lizards, which are supplemented with other small reptiles and invertebrates. Oviparous, laying 1–3 parchment-shelled eggs in a clutch.

Brigalow Scaly-foot ■ *Paradelma orientalis* SVL 180mm
(Queensland Snake-lizard)

DESCRIPTION Moderately robust, smooth-scaled, glossy, 'snake-like' lizard, with tail twice length of body. Brownish to bluish-grey above, with milky sheen, and with thick cream to yellow bar across nape, which is bordered behind with thinner blackish bar. Belly whitish. Forelimbs absent and hindlimbs reduced to small flaps. **DISTRIBUTION** Brigalow Belt of south-eastern Qld, and near coastal islands. **HABITAT AND HABITS** Found in open forest and woodland, generally dominated by Brigalow and other *Acacia*

spp., where it shelters under rocks (generally sandstone), logs and loose bark, or in leaf litter or grassy tussocks. Mostly nocturnal, foraging predominantly on the ground for small invertebrates, such as spiders, but also climbing trees to feed on sap. When provoked, mimics a small venomous snake by rearing up head and forebody, flicking tongue in and out, and even pretending to strike.

Common Scaly-foot ■ *Pygopus lepidopodus* SVL 250mm
(Southern Scaly-foot; Common Scaly Foot)

DESCRIPTION Moderately robust, 'snake-like' lizard, with strongly keeled dorsal scales and tail twice length of body (SVL). Highly variable, with colours including uniform greyish-brown, brown or reddish-brown above, more greyish on head and tail, or patterned with numerous dark, pale-edged scales, giving longitudinally streaked or striped pattern. Head and neck occasionally have conspicuous, longitudinally aligned streaks and paler lips, with darker barring. Underparts pale grey with darker spots and flecks. Forelimbs absent and hindlimbs reduced to large flaps. **DISTRIBUTION** Southern mainland Australia from south-eastern Qld, through eastern and central NSW, Vic and southern SA, to central-western WA. **HABITAT AND HABITS** Occurs in wide variety of dry and wet habitats, including coastal forests, woodland, coastal heaths, arid shrubland and grassland, with a rocky sandstone or sandy substrate. Largely terrestrial, foraging in and around low vegetation predominantly for spiders, but also for other invertebrates. Oviparous, laying 2 elongated, parchment-shelled eggs in a clutch.

Eastern Hooded Scaly-foot ■ *Pygopus schraderi* SVL 200mm
(Eastern Scaly-foot)

DESCRIPTION Moderately robust, 'snake-like' lizard, with strongly keeled dorsal scales, blackish blotch under eye and tail twice length of body (SVL). Variable in colour. Pale grey or yellowish-brown to reddish-brown above, darker and hooded on head (more noticeable in younger individuals), and with darker brown and paler mottling forming complex reticulated pattern along back and tail. Belly whitish to light grey, occasionally with some darker streaks and flecks. Forelimbs absent and hindlimbs reduced to large flaps. **DISTRIBUTION** Drier parts of eastern Australia, including western NT, western SA, north-western Vic, southern and western NSW, and Qld (except Cape York Peninsula and south-east). **HABITAT AND HABITS** Occurs in wide variety of drier habitats, including forests, woodland, shrubland, grassland and stony plains, where it is generally crepuscular and nocturnal, foraging on the ground for insects and other small invertebrates. Oviparous, laying 2 elongated, parchment-shelled eggs in soil. When provoked, mimics a small venomous snake by rearing up head and forebody, flicking tongue in and out, and even pretending to strike.

Eastern Three-lined Skink ■ *Acritoscincus duperreyi* SVL 70mm
(Three-lined Skink)

DESCRIPTION Smooth scaled, slender skink with medium-length tail. Silvery-grey to greyish-brown above, with blackish vertebral stripe and prominent thin white stripe on each side. Belly whitish, usually with orange flush on throat. **DISTRIBUTION** South-

western Australia, including Tas and islands in Bass Strait, from Adelaide and Kangaroo Island SA, through Victoria, to south-eastern NSW and Tas. **HABITAT AND HABITS** Semiarboreal; found in most grassy habitats and trees. Diurnal and feeds on invertebrates. Oviparous, laying around 5 eggs in a clutch, and occasionally doing so in association with other females of same species.

Red-throated Skink ■ *Acritoscincus platynotus* SVL 70mm
(Fence Skink)

DESCRIPTION Smooth scaled, with tail longer than body. Top of head coppery, and often with an orange flush on throat. Silvery-grey to greyish-brown above, with black vertebral

stripe and thin white stripe on outer side from snout to tail. Belly whitish. **DISTRIBUTION** South-east mainland, from far south-eastern Qld, through eastern NSW, to north-eastern Vic. **HABITAT AND HABITS** Found in dry forests, woodland, grassland and heaths, often in association with rocky outcrops, typically on slopes. Feeds mainly on invertebrates such as ants, and eggs of other skinks. Oviparous, laying up to 10 eggs in a clutch.

Highlands Forest-skink ■ *Anepischetosia maccoyi* SVL 50mm

DESCRIPTION Smooth, glossy scaled skink with elongated body and narrow, tapering tail that is same length as body (SVL). Short forelimbs and hindlimbs, all with 5 digits. Rich brown to dark greyish-brown, with light and dark flecks on dorsal, and narrow blackish-brown vertebral stripe, usually broken or obscure and sometimes with yellowish-brown bar above. Sides light grey or brown, with light and dark mottling. Brown spots on white throat. Lips white with black bars, and belly cream to yellow. **DISTRIBUTION** South-eastern Australian mainland, from western Vic to south-eastern NSW. **HABITAT AND HABITS** Rainforests and wet forests, where it is found in dense leaf litter or under rocks and logs. Nocturnal, emerging at dusk to feed within moist soil. Oviparous, laying 4 eggs in a clutch.

Short-necked Worm-skink ■ *Anomalopus brevicollis* SVL 80mm

DESCRIPTION Long, slender, 'worm-like' skink with short neck and no limbs. Body pale brown above with darker bluish-brown on head and tail. Dark speckles on each body scale form dotted longitudinal stripes. Underparts whitish, with brown spots on throat. Snout rounded, and hidden ear openings. **DISTRIBUTION** Coast and ranges of central eastern Qld. **HABITAT AND HABITS** Secretive burrowing skink found in variety of habitats, including monsoon rainforests, vine thickets and dry forests, and generally more abundant in areas where neighbouring habitats overlap. Shelters in crevices, or under rocks or fallen timber, and burrows within leaf litter and soft soils, where it is thought to feed on small arthropods. Oviparous, laying up to 2 eggs per clutch.

Speckled Worm-skink ■ *Anomalopus gowi* SVL 110mm

DESCRIPTION Long, slender, 'worm-like' skink, with limbs absent. Body light greyish-brown to rich brown above, occasionally with darker brown band across head, and blackish tip on tail. Numerous darker spots, becoming large and more concentrated on tail. Snout

rounded and external ear openings absent, with only shallow depressions visible. **DISTRIBUTION** North-eastern Qld, south of Cape York Peninsula. **HABITAT AND HABITS** Occupies woodland and dry tropical to subtropical rainforests, where it shelters under rocks and logs. Generally crepuscular; active in the hours before and after dawn and dusk. Oviparous, and presumed to lay around 2–3 eggs in a clutch.

Two-clawed Worm-skink ■ *Anomalopus leuckartii* SVL 120mm
(Burrowing Skink)

DESCRIPTION Elongated, smooth-scaled, cylindrical body, and medium-length, tapering tail that is slightly shorter than length of body. Small limbs with 2 digits on front pair; hindlimbs reduced to stumps. Greyish-brown to purplish-brown above, with or without

light yellow transverse bar on rear of head, and pale pink or creamish on belly. Lower eyelids movable and ear openings reduced to shallow depressions. **DISTRIBUTION** South-eastern Qld and north-eastern NSW. **HABITAT AND HABITS** Found in forests and woodland with either moist or dry, soft, crumbling soils and dense leaf litter. Fossorial within soil and leaf litter at bases of trees, where it hunts for small invertebrates. Oviparous, and presumed to lay around 2–3 eggs in a clutch.

Five-clawed Worm-skink ■ *Anomalopus mackayi* SVL 110mm
(Long-legged Worm-skink)

DESCRIPTION Smooth-scaled burrowing skink with medium-length, tapering tail. Reduced limbs have 3 digits on front and 2 at rear. Greyish-brown above, with rows of elongated dark spots down body, and yellowish-green underparts with numerous dark spots and flecks. Patterning generally absent in southern regions. **DISTRIBUTION** Inland areas of south-eastern Qld and north-eastern NSW. **HABITAT AND HABITS** Found in woodland and grassland, and in adjacent disturbed agricultural areas. Shelters under objects on the ground, and feeds in the early morning and evening on small arthropods, including termites. Oviparous, laying about 3 eggs in a clutch, probably in spring.

Three-clawed Worm-skink ■ *Anomalopus verreauxii* SVL 170mm
(Verreaux's Skink)

DESCRIPTION Elongated, smooth-scaled, 'snake-like' burrowing skink, with cylindrical body and medium-length tail that tapers at tip. Brown to grey above with creamy-yellow band on head, which is more distinctive on the darker juveniles, and resembles markings of young crowned snakes *Cacophis* spp. Small limbs, with 3 digits on forelimbs and greatly reduced styliform hindlimbs each with a single toe. **DISTRIBUTION** Central-eastern Qld and north-eastern NSW. **HABITAT AND HABITS** Secretive, spending most of its time under foliage, rocks or logs on the ground, within wet forests, rainforest margins and coastal shrubland. Nocturnal, foraging on the ground or in ground litter for invertebrates, including worms. When disturbed, burrows deeply into soft soil. Oviparous, laying soft-shelled eggs in spring.

Major Skink ▪ *Bellatorias frerei* SVL 180mm

DESCRIPTION Solid glossy pale to rich brown above, with darker pale-edged scales producing broken longitudinal pattern. Upper sides darker, normally sharply contrasting with paler lower sides, and with pale spots and blotches. Head moderately broad with

some dark flecking. Belly white to yellow. **DISTRIBUTION** Coastal eastern Australia, from Cape York Peninsula and islands, Qld, to north-eastern NSW. **HABITAT AND HABITS** Found around rocky outcrops in well-vegetated areas, rainforests, vine thickets, forests and woodland, where it lives in communities in complex burrow systems. Diurnal; often seen basking at edge of open forest or rainforest, and forages for invertebrates, mice, other lizards and vegetable matter. Viviparous, giving birth to up to 9 live young.

Land Mullet ▪ *Bellatorias major* SVL 300mm

DESCRIPTION Australia's largest skink. Robust, glossy body with 'fish-like' head, medium-length tail and low-keeled scales. Blackish-brown to black above, and whitish to yellowish-orange underneath. Juveniles more bluish than adults, with scattered small white spots on sides. **DISTRIBUTION** Coastal and near coastal south-eastern Qld and north-eastern

NSW. **HABITAT AND HABITS** Occurs in coastal rainforest margins and wet forests with associated open areas, where it can be seen basking in patches of sunlight, retreating loudly to a burrow under a nearby tree if disturbed. Often inhabits disturbed areas with introduced weeds, including blackberry *Rubus* spp. and lantana *Lantana camera*, and found in well-vegetated suburban gardens. Feeds on invertebrates, forest fruits and cultivated vegetable scraps in compost heaps. Viviparous, giving birth to up to 9 live young.

Cone-eared Calyptotis ▪ *Calyptotis lepidorostrum* SVL 55mm

DESCRIPTION Glossy, smooth-scaled skink with elongated body and long, tapering tail. Brownish above with 4 longitudinal rows of small dark brown spots, and with darker brown stripe that extends from snout, through eye and down upper side of body. Remainder of sides paler brown with whitish spots and darker brown marbling. Limbs small with 5 digits

on each, and pinkish-orange wash on rear limbs, extending down tail. Belly whitish to yellowish, occasionally with pinkish-orange on chest and throat. Ears marked by shallow depressions. **DISTRIBUTION** Coastal and near coastal south-eastern Qld. **HABITAT AND HABITS** Burrows through leaf litter and coarse, woody debris on rainforest floors, foraging for invertebrates. Oviparous, laying around 3 eggs in a clutch.

Red-tailed Calyptotis ▪ *Calyptotis ruficauda* SVL 55mm

DESCRIPTION Smooth, glossy-scaled skink with light brown, medium-length tail. Brown above with dark brown to black spots forming longitudinal lines, and darker line from snout to tail, along both edges of dorsal surface. Sides whitish to light brown, with white-and-

black spots. Limbs small with 5 digits on each, and pinkish-orange flush to hindlimbs and sides of tail. Dark bars on lips. Belly whitish. Ear opening large and vertical. **DISTRIBUTION** Lower north coast and adjacent ranges of NSW. **HABITAT AND HABITS** Found in wet and dry forests and rainforests, where it burrows in moist soil under logs, rocks and leaf litter. Oviparous, laying up to 6 (average 3) eggs in a clutch, with clutch sizes relating to body size.

Scute-snouted Calyptotis ■ *Calyptotis scutirostrum* SVL 50mm

DESCRIPTION Glossy, smooth-scaled skink with elongated body and medium-sized, tapering tail. Brownish above and sometimes with 4 rows of small black dorsal spots. Brown on flanks, with white spots, and lips with dark barring. Limbs small, with 5 digits

on each and pinkish-orange wash on hindlimbs and sides of tail. Belly whitish or yellow, with brown spotting on throat. **DISTRIBUTION** Coastal and near coastal south-eastern Qld and north-eastern NSW. **HABITAT AND HABITS** Found in rainforests and wet sclerophyll forests, preferring moist soils, where it burrows under logs and surface litter, foraging for small invertebrates. Oviparous, laying 2–5 (average 4) eggs in a clutch, with clutch sizes relating to body size of female.

Broad-templed Calyptotis ■ *Calyptotis temporalis* SVL 35mm

DESCRIPTION Smooth, glossy-scaled skink with medium-length tail, and small limbs with 5 digits on each. Brown above with dark brown spots forming 4 longitudinal lines, and with distinctive dark brown stripe from snout, through eye and along sides of tail. Sides of body pinkish with pinkish-orange flush on hindlimbs and sides of tail. Ear openings large and lips have white spots. **DISTRIBUTION** Coast and ranges of central-eastern Qld. **HABITAT AND HABITS** Found in rainforests and adjacent wet sclerophyll forests of the coast and ranges. Burrows under logs, rocks and leaf litter, where it forages for small invertebrates. Oviparous, laying around 2 eggs in a clutch.

Lined Rainbow-skink ■ *Carlia jarnoldae* SVL 45mm
(Jewel Rainbow Skink)

DESCRIPTION Robust body with tail slightly longer than body (SVL). Breeding males brown above with 4–6 black stripes from neck to base of tail. Reddish-brown speckled limbs with 4 digits on forelimbs and 5 digits on hindlimbs. Upper sides have small blue spots, and lower sides have broad bright orange stripe. Throat and lips greenish. Females dark brown above with pale coppery-brown head, white and blackish flecks, and black lateral stripe extending from snout to tail. Belly creamish. **DISTRIBUTION** North-eastern Qld. **HABITAT AND HABITS** Found in forests and woodland, where it is terrestrial, feeding on small invertebrates. Oviparous, laying 2 eggs in a clutch.

Closed-litter Rainbow-skink ■ *Carlia longipes* SVL 70mm

DESCRIPTION Robust body with long, tapering tail and movable eyelid containing transparent window. Front and rear limbs have 4 digits. Pale brown to reddish-brown above, paler on head, occasionally with scattered dark spots on back, and sides with lower lateral zone bright orange. Young individuals have blackish upper lateral zone. Adult males have black stripe on snout, becoming broader, and extending to neck. Ear openings lined with sharp spines. **DISTRIBUTION** North-eastern Australia, including north-eastern NT and northern Qld. **HABITAT AND HABITS** Occurs in dry forests to humid woodland and rocky areas, where it actively forages on the ground in leaf litter and on fallen timber for small invertebrates. Oviparous, laying 2 eggs in a clutch, with up to 2 clutches in a year.

Subadult   *Adult*

Shaded-litter Rainbow-skink ■ *Carlia munda* SVL 40mm

DESCRIPTION Robust skink with highly variable colour. Brown to greyish-brown with light dashes and dark spots above, and narrow white stripe running from snout to top of ear, and from bottom of ear to forelimb. Sexually active males have greenish on head, blue

throat and orange-red sides. Underparts whitish. Forelimbs have 4 digits, and hindlimbs 5. **DISTRIBUTION** Northern Australia, from north-east WA coast, through NT, to northern and eastern Qld. **HABITAT AND HABITS** Found in dry forests, woodland, rainforest margins, mangroves, shrubland and sandy grassland. Terrestrial; seen foraging among leaf and ground litter, feeding on small invertebrates, waving its tail. Oviparous, laying 2 eggs in a clutch.

Open-litter Rainbow-skink ■ *Carlia pectoralis* SVL 50mm

DESCRIPTION Robust body with tail around same length as body (SVL). Brown above with head a paler bronzy-brown. Greyish-brown to reddish-brown on back, with light and dark flecks. Lower sides greyish with small light spots. Sexually active males have bright orange flush or stripes on sides. Females and young adults lack bright colours and have stripe from snout to back legs. Belly whitish, with mature males having bluish on face, throat and lower neck. **DISTRIBUTION** Eastern Qld, from base of Cape York Peninsula to NSW border. **HABITAT AND HABITS** Found in dry, open forests and humid woodland, where it forages on the ground for small invertebrates. Oviparous, laying 2 eggs in a clutch.

Breeding male

Female

Black-throated Rainbow-skink ■ *Carlia rostralis* SVL 70mm

DESCRIPTION Robust body with strongly tapering tail that is slightly longer than body length. Brown with some small spots and flecks above; grey-brown to olive-brown head, and black stripe, bordered by white, running from head to front limbs. Forelimbs have 4 digits, and hindlimbs 5. Sides, between limbs, orange to rusty-brown. **DISTRIBUTION** Lower parts of Cape York Peninsula, northern Qld. **HABITAT AND HABITS** Found in wetter forests and woodland, but absent from rainforests, where it actively forages in leaf litter and low vegetation for small invertebrates, including spiders. Oviparous, laying 2 eggs in a clutch.

Orange-flanked Rainbow-skink ■ *Carlia rubigo* SVL 45mm

DESCRIPTION Robust body with medium-length tail and keeled dorsal scales. Rich metallic-brown above, becoming more greyish towards tail, and with orange-brown stripe along sides. Breeding males have rusty-orange wash that covers forelimbs, sides and back, and bluish throat. Pale brown from hindlimbs to tip of tail. Forelimbs have 4 digits, hindlimbs 5. Underparts creamish. **DISTRIBUTION** Eastern and central Qld, including offshore islands, south of Cape York Peninsula. **HABITAT AND HABITS** Occupies dry, open forests, grassland and rocky areas. Actively forages on the ground within grassy and rocky areas for small invertebrates, including spiders. Oviparous, laying 2 eggs in a clutch, and often having more than 1 clutch in a season.

Robust Rainbow-skink ■ *Carlia schmeltzii* SVL 60mm

DESCRIPTION Robust body with slender tail longer than body. Grey-brown or olive-brown above and pale bronze on head, with scattered flecks over coppery-brown to greyish-brown above. Forelimbs have 4 digits, hindlimbs 5. Broad black stripe runs down back, with lower lateral zone mottled in light brown. Sexually active males have orangey-red flush between limbs. Throat white with speckles on sides. Belly whitish. **DISTRIBUTION**

Northern and eastern Qld (except northern Cape York Peninsula), south to far north-eastern NSW. **HABITAT AND HABITS** Occupies dry forests to humid woodland, where it forages on the ground and in rocky areas for small invertebrates. Oviparous, laying 2 eggs in a clutch, often with more than 1 clutch in a season.

Brown Bicarinate Rainbow-skink ■ *Carlia storri* SVL 45mm
(Storr's Rainbow-skink)

DESCRIPTION Moderate body with slender tail slightly longer than body. Brown or pale olive-brown above, with both males and females having narrow white dorsolateral stripe. Females have pale brown vertebral stripe, and white or cream midlateral stripe, while

sexually active males have orange flush on sides between limbs. Forelimbs have 4 digits, hindlimbs 5. Underparts whitish. **DISTRIBUTION** Mainland and islands of north-eastern Qld. **HABITAT AND HABITS** Found in dry forests, tropical woodland, rainforest fringes and coastal shrubland. Actively forages in shaded areas within leaf litter and low grasses for small invertebrates. Oviparous, laying 2 eggs in a clutch, often with more than 1 clutch produced in a year.

Southern Rainbow-skink ■ *Carlia tetradactyla* SVL 60mm
(Four-fingered Skink)

DESCRIPTION Moderately stout-bodied, smooth-scaled skink with weakly keeled scales and long, tapering tail. Grey to rich dark brown above, with light and dark dashes that run from neck to base of tail on males and to tip of tail on females. Sexually active males have orange longitudinal stripes on sides. Creamish to white throat and whitish belly. Forelimbs have 4 digits, hindlimbs 5. **DISTRIBUTION** Inland and some coastal areas of south-eastern Australia, from southern Qld to central-southern NSW. **HABITAT AND HABITS** Found in dry forests, grassy woodland and disturbed pastures, where it shelters at night under leaf litter, logs and rocks, or within dense vegetation. Diurnal, hunting during the day for small invertebrates. Tail waved sideways during feeding, perhaps as an aid to hunting, by luring prey closer, or alternatively to protect head and body from predators. Oviparous, laying around 2 eggs per clutch.

Female

Breeding male

Lively Rainbow Skink ■ *Carlia vivax* SVL 45mm
(Lively Rainbow-skink; Tussock Rainbow-skink)

DESCRIPTION Moderately robust, medium-length body with slender tail. Breeding males have single reddish stripe along side. Brown above, paler on head, with dark-edged, pale dorsal flecks and pale dorsolateral line. Females and young males have pale brown stripe from neck to tail, bordered below in female by thin creamish white stripe, starting under eye and ending at hindlimb. Whitish or bluish below, with darker speckling on throat. Forelimbs have 4 digits, hindlimbs 5. **DISTRIBUTION** Eastern mainland, from northern Qld to lower north coast of NSW. **HABITAT AND HABITS** Found in dry forests and woodland, where it actively forages on the ground for small invertebrates, including spiders. Oviparous, laying 2 eggs in a clutch, often with more than 1 clutch laid in a year. Populations are severely impacted by fire, and do not fully recover until an area is fully revegetated.

Female

Breeding male

Northern Barsided Skink ■ *Concinnia brachysoma* SVL 75mm

DESCRIPTION Moderately robust body with medium-length, slender tail and long fourth toe on hindfeet. Pale brown to grey-brown above, with numerous black speckled markings from nape to tip of original tail. Upper part of sides dark brown with uneven lower edge, where it meets paler lower sides, and with numerous black blotches along rear portion.

Belly creamish with speckled tan markings on throat and chest. Lips barred and lower eyelid movable. **DISTRIBUTION** Coast and ranges of eastern Qld, from mid Cape York Peninsula to NSW border. **HABITAT AND HABITS** Agile skink of rocky areas in rainforests, wet forests, subtropical woodland and closed shrubland, where it spends most of its time in trees and in rocky areas. Diurnal, in shaded areas, and crepuscular, foraging for small invertebrates. Ovoviviparous, giving birth to 2–5 (average 4) live young.

Dark Barsided Skink ■ *Concinnia martini* SVL 70mm
(Dark Bar-sided Skink)

DESCRIPTION Moderately robust skink with medium-length, slender tail, movable lower eyelid and long fourth toe on hindfeet. Brown to grey-brown above, with black speckled markings along length of body and tail. Upper part of sides dark brown, with uneven lower edge where it meets paler whitish lower sides, and with numerous black blotches along rear portion. Lips barred and belly creamish with dark brown markings on

throat. **DISTRIBUTION** Coast and ranges of central eastern Australia, from northern NSW to southern Qld. **HABITAT AND HABITS** Found in rocky areas and clearings in rainforests, vine thickets, open wet forests and woodland, and occasionally enters adjacent suburban gardens and houses. Generally arboreal, foraging on logs and tree stumps for small invertebrates, but also found sheltering under rocks at night. Ovoviviparous, giving birth to 2–6 (average 4) live young.

Prickly Forest Skink ■ *Concinnia queenslandiae* SVL 80mm

DESCRIPTION Moderately robust skink with strongly keeled scales, strong limbs with 5 digits on each, and moderately long, tapering tail. Dull brown to blackish above, with thin, irregular light transverse bands on back and sides, most prominent on flanks, and generally obscure in adults. Underparts creamish with brown flecks, becoming more concentrated around vent area. Head has large ear openings, smooth scales on face and snout, and whitish spots on lips. **DISTRIBUTION** South-eastern Cape York Peninsula Qld. **HABITAT AND HABITS** Found deep in rainforest, where it normally occurs in a partially dormant state within and under rotting logs on the rainforest floor, remaining in the same area and often sheltering under the same log for several years. Feeds nocturnally on invertebrates. Viviparous, giving birth to around 3 live young late in wet season.

Barred-sided Skink ■ *Concinnia tenuis* SVL 85mm
(Bar-sided Forest-skink; Bar-sided Skink)

DESCRIPTION Smooth-scaled skink with long, slender limbs with 5 digits on each, and with fourth toe of hindlimbs longer that the rest. Pale brown to silvery-brown above, with black blotches along length of body and tail. Upper part of sides dark brown, with uneven lower edge where it meets paler creamish lower sides, and with numerous black blotches along rear portion. Underparts creamish, with dark brown markings on throat. **DISTRIBUTION** Coast and ranges of eastern Australia, from central Qld to southern NSW. **HABITAT AND HABITS** Occurs on rocky slopes in rainforests and open forests, and in heavily forested gardens in northern part of its range, and woodland in south, where it is active in trees and within rock crevices. Mainly diurnal and crepuscular, but can be active at night, foraging in shade for invertebrates, including spiders, ants and insect larvae, and some berries. Ovoviviparous, giving birth to 3–7 (average 5) live young in a litter.

Inland Snake-eyed Skink ▪ *Cryptoblepharus australis* SVL 45mm

DESCRIPTION Slender-bodied, smooth-scaled skink with fused lower eyelid that forms transparent cover over eye. Predominantly grey to grey-brown above, with complex, longitudinally aligned dorsal pattern of black flecks, which is flanked on either side by uneven silver-grey dorsolateral stripe from eye to tail. Head similar in colour to vertebral

zone, or more coppery coloured. Underparts off-white. **DISTRIBUTION** Inland Australia, including south-western WA, southern NT, southern and western Qld, central and western NSW and SA. Reaches coast in mid-SA. **HABITAT AND HABITS** Found in drier open woodland, mallee, acacia scrubland, spinifex grassland, and adjacent houses and suburban gardens, often on hills or near watercourses, but also on plains. Forages during the day on trees for small invertebrates, including cockroaches, beetles, spiders and termites. Oviparous, laying 2 parchment-shelled eggs.

Metallic Snake-eyed Skink ▪ *Cryptoblepharus metallicus* SVL 45mm
(females typically slightly larger than males)

DESCRIPTION Smooth-scaled, cryptically patterned skink, with slightly flattened body and long, slender, tapering tail. Metallic-grey to greyish-brown with black flecks above,

and with indistinct silvery longitudinal dorsolateral stripe from eye to tail. Head more copper coloured, with fused lower eyelid, containing clear window in centre that forms protective cover over eye. Underparts whitish. **DISTRIBUTION** Northern and eastern mainland Australia, from Kimberley region WA, through northern NT to south-eastern Qld. **HABITAT AND HABITS** Found in dry forests, woodland, shrubland, grassland and adjacent gardens. Diurnal and arboreal, foraging mostly on rough-barked trees and, less commonly, on rocks for small invertebrates. Oviparous, laying 2 eggs in a clutch, with up to 2 clutches laid in a year.

Ragged Snake-eyed Skink ▪ *Cryptoblepharus pannosus*
SVL 40mm (females typically larger than males)

DESCRIPTION Smooth-scaled, with flattened body, and with fused lower eyelid that forms transparent cover over eye. Grey to greyish-brown or blackish above, with numerous irregular black flecks and streaks above that form longitudinally aligned dorsal pattern from nape to tail, which is bordered on each side by obscure paler grey, ragged-edged dorsolateral stripe that starts at eye. Sides similarly patterned to back, and underparts off-white.
DISTRIBUTION Inland eastern mainland to eastern SA and far north-western NT. Reaches coast around Gulf of Carpentaria and parts of eastern and southern limits.
HABITAT AND HABITS Found in dry forests, woodland, shrubland and grassland, normally in vicinity of watercourses, where it is typically arboreal. Actively forages during the day, on trees or in rocky areas, for small invertebrates. Oviparous, laying 2 eggs in a clutch, with breeding recorded in most months of the year.

Elegant Snake-eyed Skink ▪ *Cryptoblepharus pulcher* SVL 35mm
(Wall Skink; Fence Skink)

DESCRIPTION Smooth-scaled, complex striped skink with long, tapering tail, and with fused lower eyelid that forms protective transparent cover over eye. Greyish-brown to brownish-black above, with narrow brownish vertebral stripe, bordered by black on either side, and with prominent silvery-grey dorsolateral stripes running from eye to tail. Black on upper sides, flecked with paler grey, and lower sides grey-brown. Underparts off-white. **DISTRIBUTION** Two subspecies. *C. p. pulcher* occurs along eastern coast and ranges from north-eastern Qld (south of Cape York Peninsula) to southern NSW. *C. p. clarus* found along coast and adjacent inland of southern WA and southern SA. **HABITAT AND HABITS** Found in range of wooded habitats, including dry, open forests and woodland, and adjacent parks and gardens, where it is active during the day, foraging on trees, fences and walls for small invertebrates. Oviparous, laying 2 eggs in a clutch.

Cream-striped Shining-skink ■ *Cryptoblepharus virgatus* SVL 40mm
(Striped Snake-eyed Skink)

DESCRIPTION Smooth-scaled, simply patterned skink with fused lower eyelid that forms protective transparent cover over eye. Greyish to blackish with broad, unpatterned, grey to grey-brown vertebral stripe, bordered on either side by black, and with prominent narrow cream dorsolateral stripes, extending from eye to tail. Head sometimes has coppery

flush. Sides blackish to greyish, occasionally with pale speckling, and with obscure pale broken line from eye to forelimbs. Underparts off-white. **DISTRIBUTION** Northern and eastern Cape York Peninsula, and north-east coast, Qld. **HABITAT AND HABITS** Native to dry forests and grassland, to humid woodland, and now common in urban areas, where it is usually arboreal, sheltering in tree crevices or under tree bark. Diurnal, feeding on invertebrates, including cockroaches, spiders and ants. Oviparous, laying 2–3 parchment-shelled eggs in a clutch.

Brown-blazed Wedgesnout Ctenotus ■ *Ctenotus allotropis*
SVL 55mm

DESCRIPTION Brown to reddish-brown above with white dorsolateral stripe from rear of eye and down base of tail, with narrow darker line above, containing numerous pale spots. Sides dark brown to blackish, with vertically aligned pale whitish-brown spots and

lower lateral pale longitudinal stripe that starts under eye. Black stripes run down limbs, and underparts creamish. Scaled movable lower eyelid. **DISTRIBUTION** Inland areas of central south-east, from southern NSW to southern Qld. **HABITAT AND HABITS** Found in arid woodland and shrubland, including mallee, eucalypt and cypress. Forages in leaf litter and low vegetation around bases of trees for insects and spiders. Oviparous. Very wary of predators and quickly moves to cover if disturbed.

Unspotted Yellow-sided Ctenotus ■ *Ctenotus ingrami* SVL 80mm

DESCRIPTION Fast-moving, slender-bodied, striped skink with long, tapering tail and scaled movable lower eyelid. Greyish-brown to olive-brown above, with black vertebral stripe and white dorsolateral stripe from above eye to base of tail. Sides black with white midlateral stripe from snout to rear leg, and continuing along tail, and white line along lower edge of side. Underparts white. **DISTRIBUTION** Mid-eastern interior, from central northern Qld to northern NSW. **HABITAT AND HABITS** Occupies dry woodland, shrubland and grassland, foraging in leaf litter and low vegetation for invertebrates, including insects and spiders, and smaller lizards. Oviparous. Very wary of predators and dashes quickly for cover when disturbed.

Bar-shouldered Ctenotus ■ *Ctenotus inornatus* SVL 95mm
(Plain Ctenotus; Plain Striped Skink)

DESCRIPTION Fast-moving, long, slender skink with scaled movable lower eyelid. Dark coppery-brown to olive-brown above, with blackish vertebral stripe (prominent in juveniles and generally absent in adults), and thin white dorsolateral stripe from eye to base of tail. Upper sides dark brown, mottled and dotted with black and pale brown, bordered below with pale midlateral stripe (most obvious in juveniles), and light grey-brown on lower sides. Underparts whitish. **DISTRIBUTION** Northern Australia from Kimberley region WA, through northern NT to Gulf of Carpentaria Qld. **HABITAT AND HABITS** Found in tropical woodland and rocky escarpments with areas of spinifex. Active during the day, foraging on the ground for insects and other arthropods. Oviparous, laying a single egg.

Gravelly-soil Ctenotus ■ *Ctenotus lateralis* SVL 85mm
(Gravelly-soil Striped Skink)

DESCRIPTION Glossy scaled, fast-moving, striped skink, with long, tapering tail and scaled movable lower eyelid. Olive-brown to reddish-brown above, with pale-margined black vertebral stripe, and narrow white dorsolateral stripe from rear of eye and down tail.

Sides dark brown with midlateral creamish-white stripe from neck to rear leg and onto tail. Limbs light red to brown, with dark brown stripes. Underparts whitish. **DISTRIBUTION** Central and western Qld interior. **HABITAT AND HABITS** Occurs in small populations on spinifex-clad stony hills and ridges, foraging on the ground during the day for insects and other arthropods. Oviparous, laying 2 eggs in a clutch.

Leonhardi's Ctenotus ■ *Ctenotus leonhardii* SVL 80mm
(Leonhard's Skink)

DESCRIPTION Moderately robust striped skink with slender tail and scaled movable lower eyelid. Pale to dark brown or rich reddish-brown, with pale-margined dark brown vertebral stripe and creamish-white dorsolateral stripe from eye to tail. Upper sides blackish brown with numerous whitish spots, bordered below by dashed pale midlateral stripe from front to rear leg, continuing to tail as solid line. Underparts whitish. **DISTRIBUTION** Wide inland distribution, from western WA, through central and northern SA and central and southern NT, to north-western NSW and eastern Qld. Reaches

coast at far north-west and north-east limits. **HABITAT AND HABITS** Occupies drier open woodland, shrubland, grassland and spinifex-dominated sandy or stony deserts. Feeds on small invertebrates, including grasshoppers, spiders and termites. Oviparous, laying up to 7 (average 3) parchment-shelled eggs in a clutch.

Eastern Ctenotus ■ *Ctenotus orientalis* SVL 80mm
(Eastern Striped Skink)

DESCRIPTION Smooth-scaled, fast-moving skink, with long, slender tail and scaled movable lower eyelid. Pale brown above with pale-margined black vertebral stripe and broader blackish margin containing series of small pale spots, bordered by pale dorsolateral stripe that extends from eye to tail. Upper sides blackish with numerous vertically aligned small cream spots and lower sides greyish-brown with diffused spots. Underparts white. **DISTRIBUTION** Southern Australian mainland from south-eastern WA, through southern SA and northern Vic, to south-western NSW. **HABITAT AND HABITS** Found in drier forests, woodland, shrubland and grassland. Active during the day, foraging on the ground for small invertebrates, and sheltering at other times in shallow burrows or under rocks. Oviparous, laying 2–6 eggs in a clutch.

Leopard Ctenotus ■ *Ctenotus pantherinus*
SVL 100mm (females generally larger than males)
(Leopard Skink)

DESCRIPTION Robust, strikingly patterned skink with long, tapering tail, and wedge-shaped head with scaled movable lower eyelid. Pale olive-brown to dark coppery-brown above, with rows of longitudinally aligned, black-edged white or yellowish spots on back, sides and hindlimbs, and dark brown stripes on forelimbs. Individuals in south-west have dark vertebral stripe. Underparts greyish-white. **DISTRIBUTION** Western, north-western, central and northern mainland, and nearby islands, to inland Qld and far north-west NSW. Absent from south-western and southern WA, southern SA, Vic, most of NSW, and eastern and northern Qld. **HABITAT AND HABITS** Occurs in arid to semi-arid spinifex grassland, drier woodland and shrubland. Active during the day, foraging on the ground for small invertebrates, including termites, spiders, ants and beetles. Oviparous, laying around 7 parchment-shelled eggs in a clutch.

Pale-rumped Ctenotus ■ *Ctenotus regius* SVL 70mm
(Royal Ctenotus; Royal Striped Skink)

DESCRIPTION Smooth-scaled, striped and spotted skink, with long, slender tail and scaled movable lower eyelid. Yellowish-brown to reddish-brown above, with thin, cream-edged black vertebral stripe and prominent cream dorsolateral stripe running from above eye to tail. Upper sides black with numerous spots, and bordered below by cream midlateral

stripe. Lower sides white with brown streaks and spots. Underparts whitish-cream. **DISTRIBUTION** Interior of central and southern mainland Australia, including southern NT, south-western Qld, western NSW, north-western Vic, and central and northern SA. **HABITAT AND HABITS** Found in drier woodland, shrubland and grassland, on clay and sandy soils. Terrestrial, feeding during the day on small insects and other arthropods. Oviparous, laying average of 3 eggs in a clutch.

Robust Ctenotus ■ *Ctenotus robustus* SVL 115mm
(Striped Skink; Eastern Striped Skink; Robust Striped Skink)

DESCRIPTION Moderately robust, smooth-scaled skink, with numerous stripes and blotches and scaled movable lower eyelid. Brown to olive-brown above, with pale-margined black vertebral line running from nape to tail and pale dorsolateral stripe from eye to base of tail. Upper sides dark brown with pale spots, and lower sides whitish with darker greyish marbling. Underparts whitish. **DISTRIBUTION** Northern and eastern

Australia, from north-western WA, through northern NT, northern and eastern Qld, NSW and Vic, to eastern SA. **HABITAT AND HABITS** Occurs in range of habitat types, including forests, woodland, shrubland, grassland, heaths and rocky outcrops. Active during the day, foraging on or close to the ground for invertebrates and small lizards concealed in leaf litter. Oviparous, laying up to 9 (average 6) eggs in a clutch, buried in soil. Fast moving and wary, dashing for cover when disturbed.

Barred Wedgesnout Ctenotus ■ *Ctenotus schomburgkii* SVL 50mm
(Schomburgk's Striped Skink)

DESCRIPTION Smooth-scaled, fast-moving, striped and spotted skink, with long, slender tail and scaled movable lower eyelid. Olive-brown to coppery-brown above, with series of 5 longitudinal black dorsal stripes and thin cream dorsolateral stripe from above eye to base of tail. Upper sides black with numerous large coppery-brown blotches, bordered below by white midlateral stripe that extends from ear to hindleg, then on to tail, and lower sides marbled olive-brown and black. Legs coppery-brown to olive-brown, streaked and blotched with black. Underparts whitish. **DISTRIBUTION** Western, central and southern mainland Australia, from central-western WA coastline, through southern NT, south-western Qld, central and western NSW and north-western Vic, to central and northern SA. Does not reach south-western WA and southern coast of WA and SA. **HABITAT AND HABITS** Found in drier woodland, shrubland and spinifex grassland on sandy soil. Active during the day, foraging on the ground for insects and other arthropods. Oviparous, typically laying 2–3 eggs in a clutch.

Spalding's Ctenotus ■ *Ctenotus spaldingi* SVL 100mm
(Straight-browed Ctenotus; Spalding's Striped Skink)

DESCRIPTION Moderately robust, smooth-scaled skink, with numerous stripes and blotches and scaled movable lower eyelid. Olive-brown to yellowish-brown above, with pale-margined black vertebral line running from nape to tail, and pale dorsolateral stripe from eye to base of tail. These dorsal stripes tend to be more obscure in eastern parts of its range. Upper sides dark brown with pale blotches, and lower sides whitish with darker greyish marbling. Underparts whitish. **DISTRIBUTION** Northern and north-eastern Australia, from WA border area, through northern NT and northern Qld, to east coast. **HABITAT AND HABITS** Occurs in range of habitat types, including drier forests, woodland, shrubland, grassy coastal dunes, heaths and rocky outcrops. Forages during the day for small invertebrates, taking cover in ground litter or in shallow burrows when threatened. Oviparous, laying around 3–4 eggs in a clutch.

Eastern Barred Wedgesnout Ctenotus ■ *Ctenotus strauchii* SVL 55mm
(Strauch's Striped Skink)

DESCRIPTION Smooth-scaled, moderately sized, striped and spotted skink, with long, slender tail and scaled movable lower eyelid. Coppery-brown to brown above, uncommonly with pale-margined black vertebral stripe, and with cream dorsolateral stripe, bordered on back and upper sides with black stripes containing numerous coppery-brownish blotches. Lower sides white with brown streaks and underparts white. Limbs coppery-brown with dark brown to black streaks and spots. **DISTRIBUTION** Inland central-eastern Australia,

including central and southern Qld, northern NSW, north-eastern SA and south-western NT. **HABITAT AND HABITS** Found in drier savannah and mallee woodland, and grassland, sheltering among leaf litter and ground debris. Appears to avoid porcupine grass, even in areas where it is abundant. Terrestrial, feeding during the day on small invertebrates. Oviparous, laying an average of 2 eggs in a clutch.

Copper-tailed Skink ■ *Ctenotus taeniolatus* SVL 65mm

DESCRIPTION Fast-moving, heavily striped skink with moderately long, orange-brown to brown tail, and scaled movable lower eyelid. Rich brown above with yellowish-edged black vertebral stripe from nape to tail, and series of thinner white-and-black stripes on either side of brown paravertebral stripes and along sides. Limbs brown to orange-brown with black stripes. Underparts white. **DISTRIBUTION** Eastern Australia, from south-

eastern Cape York Peninsula Qld, through eastern NSW, to northern Vic. **HABITAT AND HABITS** Found in dry forests, woodland, shrubland, heaths and open areas, such as coastal sand dunes and rocky outcrops. Shelters in rock crevices and under logs. Terrestrial, feeding during the day on invertebrates, including spiders, ants, beetles and worms. Oviparous, laying up to 7 (average 4) eggs per year in a single clutch, buried in soil.

Tasmanian She-oak Skink ■ *Cyclodomorphus casuarinae* SVL 165mm

DESCRIPTION Elongated body with short limbs and moderately long tail. Variable in colour and pattern. Generally greyish to dark reddish-brown above, with obscure longitudinal lines or transverse bars on back. Sides have darker vertical barring, with some paler spots or an obscure reticulated pattern. Underparts generally grey or greenish, occasionally with a yellowish wash, and with darker transverse barring from chest to tail. Some individuals are unpatterned. **DISTRIBUTION** Broadly distributed in Tasmania and nearby islands. **HABITAT AND HABITS** Found in dry forests, woodland, heathland, tussock grassland and sandy dunes, where it forages for snails, insects and small vertebrates. Nocturnal and crepuscular; takes cover during the day in leaf litter, and under rocks and fallen debris. Viviparous, giving birth to 2–7 live young.

Colour and patterning can vary between individuals, and the original tail, once lost, is regrown

Pink-tongued Lizard ■ *Cyclodomorphus gerrardii* SVL 200mm
(Pink-tongued Skink)

DESCRIPTION Smooth, glossy scaled skink, with large head and long, prehensile tail up to one and a half times body length (SVL). Light grey to pale brown above with strong to obscure brown, to blackish, angled transverse bands; more distinct in juveniles than adults and may be absent in some individuals. Head with or without variable darker spots and stripes, and tongue normally pink. Underparts brownish. **DISTRIBUTION** Coastal plains, ranges and eastern slopes of eastern Australia, from around Cairns Qld to Blue Mountains NSW. **HABITAT AND HABITS** Generally inhabits wetter forests, including rainforests, moist woodland and adjacent lush suburban gardens.

Active during the day, foraging around rocky areas and vegetation for molluscs and small arthropods. Viviparous, giving birth to up to 25 live young in a single litter.

Adult with pink tongue exposed　　　*Bands can be obscure or absent*

Mainland She-oak Skink ■ *Cyclodomorphus michaeli* SVL 165mm
(Eastern She-oak Skink)

DESCRIPTION Elongated body with short limbs and moderately long tail, up to about one and a half times length of body (SVL). Generally greyish to dark reddish-brown above; paler with grey on head, with obscure longitudinal lines or transverse bars on back.

Sides have darker vertical barring, with some paler spots or obscure reticulated pattern. Underparts generally grey or greenish, occasionally with yellowish wash, and with darker transverse barring from chest to tail. Some individuals unpatterned. **DISTRIBUTION** South-eastern mainland from north-eastern Vic to northern tablelands NSW. **HABITAT AND HABITS** Wet forests, woodland, coastal heathland and moist grassland. Crepuscular and nocturnal, foraging on the ground in open areas and around edges of vegetation for small invertebrates. Viviparous, giving birth to around 7 live young in a litter.

Saltbush Slender Blue-tongue ■ *Cyclodomorphus venustus* SVL 100mm

DESCRIPTION Medium-sized, robust skink, with slender head and tail about same length as body (SVL). Greyish to brown above, with black markings on scales forming speckled transverse pattern. Sides more pinkish, with large black blotches on neck and

anterior sides, and underparts cream to yellowish, occasionally with darker speckled cross-bands. **DISTRIBUTION** Inland central-southern mainland, including far south-western Qld, western NSW and eastern SA. **HABITAT AND HABITS** Found in open grassland and shrubland with heavy, cracking clay soils and gibber plains. Crepuscular; forages in the mornings and evenings for small invertebrates, including spiders, beetles, snails, cockroaches and grasshoppers, and small lizards. Shelters at other times in deep soil cracks and under dense ground litter. Viviparous.

Cunningham's Skink ■ *Egernia cunninghami* SVL 250mm

DESCRIPTION Large, robust skink with prominent keeled scales on back and tail, and short legs. Variable colouration and patterning. Brown, reddish-brown or black above, often with numerous scattered paler spots and flecks. Underparts whitish with darker mottling or banding on throat. Individuals in southern parts of range tend to be darker and more prominently patterned than elsewhere. **DISTRIBUTION** South-eastern Australian mainland along Great Dividing Range and associated slopes from south-eastern Qld, through NSW to central Victoria. Also in Mount Lofty Ranges and Fleurieu Peninsula SA. **HABITAT AND HABITS**

Generally associated with rocky areas in forests and open woodland, where it is active from dawn to dusk, sheltering during the night in rock crevices. Largely omnivorous, feeding on vegetable matter, including fruits, leaves and seeds, various invertebrates and occasionally small lizards. Viviparous, with up to 8 (average 6) young in a litter. Often seen basking on rocks.

Hosmer's Skink ■ *Egernia hosmeri* SVL 180mm

DESCRIPTION Robust, sharply keeled skink with short, thickened, tapering tail and short snout. Variable colouration and patterning. Pale brown or yellowish-brown to reddish-brown above, with numerous scattered pale and dark blotches on head, back and tail, being most concentrated on head.

Underparts white or yellowish. **DISTRIBUTION** Inland areas of north-eastern Australia from north-western NT to north-eastern Qld, south of Cape York Peninsula. **HABITAT AND HABITS** Found in rocky areas in dry woodland. Active during the day, foraging around rocky outcrops and fallen timber for vegetable matter and small invertebrates, and sheltering at other times in rock crevices and under large rocks. Viviparous, with 1–4 (average 2) live young in a litter.

Yakka Skink ■ *Egernia rugosa* SVL 220mm

DESCRIPTION Solidly robust brown skink with broad dark brown to black longitudinal dorsal stripe, bordered on each side by paler dorsolateral stripe. Sides generally brownish with paler and darker mottling. Underparts yellowish-orange. Tail short and thickened at base, limbs short and stocky, and head has vertical external ear openings covered with large

scales. **DISTRIBUTION** Coast and inland areas of eastern Qld, from Cape York Peninsula to south-east of state. **HABITAT AND HABITS** Occurs on rocky outcrops within drier woodland, sheltering within communal burrows that are constructed in mounds of earth or piles of timber, or disused burrows of rabbits. Predominantly diurnal, foraging on the ground for invertebrates, and fruits and tender leaves of plants. Viviparous, with 2–3 live young in a litter. Secretive, remaining mostly concealed by dense vegetation, and quick to retreat to safety of nearby burrow if disturbed.

Black Rock Skink ■ *Egernia saxatilis* SVL 135mm

DESCRIPTION Large, obscurely patterned skink with moderately depressed body and sharply keeled scales. Two geographically isolated subspecies, with *E. s. saxatilis* (Warrumbungle Mtns) being comparatively paler and with broken longitudinal lines of darker dashes along back, and dark vertical bars and blotches on sides. Throat and lips

whitish to grey with black blotches, and underparts yellow to orange. *E. s. intermedia* mostly black. **DISTRIBUTION** Ranges of south-eastern mainland Australia, from northern NSW to western Vic. **HABITAT AND HABITS** Found in forests, woodland and rocky outcrops, in crevices, on large rocks or on tree stumps, in small family groups. Diurnal, foraging around rocks and in trees for insects and other invertebrates, supplemented with some plant matter. Viviparous, giving birth to up to 5 (average 2) live young in a litter.

Gidgee Skink ■ *Egernia stokesii* SVL 190mm
(Stokes' Skink, Spiny-tailed Skink)

DESCRIPTION Large, robust skink with sharply keeled scales, short tail and short legs. Yellowish-brown to reddish-brown above, with numerous dark and light flecks and blotches that create obscure transverse pattern, which is most conspicuous on flattened, spiny tail. Underparts white to yellowish. **DISTRIBUTION** Arid to semi-arid Australia, from south-western Qld and far north-western NSW, through eastern and northern SA and southern NT, to eastern and western WA (absent from central WA), and on adjacent islands off central western WA coast. **HABITAT AND HABITS** Found among rocky outcrops in arid to semi-arid, open woodland, shrubland and grassland, where it is saxicolous and semi-arboreal. Diurnal, sheltering in crevices and under boulders where it basks. Feeds mainly on fruits and soft leaves, but also forages for small insects and other vertebrates, including cockroaches, grasshoppers, crickets and moths, supplemented in adults with some fruits and vegetation. Viviparous, giving birth to up to 8 (average 5) live young.

Tree Skink ■ *Egernia striolata* SVL 120mm
(Striated Skink)

DESCRIPTION Scales smooth or bluntly keeled, and moderately flattened body and slender tail. Grey to dark olive-brown with broad, paler greyish dorsolateral stripe from head to base of tail; lower sides of neck and lips white. Underparts whitish, with brown flecks on throat and chest, and with yellowish or orange flush. **DISTRIBUTION** Eastern and south-eastern Australia, from north-eastern Qld, through NSW and northern and western Vic, to southern SA. Absent from coastal NSW and Vic. **HABITAT AND**

HABITS Typically in forests, woodland, shrubland and grassland; also in rocky outcrops in some areas of range, where it shelters individually or in small groups in hollows or under loose bark. Mostly arboreal, but can also be seen basking on rocks. Active during the day, feeding mostly on invertebrates such as beetles, ants, spiders and moths, supplemented largely with plant matter and occasionally small lizards. Viviparous, with up to 6 (average 4) live young in a litter. Larger females produce larger litters than smaller ones.

Narrow-banded Sand-swimmer ■ *Eremiascincus fasciolatus*

SVL 85mm (females generally larger than males)
(Eastern Narrow-banded Skink; Thick-tailed Skink)

DESCRIPTION Glossy scaled, moderately robust skink, with long, thickened, tapering tail and movable scaly lower eyelids. Pale yellow to golden-brown above, with numerous narrow darker brown transverse bands on body and tail, which can be either strong or obscure and are narrower on tail than on body. Bands number 10–19 between nape and hips, and 35–40 on tail. Flanks and underparts whitish. **DISTRIBUTION** Central & eastern Qld. **HABITAT AND HABITS** Typically found in wide variety of arid habitats, and usually prefers sandy or loamy soils, with areas of spinifex. Burrowing, nocturnal skink

that shelters under logs, stones or leaf litter. Crepuscular and nocturnal, foraging on the ground for invertebrates, such as beetles, grasshoppers and spiders, supplemented with lizards, including geckoes, skinks and blind snakes. Oviparous, laying an average of 4 eggs in a clutch, between October and February.

Broad-banded Sand-swimmer ■ *Eremiascincus richardsonii* SVL 105mm

DESCRIPTION Glossy scaled, moderately robust skink, with long, thickened, tapering tail and movable scaly lower eyelids. Pale yellow to golden-brown above, with numerous darker brown transverse bands on body and tail, which can be either strong or obscure, and are narrower on tail than on body. Bands number 8–14 between nape and hips, and 19–32 on tail. Flanks and underparts whitish. **DISTRIBUTION** Central and western

inland Australia, from coastal western WA, through NT and SA, to western Qld, western NSW and north-western Vic. Absent from southern and northern coasts. **HABITAT AND HABITS** Found in range of drier habitats, including woodland, shrubland and grassland, with sandy and loamy soils and areas of harder or rocky ground. Forages at night for invertebrates, including beetles, grasshoppers and spiders, and occasionally small lizards, including geckoes, skinks and blind snakes. Oviparous, laying around 4 eggs in a clutch, between October and February.

Yellow-bellied Water-skink ■ *Eulamprus heatwolei* SVL 100mm
(Yellow-bellied Water Skink)

DESCRIPTION Glossy, moderately robust skink with relatively long rear legs. Coppery-brown to olive-brown above, with numerous black flecks on head, back and base of tail, and yellowish dorsolateral stripe from above eye to mid-body. Sides, including sides of tail, black with numerous cream blotches, becoming more concentrated on tail, and flanks yellowish-cream with dark grey marbling. Cheeks normally with white spots, and limbs olive-brown with black blotches and lines. Belly yellowish and throat white with black blotches. **DISTRIBUTION** Uplands of south-eastern mainland Australia from central Vic to tablelands of north-eastern NSW. **HABITAT AND HABITS** Terrestrial inhabitant of forests, woodland and grassland, usually found in association with moist habitats such as margins of swamps, lagoons and creeks. Feeds on various invertebrates and small vertebrates such as fish, frogs and small reptiles. Viviparous, giving birth to up to 8 young in a litter.

Eastern Water-skink ■ *Eulamprus quoyii* SVL 110mm

DESCRIPTION Glossy, robust skink with long, slightly laterally flattened tail, and relatively long rear legs. Metallic-brown to olive-brown above, with scattered black flecks on back and base of tail, and yellowish dorsolateral stripe from above eye to rump. Sides black with scattered cream flecks, becoming more concentrated on base of sides of tail, and flanks yellowish-cream with dark grey spotting and marbling. Limbs olive-brown with black spots, belly yellowish and throat white with black longitudinal lines, often extending onto chest. **DISTRIBUTION** Ranges, slopes and lowlands of eastern Australia, from coastal north-eastern Qld, to southern NSW and through central NSW along Murray-Darling river drainage systems, to south-eastern SA. **HABITAT AND HABITS** Occurs in most wet habitats, including rainforests, wet and dry sclerophyll forests, woodland and heaths, particularly in rocky areas around edges of creeks, rivers and swamps. Diurnal; usually seen basking on rocks, and forages among riverine vegetation for invertebrates, including worms, water beetles, aquatic larvae, tadpoles, small frogs, fish, snails and smaller lizards. Viviparous, giving birth to up to 9 young in a litter.

Southern Water-skink ■ *Eulamprus tympanum* SVL 90mm
(Southern Water Skink; Dreeite Water Skink; Water Skink)

DESCRIPTION Glossy, moderately robust skink, with slightly depressed tail and relatively long rear legs. Olive-brown above with numerous black flecks on head, back and base of tail. Sides, including sides of tail, black with scattered olive-brown blotches, becoming more concentrated on tail, and flanks olive-grey with blackish marbling. Limbs olive-brown with black blotches. Belly and throat grey, marbled and spotted with black. **DISTRIBUTION** South-eastern Australia, from north-eastern NSW, through central and southern Vic, to south-eastern SA and Fleurieu Peninsula. **HABITAT AND HABITS** Occurs in open forests, woodland, shrubland and grassland. Most commonly seen in moist

habitats along small creeks, where it basks on rocks and logs. Diurnal; feeds on invertebrates, including spiders and snails, tadpoles, small frogs, other lizards and a small amount of plant matter. Females give birth to up to 8 young. Takes to refuge in the water when alarmed.

Black-tailed Bar-lipped Skink ■ *Glaphyromorphus nigricaudis* SVL 85mm
(Black-tailed Skink)

DESCRIPTION Robust, smooth-scaled, long-tailed skink, with a movable, scaly lower eyelid and moderately long limbs. Golden brown to dark brown above, with blackish spots on forebody, along flanks, legs and original tail; spots on neck arranged in transverse rows and often form continuous bands. Lips barred with brownish-grey and cream, ear opening oval and underparts yellowish-cream. **DISTRIBUTION** North-eastern Australia, including

north-eastern NT and Cape York Peninsula Qld. **HABITAT AND HABITS** Found in wide range of moist habitats, including rainforests, vine scrubs, gallery forests, tropical woodland and coastal heaths, where it tends to occupy margins and riparian zones. Shelters during the day under rocks, fallen timber and dense leaf litter, emerging at night to forage for small invertebrates. Mainly egg laying, but viviparous in some southern areas.

Fine-spotted Mulch-skink ▪ *Glaphyromorphus punctulatus* SVL 65mm

DESCRIPTION Glossy, smooth-scaled, long-bodied skink, with long tail and movable, scaly lower eyelid, and small limbs with 5 digits on each. Uniformly yellowish-brown to rich brown above, with fine black-brown flecks on flanks, and occasionally with scattered

brown flecks on back. Lips white with black bars, and underparts cream to yellowish with dark brown spots on throat and chin. **DISTRIBUTION** Coast and adjacent inland of central eastern Qld. **HABITAT AND HABITS** Occurs from dry forests to humid woodland. Forages at night in leaf litter for small invertebrates, and shelters during the day under rocks and fallen debris. Oviparous, laying a clutch of around 3 eggs.

Rainforest Cool-skink ▪ *Harrisoniascincus zia* SVL 55mm

DESCRIPTION Small, short-limbed skink with 5 digits on each limb, and with movable lower eyelid containing small transparent disc. Brown to blackish-brown above, with numerous blackish and pale brown flecks on nape, back and original tail. Faint dorsolateral stripe from head to tail, upper sides blackish-brown and lower sides brown flecked with pale brown. Underparts white or yellow with black flecks on throat. **DISTRIBUTION** South-eastern Qld and north-eastern NSW. **HABITAT AND HABITS** Found in upland rainforests and cool, wet forests, where it is highly secretive, but can be seen basking in patches of sunlight at edges of clearings. Fossorial, foraging within loose soil and leaf litter for small invertebrates. Oviparous, with an average of 5 eggs in a clutch.

Lowlands Earless Skink ■ *Hemiergis peronii* SVL 65mm

DESCRIPTION Smooth-scaled skink with elongated body and short limbs, each with 3–4 small digits, and movable lower eyelid with transparent disc. Brown to olive-brown above with thin line of longitudinally aligned blackish dots on back and tail, and thin blackish dorsolateral stripe from eye to tail, sometimes bordered above with yellowish-brown. Sides have obscure variegated pattern and underparts yellow with each scale spotted with dark brown. Lips pale, spotted with brown, and ear openings usually absent. **DISTRIBUTION** Coast and near coastal interior, and offshore islands along southern Australia, from south-

west WA, through southern SA, to south-western Vic. **HABITAT AND HABITS** Found in dry sclerophyll forests associated with offshore islands, coastal heaths and shrubs. Fossorial, often burrowing under rotting logs and rarely venturing out into the open air. Viviparous, with around 3 live young in a litter; females able to store sperm from mating in autumn until they ovulate in the following spring.

Eastern Three-toed Earless Skink ■ *Hemiergis talbingoensis* SVL 65mm

DESCRIPTION Smooth-scaled skink with elongated body and small limbs, each with 3 small digits, and with medium-length, thickened tail that is narrower than body and tapers to pointed tip. Brown to blackish-brown above with thin, longitudinally aligned dashes or stripes on back and tail. Face and sides grey with black marbling, and underparts yellowish.

DISTRIBUTION South-eastern Australian mainland, from south-eastern Qld, through eastern NSW, to western Vic. (SA populations now considered a separate species, *H. decresiensis*.) **HABITAT AND HABITS** Found in wet and dry forests and woodland, where it is active at night, foraging for small invertebrates in leaf litter and loose soil. Shelters at other times under rocks and logs. Oviparous, laying around 4–5 eggs in a clutch. Occurs at higher altitudes in north of its range.

Dark-flecked Garden Sunskink ■ *Lampropholis delicata* SVL 45mm
(Grass Skink; Delicate Skink)

DESCRIPTION Smooth-scaled skink with moderately sized limbs, each with 5 digits, and movable lower eyelid that contains a transparent disc. Greyish-brown to rich coppery-brown above, more copper coloured on head and nape, normally with indistinct dark vertebral stripe and scattered fine darker brown flecks. Thin pale yellowish-brown dorsolateral stripe from neck to tail, and variably with white midlateral stripe from neck to rear leg. Underparts whitish. **DISTRIBUTION** Tasmania, and eastern and south-eastern mainland from north-eastern Qld (south of Cape York Peninsula), through eastern NSW and southern Vic, to southern SA. **HABITAT AND HABITS** Occurs in variety of habitats, from rainforests, dry and wet forests and open woodland, to coastal heaths, moist grassland and suburban gardens. Diurnal, actively foraging on the ground for insects and other small invertebrates, including ants, spiders, flies, moths and worms. Oviparous, laying around 3–4 eggs in communal nest with other females. Nests can contain over 200 eggs, and laying can occur more than once in a year.

Pale-flecked Garden Sunskink ■ *Lampropholis guichenoti* SVL 45mm
(Garden Skink)

DESCRIPTION Smooth-scaled skink with moderately sized limbs, each with 5 digits, a movable lower eyelid that contains a transparent disc, and a long, slender tail. Brown to brownish-grey above, more coppery on head; obscure dark brown vertebral stripe from neck to tail, with scattered dark flecks and whitish scales arranged in longitudinal row. Sides blackish-brown with dark broad dorsolateral stripe from ear to tail, occasionally bordered below with whitish midlateral line. Underparts white to pale grey, usually with some brown speckling. **DISTRIBUTION** South-eastern mainland Australia, from south-eastern Qld, through eastern NSW and Vic, to south-eastern SA. **HABITAT AND HABITS** Occurs in range of habitats, from rainforest fringes, dry and wet forests, and open woodland, to coastal heaths, moist grassland and suburban gardens. Diurnal, actively foraging on the ground for small invertebrates, including spiders, ants, flies, moths and worms. Oviparous, laying around 3–4 eggs in communal nest with other females. Nests can contain over 200 eggs, and laying can occur more than once in a year.

South-eastern Slider ■ *Lerista bougainvillii* SVL 70mm
(Bougainville's Skink)

DESCRIPTION Smooth-scaled, long-bodied skink with small, distinct external ear openings and small limbs with 5 digits on each. Grey to brown above with numerous small, dark brown dots, arranged in longitudinal rows. Upper sides have broad black lateral stripe from snout to base of tail; lower sides creamish with blackish spots and streaks. Tail yellowish or orange-brown, with darker brown spots and mottling. Underparts creamish. **DISTRIBUTION** Slopes, ranges and coastal plains of northern Tas and islands of Bass Strait, and south-eastern and southern mainland, from northern-eastern and central NSW, through Vic, to south-eastern SA. **HABITAT AND HABITS** Found in forests, woodland,

heaths, shrubland and rocky outcrops. Feeds during the day on small invertebrates, including termites, ants, spiders and insect larvae. At night, shelters in soft soil under rocks and logs. Oviparous, viviparous and ovoviviparous, within its range, giving birth to average of 3 live young in Tasmania, and laying up to 4 eggs on mainland Australia.

Eastern Mulch-slider ■ *Lerista fragilis* SVL 60mm

DESCRIPTION Smooth-scaled, long-bodied skink with small, distinct external ear openings, small limbs with 3 digits on each and movable lower eyelid. Greyish-brown to olive-brown above, with each scale having small dark centre, giving longitudinal pattern

along back. Upper sides have black stripe between snout and tail; lower sides pale greyish with dark scales forming fine lines. Tail reddish, especially in juveniles, and underparts whitish with dark flecks. **DISTRIBUTION** Central and south-eastern Qld. **HABITAT AND HABITS** Found in dry forests to humid woodland. Active at night, foraging on the ground or in loose soil and leaf litter, for small invertebrates. Oviparous, laying 2 eggs in a clutch.

Southern Sandslider ■ *Lerista labialis* SVL 60mm

DESCRIPTION Robust, 'snake-like' skink, with forelimbs absent and hindlimbs with 2 digits. Pale brown to reddish-brown above, with dark brown spots forming pair of longitudinal lines from nape to tail, and broad, dark brown stripe along upper side from snout to tail. Lower sides and underparts whitish. **DISTRIBUTION** Arid inland, from western Qld and western NSW, through central and southern NT and SA, to western and central WA. Also on Abrolhos Island off WA coast. **HABITAT AND HABITS** Found in range of arid habitats, including sandy spinifex deserts, arid scrubland and sandy coastal dunes, where it shelters in loose soil under logs, rocks and termite mounds. Nocturnal, burrowing through soft substrate and emerging to feed on the surface for insects, including ants and termites. Oviparous, laying 2 eggs in a clutch.

Eastern Robust Slider ■ *Lerista punctatovittata* SVL 100mm

DESCRIPTION Robust, smooth-scaled, long-bodied skink. Forelimbs greatly reduced, with 1–2 digits; hindlimbs longer, with 3 digits. Movable lower eyelid. Yellowish-brown, pinkish-brown or pale brown above, sometimes with dark edges on scales forming series of longitudinal lines, and paler sides. Tail greyish, flushed with pink, and heavily spotted above and below with dark brown. Head shields defined with dark brown, and lips barred cream and brown. Underparts white to yellowish. **DISTRIBUTION** Inland of central and southern Qld, central and western NSW, north-western Vic and western SA. **HABITAT AND HABITS** Occurs in drier woodland, shrubland and grassland. Forages during the night, on the ground or in loose soil and leaf litter, for small invertebrates. Oviparous, laying around 3–4 eggs in a clutch.

Timid Slider ■ *Lerista timida* SVL 45mm
(Wood Mulch Slider)

DESCRIPTION Smooth-scaled skink with an elongated body, variably sized short limbs, each with 3 digits, and fused lower eyelid. Bronze-brown to brownish-grey above with either small blackish spots forming series of longitudinal lines, or series of longitudinal dorsal stripes. Upper sides have blackish-brown stripe from snout to tail; creamish to pale grey on lower sides, with dark margins on scales forming reticulated pattern. Underparts whitish. **DISTRIBUTION** Arid and semi-arid Australian mainland, including southern and central Qld, central and western NSW, northern Vic, central and northern SA, southern NT, and western

and central WA. **HABITAT AND HABITS** Found in drier woodland, shrubland and grassland. Shelters under rocks and logs, emerging to forage during the night, either on the surface of the ground or within loose soil and leaf litter, for insects, including ants and termites. Oviparous, laying 2 eggs in a clutch.

Outcrop Rainbow-skink ■ *Liburnascincus mundivensis* SVL 55mm
(Outcrop Rock-skink)

DESCRIPTION Small, moderately flattened skink. Well-developed limbs, with 4 digits on front pair and 5 on rear, and long, slender tail. Dark greyish-brown to blackish above and

on sides, with scattered paler flecks and faint pale dorsolateral stripe. Coppery flush on neck and head, and round external ear openings. Underparts whitish. **DISTRIBUTION** Eastern Qld. **HABITAT AND HABITS** Found in dry forests to humid woodland. Active during the day, foraging in rocky areas for small insects and other arthropods, or basking in patches of sunlight. Oviparous, laying 2 eggs in a clutch, with more than 1 clutch possible in a year.

Desert Skink ■ *Liopholis inornata* SVL 85mm
(Desert Egernia; Rosen's Skink; Unadorned Desert-skink)

DESCRIPTION Moderately sized, cryptically patterned skink with thickened, tapering tail, and strong long legs and toes. Pale brown to rich reddish-brown above; edges of scales form narrow, dark brown longitudinal patterning with scattered white and brown spots from nape to tail. Sides patterned with white and dark brown, and sides of head with dark brown barring on lips and cheeks. Underparts white. **DISTRIBUTION** Arid to semi-arid southern Australia, from southern inland WA, through southern NT and SA, to south-western Qld, western and central NSW, and north-western Vic. **HABITAT AND HABITS** Occurs in mallee woodland, shrubland and grassland with sandy or stony soils, where it feeds during the day on small invertebrates, including spiders, centipedes and ants, and small lizards. Viviparous, with up to 4 (average 2) young in a litter, and 1–2 litters in a year.

Eastern Ranges Rock-skink ■ *Liopholis modesta* SVL 110mm
(Modest Skink)

DESCRIPTION Fast-moving, robust skink with well-developed limbs and thick, tapering tail. Olive-grey to brown above, with edges of scales forming narrow, dark brown longitudinal patterning from nape to tail. Sides greyish-brown with faint reticulated pattern. Lips, cheeks and anterior flanks have white spots. Underparts whitish. **DISTRIBUTION** South-eastern Qld, north-eastern NSW and isolated areas of central NSW. **HABITAT AND HABITS** Occurs in dry forests to humid woodland, where it is active during the day, foraging on the ground around rock areas and fallen logs for insects and other small invertebrates. Shelters in social family groups of 2–6 individuals, in complex burrow system with numerous interconnecting tunnels and several entrances. Viviparous, with 1–5 (average 3) live young in a litter.

White's Skink ■ *Liopholis whitii* SVL 115mm

DESCRIPTION Fast-moving, robust, smooth-scaled skink, with well-developed limbs and long, tapering tail. Highly variable in colour and pattern. Reddish-brown to dark brown, with reddish-brown vertebral stripe and blackish longitudinal dorsal stripes, cream dashed, or unpatterned with just a few scattered blackish spots. Sides paler greyish and speckled with light and dark spots, and with 1–2 dark-edged pale spots vertically above front limbs.

Underparts white to pale grey. **DISTRIBUTION** Tasmania and islands of Bass Strait, and southern and eastern mainland, from south-western Qld, through eastern NSW and Vic, to central southern SA. **HABITAT AND HABITS** Occupies dry forests, woodland, heaths and grassland. Active during the day, foraging on the ground for invertebrates, including ants, crickets, spiders and beetles, as well as eating fruits, berries, flowers and soft shoots. Often seen with other members of its species. At night shelters in burrows under rocks. Viviparous, typically with 3–4 young in a litter, and a single litter in a year.

Eastern Mourning Skink ■ *Lissolepis coventryi* SVL 100mm
(Swamp Skink)

DESCRIPTION Moderately robust, smooth-scaled skink with well-developed limbs, with 5 digits on each, and fourth toe longer than rest; distinct ear lobules. Greenish-brown to olive-brown above, with black edges of scales creating variable two-toned pattern, and 2 longitudinal dorsolateral black stripes from nape to base of tail. Upper sides black with scattered yellowish-green spots, and lower sides reticulated black and olive-green. Head

has black blotches and lips have white bars. Underparts whitish, with olive-green wash on throat. **DISTRIBUTION** Coast and ranges of far south-eastern NSW, through southern Vic, to far south-western SA. **HABITAT AND HABITS** Found in coastal and near coastal swamps, marshes and lagoons. Active during the day, foraging on the ground for small invertebrates, including beetles and worms, and plant material. Viviparous, with average of 3 young in a litter.

Tree-base Litter-skink ▪ *Lygisaurus foliorum* SVL 35mm, TL 80mm
(Iridescent Litter-skink; Tree Base Litter Skink)

DESCRIPTION Slender, smooth-scaled skink with relatively short limbs, 5 digits on rear limbs and 4 on front ones, and partially or fully fused lower eyelid, forming transparent covering over eye. Brown above with numerous light brown and darker brown flecks, white-flecked sides and limbs, and contrasting orange-brown hindlimbs and tail. Lips white with brown barring, and underparts whitish with scattered dark brown spots. **DISTRIBUTION** Eastern Australia, from north-eastern Qld (south of Cape York Peninsula) to around Sydney NSW. **HABITAT AND HABITS** Favours moist forests, open woodland and heaths. Active within partly shaded areas from dawn to dusk, foraging in leaf litter on the ground for insects and other arthropods. Oviparous, laying 2 eggs in a clutch.

Common Dwarf Skink ▪ *Menetia greyii* SVL 35mm
(Grey's Menetia, Grey's Skink)

DESCRIPTION Very small, slender skink with well-developed, short limbs, 5 digits on rear limbs and 4 on front ones, and fully fused lower eyelid, forming transparent covering over eye. Bronzed grey-brown above, with 4 thin, broken, black-dashed longitudinal lines from head to tail, and black dorsolateral stripe starting at snout, becoming broader behind eye and continuing to tail. White midlateral stripe, with grey-brown lower side and yellowish-cream underparts. Lips paler, with brown flecks, similar on chin, and throat whitish with darker brown lines. **DISTRIBUTION** Throughout mainland Australia, although absent from Cape York Peninsula Qld, eastern and south-eastern coasts, and central northern WA. **HABITAT AND HABITS** Occurs in large range of habitats, including dry forests, temperate-tropical woodland, mallee, arid scrubland and grassland. Active during the day, foraging in leaf litter for insects and other small arthropods. Oviparous, laying an average of 2 eggs in a clutch.

Saltbush Morethia Skink ▪ *Morethia adelaidensis* SVL 50mm
(Saltbush Skink)

DESCRIPTION Small, smooth-scaled skink with 5 digits on each limb, long, slender tail, and fused lower eyelid forming clear covering over eye. Greyish-brown to olive-brown above with longitudinally aligned pattern of dark brown spots and dashes, and thin pale cream dorsolateral stripe. Sides have fragmented dark brown upper lateral stripe; lower

sides white with dark brown streaks. Underparts whitish, with sexually active males having orange flush. **DISTRIBUTION** Southern Australian mainland from south-western WA, through southern and eastern SA, to north-western Vic, western NSW and south-western Qld. **HABITAT AND HABITS** Occurs in dry woodland, shrubland and grassland. Active during the day, foraging on the ground for small invertebrates. Oviparous, laying around 3 eggs in a clutch.

Boulenger's Snake-eyed Skink ▪ *Morethia boulengeri* SVL 55mm
(South-eastern Morethia Skink; Boulenger's Skink)

DESCRIPTION Small, smooth-scaled skink with 5 digits on each limb, long, slender tail and fused lower eyelid, forming clear covering over eye. Greyish-brown, olive-brown or reddish-brown, with longitudinally aligned blackish flecks. Upper sides blackish and lower sides pale grey, the two separated with white midlateral stripe. Underparts white, with sexually active males having reddish flush on throat, and base of tail has coppery wash.

Belly white. **DISTRIBUTION** Southern and eastern mainland Australia, including central and southern Qld, southern NT, western WA, SA, northern Vic and NSW. Absent from the coast throughout the majority of its range. **HABITAT AND HABITS** Occurs in dry forests, woodland, shrubland and grassland, where it is active during the day, foraging on the ground for small invertebrates. Oviparous, laying an average of 3 eggs in a clutch, with 1–2 clutches laid in a year.

Fire-tailed Skink ■ *Morethia taeniopleura* SVL 40mm
(Eastern Fire-tailed Skink)

DESCRIPTION Small, smooth-scaled skink with 5 digits on each limb, long, slender tail and fused lower eyelid, forming clear covering over eye. Uniform coppery-brown to greyish-brown above, with small, scattered dark brown to black flecks, and distinct white dorsolateral stripe from snout to base of rear limbs. Sides have broad black stripe, bordered below with broad white stripe. Tail reddish-brown to reddish-orange, and underparts whitish. **DISTRIBUTION** Coast and adjacent inland of eastern Queensland. **HABITAT AND HABITS** Occurs in dry forests, open woodland and rocky ridges, where it is active during the day, foraging on the ground for small invertebrates. Oviparous, laying an average of 2 eggs in a clutch.

Southern Forest Cool-skink ■ *Carinascincus coventryi* SVL 50mm
(Coventry's Skink)

DESCRIPTION Slender skink with slightly keeled scales, well-developed limbs, 5 digits on hindlimbs and 4 on front ones, and movable lower eyelid containing clear transparent disc. Uniform dark brown above, occasionally with blackish flecks, with pale coppery-brown dorsolateral stripe from neck to tail, and sides flecked with blackish and cream. Underparts creamish with scattered blackish flecks. **DISTRIBUTION** South-eastern mainland Australia, from around Sydney NSW, to central western Vic. **HABITAT AND HABITS** Normally associated with wet forests and woodland, but also in mixed forests and grassland. Active during the day in both shaded and sunny areas, foraging in fallen tree litter for small invertebrates. Viviparous, laying up to 7 (average 3) young in a litter.

Metallic Cool-skink ■ *Carinascincus metallicus* SVL 60mm
(Metallic Skink)

DESCRIPTION Slender skink with weakly keeled scales, well-developed limbs, 5 digits on hindlimbs and 4 on front ones, movable lower eyelid containing clear transparent disc, and long, slender tail. Variable in colour. Generally brownish above with or without

longitudinally aligned dark brown and pale brown flecks, and obscure pale dorsolateral stripe. Upper sides blackish-brown with obscure pale flecks; lower sides mottled grey with pale flecks, with whitish midlateral stripe from ear to rear legs. Underparts whitish flecked with brown. **DISTRIBUTION** Tas and central southern Vic. **HABITAT AND HABITS** Occurs in wide range of habitats, including forests, woodland, coastal heaths and grassland. Active during the day, foraging on the ground for small invertebrates. Viviparous, with up to 8 (average 4) young in a litter.

Ocellated Skink ■ *Carinascincus ocellatus* SVL 85mm

DESCRIPTION Slender, smooth-scaled skink with well-developed limbs, 5 digits on hindlimbs and 4 on front ones, movable lower eyelid containing clear transparent disc, and medium-length, slender tail. Olive-brown to rich coppery-brown above, paler on head

and tail, with numerous yellowish-cream flecks and blotches, often merging together to form variegated pattern. Sides similar, but with fewer spots, and underparts whitish to pale grey, occasionally with dark brown markings on throat. **DISTRIBUTION** Northern and eastern Tas. **HABITAT AND HABITS** Found in dry forests to humid woodland. Active during the day, foraging on the ground and in rocky outcrops for range of small invertebrates, supplemented with fruits of cheese berry plants *Cyathodes* spp. Viviparous, with average of 3 young in a litter, and producing a single litter in a year.

Ornate Soil-crevice Skink ■ *Notoscincus ornatus* SVL 35mm

DESCRIPTION Small, smooth-scaled skink with moderately developed limbs, each with 5 digits, fused lower eyelid containing transparent disc that covers eye, and medium-length tail. Coppery-brown or olive-brown above with or without vertebral line of dark brown spots, often more noticeable on tail, and with thin whitish dorsolateral stripe from snout to tail. Sides have broad lateral black stripe from eye to hindlimbs, bordered below with white lower lateral stripe. Underparts whitish with darker streaks on throat and lips marked faintly with brown. **DISTRIBUTION** Northern Australia, from western WA, through NT, to northern Qld, except Cape York Peninsula. **HABITAT AND HABITS** Found in dry woodland, shrubland and grassland, where it is active during the day, foraging on the ground for small invertebrates. Oviparous, laying around 2–3 eggs in a clutch.

Black upper lateral zone may be solid or broken into a series of blotches

Kinghorn's Snake-eyed Skink ■ *Proablepharus kinghorni* SVL 45mm
(Red-tailed Soil-crevice Skink)

DESCRIPTION Glossy, smooth-scaled skink with moderately sized limbs, each with 5 digits, small external ear openings, and partially fused lower eyelid containing transparent disc that covers eye, but with slit at top of eye. Pale grey or pale brown, with darker edges on scales forming series of alternating white and brown spotted longitudinal stripes from head to tail. Tail dull to bright reddish, rear limbs brown and front limbs greyish-white. Underparts whitish. **DISTRIBUTION** Central eastern Australia, from central western NT, through south-western Qld, to north-western NSW. **HABITAT AND HABITS** Favours black soil plains and tussock grassland on red sandy soil, where it shelters under leaf litter or fallen timber, or in soil crevices. Feeds on invertebrates that it finds in cracking clay soils during daylight. Oviparous, laying up to 4 eggs in a clutch.

Southern Grass Skink ■ *Pseudemoia entrecasteauxii* SVL 60mm
(Grass Skink; Tussock Cool-skink)

DESCRIPTION Medium-sized, slender, smooth-scaled skink with well-developed limbs, each with 5 digits, and with movable lower eyelids containing transparent disc. Variable colouration. Olive-brown to coppery-brown above, patchy blackish laterodorsal stripe, and greyish dorsolateral stripe from eye to tail. Sides darker, often with paler flecking. Older adults often with obscure pattern. Underparts greyish-white, with breeding males having red wash on throat and chest. **DISTRIBUTION** Tas and islands of Bass Strait, and south-eastern mainland, from north-eastern NSW, through southern Vic, to south-eastern SA. **HABITAT AND HABITS** Occupies forests and grassland, where it is active during the day, foraging in grasses or under dense ground for small invertebrates, or basking on logs and rocks. Viviparous, giving birth to up to 8 (average 4) young in a litter.

Breeding male

Female

Tussock Skink ■ *Pseudemoia pagenstecheri* SVL 65mm

DESCRIPTION Small, smooth-scaled, striped skink, with moderately short limbs and movable lower eyelid containing transparent disc. Grey to olive-brown above, with thin black vertebral stripe, occasionally dark longitudinal line on either side of back, and narrow yellowish dorsolateral stripe. Upper sides dark brown and lower sides greyish, and pale yellow, or orange in males, pale midlateral stripe from behind ear to tail. Sides of neck and lips grey with some dark brown markings. Underparts whitish-grey to yellowish. **DISTRIBUTION** Tas and islands of Bass Strait, and south-eastern mainland, from north-eastern NSW to western Vic. **HABITAT AND HABITS** Found in forests, woodland and grassland. Shelters at night in bases of grassy tussocks, and forages in tussocks and on the ground in leaf litter for small invertebrates. Viviparous, giving birth to up to 11 (average 4–5) young in a litter.

Glossy Grass Skink ■ *Pseudemoia rawlinsoni* SVL 60mm
(Swampland Cool-skink)

DESCRIPTION Medium-sized, slender, smooth-scaled skink with well-developed limbs, each with 5 digits, and with movable lower eyelid containing transparent disc. Olive-grey to brown above with dark brown vertebral stripe from nape to tail, and black laterodorsal stripe and creamish dorsolateral stripe. Sides dark brown with white midlateral stripe. Underparts whitish-grey. **DISTRIBUTION** North-eastern Tas and Cape Barren Island and south-eastern mainland, from south-eastern NSW, through central Vic, to south-eastern SA. **HABITAT AND HABITS** Favours wet areas, including swamps and marshes, where it is active during the day, foraging on the ground for small invertebrates. Viviparous, giving birth to up to 8 (average 6) young in a litter.

Trunk-climbing Cool-skink ■ *Pseudemoia spenceri* SVL 60mm
(Spencer's Skink)

DESCRIPTION Medium-sized, slender, weakly keeled skink with well-developed limbs, each with 5 digits, and with movable lower eyelid containing transparent disc. Coppery-brown to blackish above, with numerous small, metallic yellowish-brown flecks and spots forming discontinuous longitudinal stripes, more concentrated on head, and with distinctive yellowish or silvery-grey dorsolateral stripe from snout to tail. Sides blackish, with numerous yellowish-brown spots and thin, silvery-grey midlateral stripe. Underparts whitish to silvery-grey. **DISTRIBUTION** South-eastern mainland Australia (above 500m), from south-eastern NSW to southern Vic. **HABITAT AND HABITS** Found in forests and woodland, where it lives in large groups. Shelters at night in rock crevices and cracks in trees, and emerges during the day to forage on trees and rocky areas for small invertebrates. Viviparous, with up to 3 young in a litter.

Dwarf Litter-skink ▪ *Pygmaeascincus timlowi* SVL 29mm
(Low's Litter Skink)

DESCRIPTION Small, slender skink with large scale in centre of top of head, short limbs with 4 digits on front pair and 5 on rear, and large, fixed, transparent disc covering eye. Dark greyish-brown above with some dark and light flecks, an iridescent sheen, and a

reddish flush in breeding males. Sides dark greyish-brown with fine dark spotting, most concentrated on flanks and tail. Underparts white, occasionally with scattered brown flecks. **DISTRIBUTION** Coast, ranges and adjacent inland of eastern Qld. **HABITAT AND HABITS** Found in dry forests and woodland, where it is rarely seen in the open, preferring instead to live in fallen leaf litter around bases of trees, where it forages for small invertebrates. Oviparous, laying 1–2 eggs in a clutch.

Three-toed Skink ▪ *Saiphos equalis* SVL 75mm

DESCRIPTION Robust, smooth-scaled, long-bodied skink with shortened, widely spaced limbs, each with 3 very short digits, and movable lower eyelid. Rich brown to greyish-brown above with dark brown, longitudinally aligned spots, and with sharply contrasting blackish-brown sides. Head has dark brown face, with yellowish spots on the cheeks and flanks; external ear openings absent. Underparts yellow to orange, with dark brown spots

on throat. Underside of tail black. **DISTRIBUTION** Coastal lowlands and adjacent ranges of eastern mainland, including south-eastern Qld and eastern NSW. **HABITAT AND HABITS** Found in rainforests, forests, woodland, heaths, grassland and adjacent suburban gardens. Active at night, foraging under rocks and logs, or in dense groundcover, for invertebrates that include beetles and their larvae, worms and centipedes. Oviparous, laying around 3 advanced eggs that hatch within 2 weeks. Often found in large numbers where it occurs.

Three-toed Snake-tooth Skink ■ *Saiphos reticulatus* SVL 195mm

DESCRIPTION Robust, long-bodied skink with shortened, widely spaced limbs, each with 3 digits, wedge-shaped snout and dark eye-patch. Yellowish-brown or grey-brown above, with numerous scattered darker brown flecks and streaks, indistinct bands, more prominent in juveniles, and blackish collar. Underparts greyish, with dark-edged scales forming reticulated pattern, and with dark brown streaks on throat. **DISTRIBUTION** Eastern Australia, from Fraser Island south-east Qld, to Crescent Head, north-east NSW. **HABITAT AND HABITS** Found in loose, fertile soils, dense leaf litter and rotting logs, and under bark of trees. Nocturnal and fossorial, hunting within loose soil mainly for worms, but will also eat beetle larvae. Oviparous, generally laying up to 6 eggs in soil under rotting timber.

Orange-tailed Shadeskink ■ *Saproscincus challengeri* SVL 55mm
(Challenger Skink)

DESCRIPTION Smooth-scaled, slender skink, with long, well-developed limbs, 5 digits on each limb, and slender, tapering tail. Yellowish-brown to greyish-brown or reddish-brown above, with light brown flecks and scattered black spots. Blackish-brown dorsolateral stripe, often fragmented, and occasionally with paler reddish margin, and tail with conspicuous creamish blotches. Sides of neck and face paler, with darker brown spots and blackish streak behind eye. Females have pale-edged, dark brown dorsolateral stripe. Underparts white to yellowish with brown spots. **DISTRIBUTION** Far south-eastern Qld and far north-eastern NSW. **HABITAT AND HABITS** Occupies wetter forests, including rainforests, where it is active from dawn to dusk, foraging on the ground or in leaf litter for insects and other small invertebrates. Shelters at other times in moist areas under rocks and logs, or in dense leaf litter. Oviparous, laying 2 eggs in a clutch.

Weasel Skink ■ *Saproscincus mustelinus* SVL 50mm

DESCRIPTION Smooth-scaled, slender skink, with long, well-developed limbs, 5 digits on each limb, and long, slender, tapering tail. Grey-brown, pale brown or dark coppery-brown above, with or without variegated pattern of light and dark brown flecks, and with indistinct pale yellowish-brown to orange-brown dorsolateral stripe. Paler on flanks, with darker brown streaks, and head with short white bar behind eye, which is edged

with blackish-brown above. Underparts whitish to yellowish with long dark streaks. **DISTRIBUTION** Coast and adjacent ranges of south-eastern mainland Australia, from northern NSW to southern Vic. **HABITAT AND HABITS** Occurs in wetter forests, including rainforests, woodland, heaths and adjacent pastures or gardens, where it shelters under logs or in timber and other vegetation. Feeds on small invertebrates. Oviparous, laying around 3–4 eggs in a communal nest, with several other females, with 1–2 clutches in a year.

Rose's Shadeskink ■ *Saproscincus rosei* SVL 60mm

DESCRIPTION Smooth-scaled, slender skink, with long, well-developed limbs, 5 digits on each limb, and slender, tapering tail. Greyish-brown to reddish-brown above, either with short, blackish vertebral line, bordered with broad bronze to orange stripes, and with numerous scattered spots and flecks of lighter and darker brown, or largely unpatterned. Broad, fragmented blackish-brown dorsolateral stripe and paler greyish flanks, spotted with

lighter and darker brown. Females have strong blackish sides with broad white or yellow midlateral stripe. Underparts white to yellowish with brown spots. **DISTRIBUTION** Coastal south-eastern Qld and north-eastern NSW. **HABITAT AND HABITS** Occurs in wetter forests, including rainforests, and dense thickets. Active from dawn to dusk, foraging on the ground or in leaf litter for insects and other small invertebrates, including cockroaches and moths. Shelters at other times in moist areas under rocks and logs, or in dense leaf litter. Oviparous, laying 2 eggs in a clutch.

Gully Skink ■ *Saproscincus spectabilis* SVL 60mm
(Pale-lipped Shadeskink)

DESCRIPTION Smooth-scaled, slender skink, with long, well-developed limbs, 5 digits on each limb, and slender, tapering tail. Brown to reddish-brown above, with scattered lighter and dark flecks, and blotches forming complex variegated pattern. Broad, ragged dark brown dorsolateral stripe, and sides with variegated pattern of lighter and darker brown with, at times, cream midlateral stripe. Tail reddish-brown, and underparts white to yellow with longitudinally aligned brownish flecks. **DISTRIBUTION** Coastal and near coastal south-eastern Qld and ranges of north-eastern NSW. **HABITAT AND HABITS** Found in wetter forests, including rainforests, where it is active from dawn to dusk, foraging on the ground for small insects and other invertebrates, and often seen basking in patches of sunlight. Oviparous, laying 2 eggs in a clutch.

Murray's Skink ■ *Karma murrayi* SVL 110mm
(Blue-speckled Forest-skink)

DESCRIPTION Robust skink with an attractive variegated pattern. Rich brown to coppery-brown above, with dark-edged scales giving flecked transverse pattern. Sides and neck paler, with numerous black flecks that combine to form larger blotches on neck. Lips creamish with black blotches, and underparts creamish with darker flecking towards outer edges. **DISTRIBUTION** Coast and ranges of south-eastern Qld and north-eastern NSW. **HABITAT AND HABITS** Found in rainforests and wet, open forests, where it is active during the day, foraging on logs and in leaf litter in open areas, or places with patches of native or exotic shrubs. Normally found sheltering under rotting logs or crevices, or basking partially exposed in filtered sunlight. Viviparous, producing 3–5 live young in a litter.

Centralian Blue-tongue ■ *Tiliqua multifasciata* SVL 280mm
(Centralian Blue-tongued Skink)

DESCRIPTION Large skink with broad head, short limbs, moderately long, tapering tail and large blue tongue. Generally greyish with numerous orange-brown transverse bands on back and tail, and broad blackish stripe from eye to above ear. Underparts creamish. Top of

head unpatterned, or with some thin blackish marks. DISTRIBUTION Western, central and northern Australia, from coastal north-western WA, through central and southern NT and northern SA, to western Qld. HABITAT AND HABITS Occurs in open woodland, shrubland and grassland. Active during the day, foraging on the ground for insect larvae and other invertebrates, such as spiders, berries, flowers and soft shoots of plants, and carrion. Viviparous, with up to 10 live young in a litter.

Blotched Blue-tongue ■ *Tiliqua nigrolutea* SVL 275mm
(Blotched Blue-tongue Lizard; Blotched Blue-tongued Skink; Southern Blue-tongue)

DESCRIPTION Large skink with broad body, short limbs, moderately long, tapering tail and large blue tongue. Generally dark brown to blackish above, with large cream, yellow or pinkish blotches on back and tail. Blotches can be loosely aligned to form transverse bands, or obscure longitudinal rows on back. Head generally pale, with greyish lips, and occasionally with indistinct eye-stripe. Underparts paler and conspicuously patterned.

Throat white. DISTRIBUTION Tas and south-eastern mainland Australia, from north-eastern SA, through Vic, to Blue Mountains NSW. HABITAT AND HABITS Found in tall, open forests, woodland, heaths, grassland and adjacent gardens, where it shelters under rocks and logs, and in dense leaf litter. Feeds on invertebrates, including snails, slugs and spiders, vegetable matter, such as berries, flowers and leaves, as well as small mice and some carrion. Viviparous, giving birth to up to 15 (average 8) live young in a litter, typically every 2 years. When threatened, tends to flatten body, open its wide mouth and stick out its large blue tongue.

Western Blue-tongue ■ *Tiliqua occipitalis* SVL 300mm
(Western Blue-tongued Skink)

DESCRIPTION Large skink with broad head, short limbs, short tail and large blue tongue. Generally greyish to yellowish-brown above; head darker and with broad blackish stripe from eye to ear. Series of broad, brownish-black transverse bands on back, which extend to whitish underparts, and have varying amounts of paler spots and blotches contained within them. Tail also banded. **DISTRIBUTION** Western and southern mainland Australia, from central-west coast of WA, through southern WA, southern NT and SA, to north-western Vic and south-western NSW. **HABITAT AND HABITS** Found in range of arid to sub-humid habitats, including woodland, shrubland, heaths and spinifex grassland, where it shelters under rocks and leaf litter, and occasionally within disused animal burrows. Diurnal, foraging on the ground for insect larvae and other invertebrates, such as spiders, berries and flowers of plants, and carrion. Viviparous, with 3–10 (average 5) large live young in a litter. When threatened, tends to flatten body, open its wide mouth and stick out its large blue tongue.

Shingleback Lizard ■ *Tiliqua rugosa*
SVL 300mm (females slightly larger than males)
(Shingleback; Shingle-back; Stumpy-tail; Stumpy-tailed Lizard; Boggi; Sleepy Lizard; Bob-tail Lizard; Two-headed Lizard; Pinecone Lizard)

DESCRIPTION Robust, rough-scaled body, with large, triangular head, short, rounded tail, short limbs and large blue tongue. Colour variable, subject to range, from orange-brown to dark brown or blackish above, often with paler head, and with paler whitish or yellowish blotches. Paler below with darker blotches. **DISTRIBUTION** Southern and eastern Australia, from coastal western and south-western WA, through southern SA and northern Vic, to central and western NSW and southern Qld. Absent from eastern and south-eastern coasts. Four subspecies within the currently adopted classification: *T. r. aspera*, southern SA, Vic, NSW and southern Qld; *T. r. konowi*, Rottnest Island, WA; *T. r. palarra*, Shark Bay area, WA; *T. r. rugosa*, south-western WA. **HABITAT AND HABITS** Found in open areas in drier forests, woodland, shrubland and grassland in semi-arid regions, where it shelters during the night under rocks or logs, or in dense leaf litter or other similar groundcover. Terrestrial, feeding mainly on vegetable matter, including tender leaves and shoots, and flowers near or on the ground, supplemented with range of invertebrates, including snails and some carrion. Viviparous, with 1–4 live young in a litter. When threatened, tends to flatten body, open its wide mouth and stick out its large blue tongue.

Eastern Blue-tongue ■ *Tiliqua scincoides* SVL 320mm (females bigger than males)
(Eastern Blue-tongue Lizard; Common Blue-tongued Lizard)

DESCRIPTION Large skink with broad head, short limbs, moderately long, tapering tail and large blue tongue. Generally silvery-grey to olive-green or brownish above, with broad dark brown to blackish, irregular transverse bands on back and tail, and sometimes with broad blackish stripe from eye to above ear. Underparts white or creamish. Colour varies with its range, with individuals in north being more brown, paler on head, with blackish bars on back and with eye-stripe reduced or absent. **DISTRIBUTION** Two subspecies: Northern Blue-tongued skink *T. s. intermedia* throughout northern Australia, from north-west WA, through northern NT, to north-western Qld; Eastern Blue-tongue *T. s. scincoides* through eastern Australia, from north-eastern Qld, through central and eastern NSW, to Vic. **HABITAT AND HABITS** Found in wide variety of habitats, generally with plenty of groundcover, where it shelters at night in dense leaf litter, or under fallen logs, rocks, or

human items such as discarded timber or corrugated iron. Diurnal, actively foraging during warmer parts of the day for molluscs, insects, plant material and some carrion. On cooler days individuals can remain inactive in their shelter site, or spend lengthy periods of time basking in sunny areas. Viviparous, giving birth to up to around 20 (average 10) live young in a litter, normally with 1 litter each year, but may miss a year if there is insufficient food available. When threatened, tends to flatten body, open its wide mouth and stick out its large blue tongue.

Ridge-tailed Monitor ■ *Varanus acanthurus* TL 650mm
(Spiny-tail Monitor)

DESCRIPTION Reddish to blackish-brown above, with numerous pale to bright yellowish spots on back and flanks forming conspicuous eye-like rings. Head with pale to bright yellowish spots and longitudinal stripes, and tail with similarly coloured or pale brown rings, occasionally fading to uniform blackish towards tip. Tail long and

slightly flattened, with prominent keels giving spiny appearance. Undersurface yellowish-cream to whitish. **DISTRIBUTION** Northern Australia, from central western WA coast, through NT, to western Qld. Also on Groote Eylandt and Wessel Group. **HABITAT AND HABITS** Found on rocky outcrops and ranges, where it shelters in deep crevices or under larger rocks. Terrestrial, feeding on invertebrates and lizards, and occasionally small mammals and eggs. Oviparous, producing around 10 eggs in a clutch, occasionally with 2 clutches in a year.

Perentie ■ *Varanus giganteus* TL 2.5m

DESCRIPTION Australia's largest lizard. Pale brown to brown above, with large, yellow, dark-edged spots on body and tail forming transverse rows, and heavy dark brown or blackish speckling. Head and throat paler, with thin dark lines forming reticulated pattern, and head with distinctive angular brow. Neck long with large, sagging throat, and long tail with yellow tip. Limbs powerful, blackish and with large yellowish-cream spots. Underparts whitish or cream. **DISTRIBUTION** Central and western Australia, from central-western WA coast in broad inland band through southern NT and northern SA, to western Qld. **HABITAT AND HABITS** Found in arid sandy deserts, gorges and rocky ranges, where it shelters in deep burrows in rocky outcrops and beneath boulders. Terrestrial, foraging over large areas for lizards, snakes, mammals, birds and invertebrates, but will also eat carrion. Food detected using large, forked tongue. Oviparous, laying around 9 parchment-shelled eggs in a clutch.

Gould's Goanna ■ *Varanus gouldii* TL 1.6m
(Sand Goanna; Sand Monitor)

DESCRIPTION Moderately robust, with long, laterally compressed tail and large, angular head with dark stripe behind eye. Yellow or reddish-brown to blackish above, with numerous large and small yellow spots and speckles, forming largely cryptic pattern of transverse rows and longitudinal lines. Belly white or yellowish with darker spots, and throat has grey streaks. End of tail pale cream to yellow and unbanded. **DISTRIBUTION** Occurs throughout most of mainland Australia, except most of southern coastline, south-west and central Qld. **HABITAT AND HABITS** Found in varied open habitats with sandy soils throughout its large range, including forests, woodland, shrubland and sandy deserts. Terrestrial, sheltering in burrows or hollow logs. Feeds on invertebrates, smaller lizards and their eggs, frogs, mammals, birds and carrion. Oviparous, laying around 7 parchment-shelled eggs in burrows. Raises itself on hindlegs and tail.

Mertens' Water Monitor ■ *Varanus mertensi* TL 1.1m

DESCRIPTION Moderately robust, with medium-length, strongly laterally compressed tail and raised dorsal ridge. Olive-brown to blackish above, with numerous small, dark-edged, creamish-yellow spots. Head slender with upwards facing nostrils and bluish bars on lips. Underparts white or pale yellow, with scattered darker spots on throat and bluish bars

on chest. **DISTRIBUTION** Northern Australia, from Kimberley region WA, through northern NT, to northern and north-western Qld. **HABITAT AND HABITS** Normally seen on rocks and logs adjacent to or overhanging rivers, creeks, lagoons and swamps, diving into the water when approached. Strongly aquatic; able to spend long periods underwater foraging for fish, frogs and crustaceans, as well as invertebrates, mammals, and lizards and their eggs. Will also feed on carrion. Oviparous, laying around 9 parchment-shelled eggs in a clutch, in nest filled with leaves.

Yellow-spotted Monitor ■ *Varanus panoptes* TL 1.4m
(Northern Sand Goanna; Floodplain Monitor)

DESCRIPTION Stocky, with powerful limbs and moderately long, laterally compressed tail. Reddish-brown to blackish above, with alternating transverse rows of larger dark brown and smaller, dark-edged, pale yellow spots.

Neck has longer longitudinal streaks and lines, with blackish stripe extending from eye to start of neck. Tail has darker banding, normally extending to tip. Underparts whitish or yellow, paler on throat, and with blackish spots. **DISTRIBUTION** Northern and western Australia, including central and western WA, and from Kimberley region WA, through northern NT, to northern and central Qld. **HABITAT AND HABITS** Occurs in wide variety of habitats, including woodland, grassland and coastal beaches, and often seen in floodplains and in vicinity of waterways. Terrestrial; feeds on variety of invertebrates, small mammals and freshwater turtle eggs, as well as carrion. Has suffered a decline as a result of eating the introduced poisonous Cane Toad *Rhinella marina*. Oviparous, laying around 11 eggs in a burrow.

Heath Monitor ■ *Varanus rosenbergi* TL 1.3m

DESCRIPTION Moderately robust, with medium-length, laterally compressed tail. Dark grey to blackish above, with fine yellow or white spotting, forming alternating wider pale and darker narrow transverse bands, which extend from neck to tip of tail, and larger yellowish blotches on sides and legs. Head long and narrow, with pale-edged dark line extending through eye and above ear, and with vertical barring on lips. Underparts whitish with dark grey reticulated pattern. **DISTRIBUTION** Southern Australia, from southern WA, through southern SA (including Kangaroo Island) and isolated areas of south-western Vic, and inland south-eastern and coastal northern NSW. **HABITAT AND HABITS** Occurs in open forests, woodland and heaths, where it digs burrows for shelter or occupies rock crevices, hollow logs or disused burrows of other animals. Largely terrestrial and diurnal, feeding mainly on carrion, reptiles, eggs, birds and small mammals. Oviparous, with up to 14 (average 12) eggs in a clutch, laid in termite mounds; clutch defended by female for up to 3 weeks.

Hatchling

Adult

Spotted Tree Monitor ■ *Varanus scalaris* TL 600mm
(Banded Tree Monitor; Spotted Tree Goanna)

DESCRIPTION Moderately robust, largely arboreal goanna, with medium-length, cylindrical tail that has strongly keeled scales on top and sides. Generally dark grey, brown or blackish above, with large, dark-centred cream spots that form irregular transverse bands on back and most of tail, and numerous smaller creamish or yellowish spots and flecks. Remainder of tail blackish. Head normally with blackish stripe from back of eye to above ear. Belly whitish. **DISTRIBUTION** Northern Australia, from Kimberley Region WA, through northern NT, to northern Qld. **HABITAT AND HABITS** Found in rainforests, forests and grassy woodland. Arboreal, but hunts both on the ground and in trees for small lizards, frogs, invertebrates and nestling birds, during the day. Shelters at night in tree-holes or under loose bark. Oviparous, with around 5–6 eggs in a clutch. When disturbed, seeks the safety of trees.

Spencer's Monitor ■ *Varanus spenceri* TL 1.2m
(Spencer's Goanna)

DESCRIPTION Heavy, thick-set goanna, with short, laterally flattened tail and rounded snout. Greyish-brown above with numerous paler and darker spots, and broad, pale yellowish-grey transverse bands on back and tail. Head darker and lips paler and barred.

Yellowish-cream below, with dark grey mottling, more prominent on throat. Well equipped for digging, with long, sharp claws. **DISTRIBUTION** Open black soil plains of north-eastern NT and central western Qld. **HABITAT AND HABITS** Terrestrial, foraging on the ground in open grassland for wide variety of prey, including venomous snakes, small lizards, small mammals, carrion and eggs. When not active shelters underground, in burrows or large cracks in soil. Oviparous, with around 20 eggs in a clutch. The only Australian goanna that is not arboreal. If threatened, gives a loud hiss and uses its short, muscular tail as a whip.

Black-headed Monitor ■ *Varanus tristis* TL 800mm
(Black-headed Goanna; Freckled Monitor)

DESCRIPTION Small, slender-bodied goanna with long, roughly cylindrical tail that is mostly blackish and with small spines in male. Greyish-brown to reddish-brown above, with dark-centred, pale greyish ocelli forming transverse rows on body and base of tail (more defined in juveniles than adults, and fade with age). Underparts greyish with

darker spots and streaks. **DISTRIBUTION** Widespread throughout Australia, except coastal and inland areas of south and south-east. **HABITAT AND HABITS** Occurs in open forests, woodland, shrubland, grassland and rocky ranges. Diurnal, generally sheltering at night within hollows, although young lizards may shelter under loose bark on trees. Feeds within rocks and in open areas on invertebrates, lizards, small mammals and birds, including their eggs and young. Oviparous, laying around 10 parchment-shelled eggs in hole that female digs in the ground, and may produce more than 1 clutch in a good season.

Lace Monitor ▪ *Varanus varius* TL 2m
(Tree Goanna)

DESCRIPTION Moderately robust goanna with long, laterally depressed tail that extends to thin, 'whip-like' end. Generally bluish-black above with numerous various-sized, creamish-yellow spots arranged in transverse bands, becoming less intense with age and almost absent in older adults. Snout and chin have yellow and black barring. In sub-humid parts of range, occasional individuals have colour pattern of wide yellow-and-black banding, known as Bell's phase. **DISTRIBUTION** Eastern Australia from southern Cape York Peninsula and eastern Qld, through central and south-eastern NSW, and eastern and northern Vic, to south-eastern SA. **HABITAT AND HABITS** Found in coastal rainforests, forests, woodland and inland ranges, where it is largely arboreal, but often forages on the ground for food, which includes carrion, mammals, birds (including eggs), reptiles, invertebrates and frogs. Oviparous, laying around 8 parchment-shelled eggs in termite nests.

SNAKES (SERPENTES)
Snakes, of the suborder Serpentes, form the second largest group of reptiles after the lizards, containing just over a third of the world's currently known species. While Australia has less than 10 per cent of these species, it is home to some of the most toxic (and potentially deadly) land and sea snakes in the world, as well as non-venomous file snakes, pythons and blind snakes.

Arafura File Snake ▪ *Acrochordus arafurae* TL 2m (females larger than males)
(Arafura Filesnake; Filesnake; Arafura Wart Snake)

DESCRIPTION Predominantly bluish-grey to dark brown above, with brown and black vertebral blotches extending down sides and onto flanks. Skin loose and baggy, covered with tiny, granular, rasp-like, keeled scales, which aid with grasping of fish after capture. Whitish below. **DISTRIBUTION** Coastal regions and waterways of northern Australia, including WA, NT and Qld, with range extending during wet season. Also found in New Guinea. **HABITAT AND HABITS** Aquatic, and usually found in slow-moving freshwater streams, lagoons and swamps, but will also enter estuarine areas and, occasionally, the sea. Feeds almost exclusively on fish, which are caught during the night using the mouth and by wrapping the body around the victim, which is then eaten whole. Breeds irregularly and males are able to store sperm for a number of years. Viviparous, producing up to 27 (average 17) live young in a single litter. Non-venomous, but able to inflict a painful bite.

Children's Python ■ *Antaresia childreni* TL 1.2m
(Banded Rock Python; Northern Brown Python)

DESCRIPTION Smooth-scaled, solid python, with narrow head that is distinct from neck and moderately sized body. Yellowish, reddish or olive-brown above, normally with irregular dark, rounded blotches, forming irregular pattern, but occasionally uniform

in colour. Belly white. **DISTRIBUTION** Tropical northern Australia, from Kimberley region WA, through northern NT, to Gulf of Carpentaria. **HABITAT AND HABITS** Found in wet and dry forests, and woodland, grassland, shrubland, rocky outcrops and urban areas. Nocturnal and terrestrial, although it is a skilled climber, and can often be seen hunting on roofs of caves. Feeds on small mammals, lizards, frogs and birds; small bats often captured in flight as they exit caves. Prey killed by constriction. Oviparous, laying up to 12 (average 7) parchment-shelled eggs. Non-venomous and generally harmless to humans.

Spotted Python ■ *Antaresia maculosa* TL 1m
(Mottled Python; Eastern Small-blotched Python; Queensland Children's Python)

DESCRIPTION Glossy, solidly built python with narrow head that is distinct from neck. Pale brown to brown above, paler on flanks, with contrasting, ragged edged, darker brown cross-bands and blotches that form wavy streaks down body. Belly whitish-cream. **DISTRIBUTION** Eastern Australia from Cape York Peninsula Qld, to northern NSW.

HABITAT AND HABITS Favours rocky slopes, outcrops, caves and ridges in wet and dry, open forests and woodland, and adjacent farmland and suburbs. Nocturnal, sheltering during the day in caves, rocky crevices and tree hollows. Both terrestrial and arboreal when hunting, foraging mainly for small mammals and reptiles, but also small birds and frogs, which are killed by constriction. Oviparous, with up to 16 eggs (average 10) laid in a clutch. Non-venomous and generally regarded as harmless to humans, but bites can cause minor lacerations or punctures, and are prone to infections.

Stimson's Python ■ *Antaresia stimsoni* TL 1m
(Large-blotched Python)

DESCRIPTION Smooth-scaled, robust python with moderate body and narrow head that is distinctive from neck. Cream to light brown above, with irregular large reddish to dark brown blotches. Undersurface whitish. Head pale brown with darker brown line through eye, and pale patch on sides of neck. **DISTRIBUTION** Central and Western Australia, from central Qld and north-western NSW, through southern NT and northern SA, to coastal WA. Absent from far north, south and south-east. **HABITAT AND HABITS**

Favours rocky outcrops and large trees in arid to semi-arid grassland, shrubland, woodland, deserts and tree-lined watercourses. Shelters during the day in rocky crevices, tree hollows, burrows and large spinifex tussocks, emerging at night to hunt for small mammals, birds, reptiles and frogs. Prey located with heat-sensing organs on its head, and killed by constriction. Oviparous, laying up to 19 (average 10) eggs in a clutch. Non-venomous.

Black-headed Python ■ *Aspidites melanocephalus* TL 2.5m
(Black-headed Rock Python)

DESCRIPTION Moderately sized, smooth-scaled python, with cylindrical body and head similar in thickness to neck. Cream, yellowish or light brown, with irregular reddish to dark brown or blackish transverse bands, occasionally with small blotches in between. Head and neck glossy black, with head lacking heat-sensory pits. Belly yellow with darker blotches. **DISTRIBUTION** Northern Australia, from east to west coasts, including north-western WA, northern and eastern NT, and central and northern Qld. **HABITAT AND HABITS** Found in wet and dry forests, woodland, shrubland and grassland with rocky

outcrops or cracking soils, where it shelters during the day in disused animal burrows or ones it digs itself. Although terrestrial, a capable climber and also able to swim to avoid danger. Feeds mainly on snakes, including venomous species, and other reptiles, supplemented with some mammals and birds. Prey generally ambushed and killed by constriction. Non-venomous and harmless to humans, but if disturbed may hiss and strike with closed mouth. Oviparous, laying up to 18 eggs in a clutch.

Woma ■ *Aspidites ramsayi* TL 2m
(Sand Python; Woma Python)

DESCRIPTION Smooth-scaled and moderately sized body, with head similar in thickness to neck. Yellowish, pale brown or light olive above, with irregular dark brown to reddish-brown transverse bands. Head yellow to brownish-orange, lacking heat-sensory pits, and often with dark mark above each eye. Belly yellow to cream, with numerous pink or dark

brown blotches. **DISTRIBUTION** Pilbara coast WA, through southern NT and northern SA, into northern NSW and southern Qld. Also in central south-west WA. **HABITAT AND HABITS** Found in arid and semi-arid hummock grassland, shrubland and woodland on sandy plains. Nocturnal and terrestrial, sheltering during the day in hollow logs, burrows, deep soil cracks and spinifex tussocks, and emerging to forage mainly for reptiles, but also small mammals and birds, which are killed by constriction before eating. Oviparous, laying up to 28 eggs (average 14) per clutch, which are incubated and protected until they hatch. Non-venomous and harmless.

Water Python ■ *Liasis mackloti* TL 2.5m
(Brown Water Python; Yellow-bellied Python)

DESCRIPTION Glossy, smooth-scaled python with reflective rainbow sheen, and with narrow head that is distinct from narrow neck. Uniformly olive-brown to dark greyish-brown above, cream to yellowish-orange on belly and flanks, with white throat and dark brown underside of tail. Lips pale olive-brown, with darker fine spotting. **DISTRIBUTION** Coastal and near coastal northern Australia, from north-western WA, through northern NT, to north-eastern Qld. **HABITAT AND HABITS** Found in freshwater lagoons, swamps, creeks and floodplains in wet and dry, open forests and woodland. Terrestrial and nocturnal, generally ambushing prey as it approaches the water, or locating it using heat-sensory pits in lower jaw. Feeds mainly on mammals,

reptiles (including small crocodiles), waterbirds and frogs, which are killed by constriction before being swallowed whole. Oviparous, laying up to 24 parchment-shelled eggs (average 10) in a clutch. Non-venomous.

Adult   *Juvenile*

Olive Python ■ *Liasis olivaceus* TL 4.8m
(Pilbara Olive Python)

DESCRIPTION Large, smooth-scaled python with robust body, and narrow head that is distinct from thinner neck. Scales are small, which contributes to glossy appearance. Uniform light brown to olive-brown or greyish above. Lips are creamish, with pale brown or light grey spotting, and belly is white or cream. **DISTRIBUTION** Two isolated distributions in northern Australia, including Pilbara region of north-western WA, and from Kimberley region WA, through northern NT, to western Qld. **HABITAT AND HABITS** Favours rocky hills, gorges and watercourses in wet and dry, open forests, shrubland and hummock grassland. Mainly nocturnal, sheltering during the day in caves, rock crevices and hollow logs, and emerging to feed on birds, reptiles (including small crocodiles), frogs and mammals up to the size of rock-wallabies. Accomplished swimmer, actively hunting in watercourses, but will also wait in hiding for animals to approach within striking distance. Prey is killed by constriction. Oviparous, laying up to 30 (average 16) eggs.

Carpet Python ■ *Morelia spilota* TL 3m

DESCRIPTION Highly variable large python. Generally, blackish, brownish or olive-green above, with greenish-yellow spots, irregular bright yellow stripes, or pale brown to olive-grey, dark-edged blotches, transverse bands and longitudinal lines. Yellowish, cream or white on undersurface. Head large and triangular, and visibly distinct from neck, with row of deep heat-sensory pits along lower jaw. **DISTRIBUTION** Throughout mainland Australia, except the arid interior, western WA and southern Vic. **HABITAT AND HABITS** Found in range of habitat types, including rainforests, open forests and woodland, riverine areas, coastal heaths, shrubland, rocky outcrops, and suburban parks and gardens. Generally nocturnal and semi-arboreal, becoming more diurnal during cooler months. Feeds mostly on small to medium-sized mammals and birds, but also on frogs and lizards. Oviparous, laying up to 50 eggs in a clutch, with female defending eggs until they hatch. Non-venomous, but can be aggressive and capable of inflicting a painful bite that is prone to infection.

Subspecies spilota cheynei   *Subspecies* spilota metcalfei   *Subspecies* spilota spilota

Green Python ▪ *Morelia viridis* TL 1.7m
(Green Tree Python)

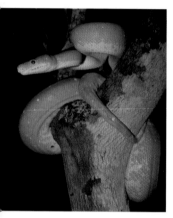

DESCRIPTION Unmistakable. Emerald-green above with a few scattered white spots on sides and longitudinal row of white or yellowish scales that follow prominent vertebral ridge. Tail tipped blue-grey. Belly cream to yellow. Young bright yellow with purplish-brown line on vertebral ridge, and with scattered purplish-brown spots and large, dark-edged white blotches and lines. **DISTRIBUTION** Eastern rainforests of far northern Cape York Peninsula, Qld. **HABITAT AND HABITS** Lowland tropical rainforests and monsoon forests. Arboreal and nocturnal, resting during the day in tree hollow or epiphytes, or sitting with body coiled over a horizontal branch. Hunts by ambushing its prey, waiting for several days at a suitable site with head and neck held in striking position, and with prehensile tail coiled around branch as an anchor. Feeds on reptiles, small mammals, frogs and birds. Oviparous, laying up to 32 eggs in a clutch. Non-venomous, but can be quite aggressive when threatened.

Australian Scrub Python ▪ *Morelia amethistina*
TL 5m (unconfirmed records of 8.5m)
(Amethyst Python; Amethystine Python; Scrub Python)

DESCRIPTION Australia's largest snake. Smooth scaled, with large head that is distinct from relatively slender neck, and with heat-sensory pits on lower jaw. Olive-yellow or greenish-grey to golden-brown above, with numerous blackish angled vertebral cross-bands and longitudinal lines on sides. Belly cream to white. Common name derives from iridescent purplish sheen on scales. **DISTRIBUTION** North-eastern Qld, from Townsville to Cape York Peninsula, and introduced population at Airlie Beach near Proserpine. **HABITAT AND HABITS** Found in rainforests, vine thickets, forests, open woodland, coastal scrub and vegetated sandy coral islands. Prey, mainly mammals up to size of a wallaby, and some birds, is located using heat-sensory pits on jaw, then killed by constriction before being swallowed whole. Oviparous, laying around 11 eggs in a clutch. Non-venomous but very aggressive.

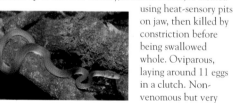

Dorsal colour can be olive-yellow, greenish-grey or golden-brown

Brown Tree Snake ▪ *Boiga irregularis* TL 2m
(Night Tiger; Eastern Brown Tree Snake; Doll's Eye Snake)

DESCRIPTION Slender, with narrow neck, distinct head and bulging eyes with vertical pupils. Two distinct colour patterns. Eastern Australian individuals orange to reddish-brown above with irregular dark cross-bands on back and sides, and cream or orange underparts. Northern Australian individuals cream above and below, with bold reddish-brown bands. **DISTRIBUTION** Coastal and sub-coastal northern and eastern Australia, from Kimberley region of WA, through northern NT, northern and eastern Qld, south to Sydney NSW. **HABITAT AND HABITS** Occurs in broad range of habitats including open forests, rainforests, mangroves, rock escarpments, coastal heaths and urban areas.

Nocturnal and arboreal, sheltering coiled up in tree hollows, caves and buildings during the day, but may also hunt on the ground. Preys mainly on birds and their eggs, but also reptiles, frogs and small mammals. Oviparous, laying 3–12 eggs in a clutch. Venomous and aggressive when threatened, but generally not considered dangerous to humans.

Northern individual

Eastern individual

Green Tree Snake ▪ *Dendrelaphis punctulatus* TL 1.6m
(Common Tree Snake)

DESCRIPTION Variable, based on distribution. Olive-green or blue-grey above in south-east, black further north-east, and yellow with blue-grey or brown head across north. Pale blue skin, which appears as flecks between body scales, visible during threat display. Typically has bright yellow throat and paler yellow underparts, but can also be greenish, bluish or white. **DISTRIBUTION** Coastal and sub-coastal northern and eastern Australia, from Kimberley region of WA, through northern NT, northern and eastern Qld, to south of Sydney NSW. **HABITAT AND HABITS** Occurs in wide range of vegetated habitats, including open forests, rainforests, mangroves and suburban gardens. Diurnal and arboreal, but also forages on the ground, sheltering during the night in tree hollows and rock crevices. Feeds mainly on frogs and birds, but also eats small reptiles and mammals. Oviparous, laying 3–12 (average 8) eggs in a clutch. Non-venomous, but flattens neck and anterior body and produces an unpleasant odour if threatened.

Dorsal colour is variable throughout range, being greenish, bluish or blackish

Slaty-grey Snake ■ *Stegonotus cucullatus* TL 1.3m (males larger than females)
(Slaty-grey Snake)

DESCRIPTION Uniform dark brown to dark grey to black above, and cream to white below, with dark flecking on edges. Head moderately sized and slightly flattened, with medium-sized, slightly protruding eyes. **DISTRIBUTION** Coast and floodplains of northern Australia, from western Arnhem Land NT, to southern Cape York Peninsula Qld. **HABITAT AND HABITS** Found in wetter habitats, from coastal dunes to rainforests, with permanent water, and suburban buildings. Nocturnal and largely terrestrial, although

will climb to avoid danger; often found sheltering under logs or rocks or in dense leaf litter. Feeds mainly on frogs, but will also eat lizards (and their eggs), small mammals, fish and smaller snakes. Oviparous, laying up to 16 (average 12) eggs in a clutch. Non-venomous and generally harmless, but aggressive if provoked and releases a pungent odour.

Keelback ■ *Tropidonophis mairii* TL 750mm
(Freshwater Snake)

DESCRIPTION Olive-brown or black above, with indistinct darker cross-bands of darker flecks, and with paler flecks of skin visible between strongly keeled scales. Head and neck grey-green to brown. Underparts cream with narrow dark bands, and often flushed with orange or pink along edge. Distinguished from venomous Rough-scaled Snake (see p. 145) by loreal scale, which is absent in Rough-scaled Snake. **DISTRIBUTION** Coastal areas of northern and eastern Australia from Kimberley region WA, through NT and Qld, to far northern NSW. **HABITAT AND HABITS** Semiaquatic, favouring moist areas, including freshwater creeks, swamps and dams, but also in forests, heaths and adjacent

suburban gardens. Active day and night, depending on temperature, and largely terrestrial, but an adept climber. Feeds on frogs and tadpoles, supplemented with fish, lizards and mammals. Preys successfully on introduced, poisonous Cane Toad *Rhinella marina*, but larger individuals are too toxic. Oviparous, laying up to 18 (average 9) eggs in a clutch. Non-venomous and generally inoffensive.

Common Death Adder ■ *Acanthophis antarcticus* TL 700mm

DESCRIPTION DANGEROUSLY VENOMOUS. Triangular-shaped head, short, stocky body and thin, pale-coloured tip to tail. Grey to reddish-brown above, usually with alternating lighter bands, and greyish-cream below. **DISTRIBUTION** Eastern Australian mainland from north-west NT, through Qld and NSW, to northern Vic, although absent from western far north and far south-east. Also found in small coastal band in southern SA and WA. **HABITAT AND HABITS** Found in wet and dry forests, woodland, grassland and

coastal heaths. Ambush predator, lying coiled and motionless, sometimes covered in leaves, twitching pale tip of tail as lure to attract prey, and using long fangs to strike inquisitive animals, including lizards, birds, frogs and mammals. Once envenomated prey is often left to die before being eaten. Ovoviviparous, giving birth to up to 40 live young during summer and early spring. Death Adder venom is neurotoxic and can be fatal to humans.

North-eastern Plain-nosed Burrowing Snake
■ *Antaioserpens albiceps* TL 350mm
(Robust Burrowing Snake)

DESCRIPTION Glossed orange to orange-brown above, with dark grey-brown head and broad black nuchal patch. Scales of upper body each with darker rear edge, giving strongly defined reticulated pattern. Underparts pale cream. **DISTRIBUTION** North-eastern Qld.

Individuals from southern Qld, formerly considered a separate population of this species, now considered to be **Warrego Burrowing Snake** *A. warro*. **HABITAT AND HABITS** Found in dry woodland and forests, where it is active at night, burrowing through loose soil and leaf litter in search of sleeping skinks. Oviparous, normally laying 3 eggs in a clutch. Venomous snake, but not aggressive and generally considered to be harmless.

Highland Copperhead ▪ *Austrelaps ramsayi* TL 1.4m
(Uplands Copperhead; Alpine Copperhead)

DESCRIPTION DANGEROUSLY VENOMOUS. Orange-brown, with darker vertebral stripes (often most noticeable in younger snakes), to dark grey-brown or blackish above. Pale cream or reddish on flanks, and cream to greyish underneath. Lips barred. **DISTRIBUTION** Highlands of eastern NSW and north-eastern Vic. **HABITAT AND**

HABITS Terrestrial. Most common in wetter areas, including swamps, marshes and riparian zones of small creeks, but also in wooded areas and cleared areas around farms. Shelters under fallen timber, rocks or dense vegetation. Hunts day or night for frogs, lizards, other snakes and insects, seemingly preferring cooler parts of the day in warmer months, and more active from spring through to late autumn. Ovoviviparous, with average of 15–20 young, and may not breed every year.

Lowland Copperhead ▪ *Austrelaps superbus* TL 1.5m

DESCRIPTION DANGEROUSLY VENOMOUS. Variable, ranging from pale brown to black above, with white edging on scales of upper lip. Young snakes are generally paler, and have obscure stripe on nape. Cream to grey underparts. **DISTRIBUTION** Lowlands of far south-eastern NSW, southern Vic, Tasmania and south-west. **HABITAT AND HABITS** Prefers wetter areas of woodland, grassland and heaths, and heavily disturbed areas, where

it actively hunts either during the day and warmer nights, for small vertebrates, such as frogs, lizards and small mammals. Ovoviviparous, giving birth to up to 30 live young. Although generally not aggressive towards humans, capable of inflicting fatal bites.

Coral Snake ■ *Brachyurophis australis* TL 400mm
(Eastern Shovel-nosed Snake)

DESCRIPTION Reddish-brown or pink above with numerous cross-bands, consisting of yellowish-white scales each edged with dark brown. Dark blackish band passing across head, through eyes, and broader second band across neck. Large frontal scale in centre of crown is longer than it is broad, and rostral scale at front of head is somewhat pointed, giving rise to alternative common name of Eastern Shovel-nosed Snake. Whitish below.
DISTRIBUTION Broad inland band from south-eastern SA, through north-western Vic and western NSW, to north-eastern NSW and south-eastern Qld coast, then extending northwards through inland Qld and

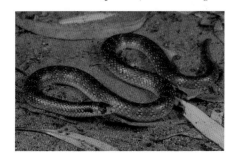

back to mid-northern Qld coast.
HABITAT AND HABITS Occupies wide variety of habitats, including open, semi-arid spinifex grassland, grassy woodland and shrubland. Active at night, burrowing through soil and leaf litter in search of small lizards and their eggs. Oviparous, laying 2–6 eggs in a clutch. Venomous, but not considered dangerous to human adults.

White-crowned Snake ■ *Cacophis harriettae* TL 450mm
(White-naped Snake)

DESCRIPTION Glossed dark bluish-grey above, with broad cream collar on nape of neck, extending through eyes and to tip of snout. Underparts pale grey. When threatened, raises body vertically and makes striking movements. **Northern Crowned Snake**
C. churchilli, in northern part of

its range, has narrower collar.
DISTRIBUTION Coastal areas from far northern NSW to central Qld. **HABITAT AND HABITS** Found in woodland, forests and gardens in adjacent areas, where it shelters during the day beneath logs and rocks, and within leaf litter, emerging at night to hunt for small skinks and their eggs. Oviparous, generally laying 4–5 eggs in a clutch. Not considered dangerous to humans.

Southern Dwarf Crowned Snake ▪ *Cacophis krefftii* TL 300mm
(Dwarf Crowned Snake)

DESCRIPTION Steely-grey to black above, with narrow yellowish-cream collar on nape of neck, flecked darker as it extends along sides of head towards snout. Underside pale

yellow, with each scale distinctly edged with black. **DISTRIBUTION** Coastal regions, east of Great Dividing Range, from central NSW to south-east Qld. **HABITAT AND HABITS** Occurs in rainforests and moist areas of open forests. Terrestrial and nocturnal, sheltering during the day under rocks, rotting logs and moist leaf litter, and emerging to feed on small skinks and other lizards. Venomous, but not considered dangerous to humans and reluctant to bite. If threatened will rear up and make striking motions with a closed mouth.

Golden-crowned Snake ▪ *Cacophis squamulosus* TL 650mm

DESCRIPTION Grey or brown above and pink below, with golden-yellow marking on top of head. Yellowish-brown line on either side of head and onto nape, converging slightly

but not meeting. Pupils elongated and vertical. **DISTRIBUTION** East coast and ranges from around Sydney, NSW, to south-eastern Qld. **HABITAT AND HABITS** Found in deeper forests in northern parts of its range and sandstone areas in south, where it shelters during the day under logs and rocks, and in leaf litter. Hunts predominantly for sleeping lizards, which are detected largely by scent, but also takes blind snakes and frogs. Oviparous, laying an average of 6 eggs in a clutch in mid-summer. Venomous, but not considered dangerous to humans. If threatened, flattens neck and makes striking actions, but rarely bites.

Eastern Small-eyed Snake ■ *Cryptophis nigrescens*
TL 850mm (size increases towards northern end of its ranges)
(Small-eyed Snake)

DESCRIPTION DANGEROUSLY VENOMOUS. Uniformly glossy blue-black or dark grey on back sides. Belly cream with grey blotches in south, and reddish-pink with dark grey flecks in north. Head flattened and eyes small and dark. Males larger than females, and with larger head. **DISTRIBUTION** Along coast and ranges of eastern Australia between southern Cape York Peninsula, Qld and south-eastern Vic. **HABITAT AND HABITS** Found in rainforests, wet and dry sclerophyll forests, woodland, coastal heaths and suburban gardens. Nocturnal, sheltering during the day beneath stones, rock crevices, loose bark and fallen logs, and emerging to forage for small terrestrial lizards and their eggs, blind snakes and small snakes. Viviparous, producing up to 7–8 live young in a litter. Venom contains myotoxins, which affect muscle tissue (including the heart).

Black-striped Snake ■ *Cryptophis nigrostriatus* TL 500mm

DESCRIPTION Reddish to orange-brown with dark brown to black vertebral stripe that covers top of head and extends to tip of long tail. Head slightly flattened, and eyes comparatively large. Underparts pale cream. **DISTRIBUTION** Coast and ranges of north-eastern Qld from Cape York Peninsula to around Gladstone. **HABITAT AND HABITS** Favours rocky outcrops in sclerophyll forests and woodland. Nocturnal, sheltering during the day under fallen logs and in leaf litter, or within cracks in the soil. Semifossorial, hunting through leaf litter and topsoil for sleeping skinks and other small lizards. Viviparous, with around 6 live young produced in a litter.

Greater Black Whipsnake ■ *Demansia papuensis* TL 1.6m
(Papuan Whip Snake)

DESCRIPTION Dark grey or black to dark brown above (particularly in eastern part of its range), with copper-coloured head, spotted with black, and long, tapering, copper-coloured

tail. Underparts dark greyish. Eye dark with discontinuous pale eye-ring, which may descend towards mouth. **DISTRIBUTION** Northern Australia from Kimberleys WA, northern NT and northern Qld. **HABITAT AND HABITS** Dry, open forests and woodland, where it is active during the day, foraging for small lizards and frogs. Oviparous, laying up to 20 eggs in a clutch. Venom composition not fully determined – even though past clinical presentations in Australia indicate that envenoming is unlikely to cause human fatalities, it should still be regarded as potentially dangerous.

Yellow-faced Whip Snake ■ *Demansia psammophis*
TL 900mm (males larger than females)

DESCRIPTION Variable, from pale blue-grey to olive or greenish-brown above, with reddish tinge on head, anterior and tail. Face generally yellowish, with yellow-edged dark line between nostrils, and eye large, encircled by pale ring. Black, comma-shaped marking from eye to mouth. Greenish-grey to yellowish underparts. **DISTRIBUTION** Broad distribution band from north-western WA, south and east through SA and far southern NT, north-western Vic, NSW and eastern Qld. **HABITAT AND HABITS** Found in wide

variety of habitat types, including open forests, arid scrubland, grassland, heaths and adjoining suburban gardens. Diurnal and terrestrial, sheltering at night beneath rocks and in crevices in the ground, and emerging to feed predominantly on lizards, which are caught with quick bursts of speed, but will also eat frogs, small snakes and lizard eggs. Oviparous, typically laying 3–9 eggs (average 6) in a clutch, and forms large communal clutches in some areas, with eggs deposited in deep soil, cracks or crevices. Although venomous, it is not considered dangerous to humans.

Crack-dwelling Whipsnake

■ *Demansia rimicola* TL 900mm (males slightly larger than females)
(Blacksoil Whipsnake)

DESCRIPTION Long, slender whipsnake. Yellow-brown to brown above, normally with darker brown spots and flecks on head, nape and back. Darker brown nape, with 2 paler cream nuchal bands. Face has cream streaks and black teardrop from eye to corner of mouth. Underparts yellow to orange-red, with dark brown marbling and pair of spots on first ventral scale of throat.

DISTRIBUTION Northern-central Australia, in diagonal band from north-eastern SA, north-western NSW and central-western Qld, through central NT to north-eastern WA. **HABITAT AND HABITS** Generally found in quite open areas, including cracking clay soils of open, wooded areas and shrubland, where it shelters under logs, in grass tussocks and in deep soil cracks or disused animal burrows. Hunts actively during the day for small reptiles. Oviparous.

Collared Whipsnake

■ *Demansia torquata* TL 600mm (males generally larger than females)
(Collared Whip Snake)

DESCRIPTION Slender. Generally greyish to olive-brown above, head darker, and nape blackish with 2 narrow pale nuchal bands. Pale-edged dark bar from front of eyes and across front of snout, and dark teardrop mark from eye to mouth, edged with pale yellow. Underparts greyish. **DISTRIBUTION** Coast and ranges of north-eastern Qld and nearby islands. **HABITAT AND HABITS** Occurs in open, wooded areas and shrubland, where it shelters under logs and flat rocks, and in crevices and ground debris. Diurnal and terrestrial, actively searching for and pursuing prey, which almost exclusively consists of lizards, including skinks and geckoes. Oviparous, normally laying 2–8 eggs (typically 4) in a clutch. Although venomous it is not considered dangerous, and is reluctant to bite.

Black Whipsnake ▪ *Demansia vestigiata* TL 1.3m
(Lesser Black Whipsnake)

DESCRIPTION DANGEROUSLY VENOMOUS. Slender-bodied with long, thin tail. Light to dark olive-brown or blackish above, with dark edging on scales more visible in lighter individuals, forming reticulated pattern (more pronounced posteriorly). Head and neck separation not clearly defined; eye large with round pupils. Underparts largely yellowish to greenish-grey, with anterior scales edged with black, and becoming reddish towards tail. Males generally larger than females, and have longer tails. **DISTRIBUTION** Coastal and near coastal areas of northern Australia, from Kimberleys WA, through NT to central east Qld. **HABITAT AND HABITS** Found in most dry areas with grassy understorey, including open forests and woodland, and adjacent urban areas. Diurnal, but more crepuscular or nocturnal on hotter days. Shelters under logs, rocks and leaf litter, in cracks and crevices, and in disused animal burrows. Hunts on the ground mainly for lizards, and some frogs, which are actively pursued. Oviparous, laying up to 13 eggs in a clutch.

Dorsal colour can range from blackish to light olive-brown

De Vis' Banded Snake
▪ *Denisonia devisi* TL 585mm (decreasing in size from south to north)
(Mud Adder)

DESCRIPTION Thick-set and slightly flattened. Yellowish-brown with loosely defined, dark brown transverse bands above and cream below. Head dark brown, speckled with lighter flecks, and lips barred with cream and brown. Eyes located towards top of head, with conspicuous pale irises. **DISTRIBUTION** Low-lying areas in central northern NSW and central southern Qld.

HABITAT AND HABITS Found in floodplains, dry forests and grassy woodland. Nocturnal, sheltering during the day under logs or stones, and in deep soil crevices, and emerging on warm nights to hunt almost exclusively for frogs. Viviparous, generally giving birth to 6–8 live young in a litter. Sluggish snake with mildly toxic venom.

White-lipped Snake ■ *Drysdalia coronoides* TL 450mm

DESCRIPTION Small, slender snake with conspicuous thin white stripe along upper lip that continues along sides of head and onto neck. Back colour variable, from pale to blackish-grey, olive-green or reddish-brown, but without pale band on nape. Belly usually salmon-pink, but can be yellowish-cream or grey. **DISTRIBUTION** Cooler regions of north-eastern NSW, south to Vic and south-western SA, and in Tas. **HABITAT AND**

HABITS Found in forested areas and tussock grassland, often in wetter habitats. Mainly nocturnal, usually sheltering during the day in dense leaf litter or under rocks and fallen logs during the day, but diurnal during colder periods, preferring areas of heavy cover. Feeds predominantly on small lizards, but also takes frogs and small mammals. Viviparous, producing up to 10 live young in a litter towards the end of summer. Venomous, with bites generally requiring administration of antivenom.

Mustard-bellied Snake ■ *Drysdalia rhodogaster* TL 400mm
(Rose-bellied Snake)

DESCRIPTION Small, moderately slender snake, with dark head and distinct yellow to orange band across nape. Uniformly olive-grey to brown above, and typically orange or yellow below. Snout rounded, and dark brown line running from snout to eye.

DISTRIBUTION Central ranges and south coast and ranges of NSW, extending to coast in the south of its distribution. **HABITAT AND HABITS** Occurs in wide range of habitats, including dry forests, woodland and heaths, generally with significant grassy understorey. Terrestrial and predominantly nocturnal, sheltering under logs or rocks, in crevices or among dense leaf litter during the day, but may also forage during this time. Feeds mainly on lizards, favouring skinks. Viviparous, with an average of 5 young per litter. Although venomous, not considered lethal to humans.

Yellow-naped Snake ■ *Furina barnardi* TL 500mm
(Barnard's Snake)

DESCRIPTION Dark brown to blackish above, darker on head, with broad pale brown or yellowish collar on nape, which becomes less noticeable with age. Scales of body obscurely edged paler. Underparts whitish. Similar **Brown-headed Snake** *Furina tristis* of northern Cape York Peninsula is longer (1m long), and broader when mature. **DISTRIBUTION**

Central inland and eastern Qld, from southern Cape York Peninsula to southern central coast. **HABITAT AND HABITS** Found in open forest, grassland, vegetated dunes and rocky outcrops. Nocturnal and terrestrial, sheltering during the day under logs, and in leaf litter and crevices, and emerging to forage for small lizards, mostly skinks. Oviparous. Venom not well known, but not thought to be dangerous to humans. If threatened by a human intruder, raises head into the air and strikes repeatedly with a closed mouth, but seldom bites.

Red-naped Snake ■ *Furina diadema* TL 400mm

DESCRIPTION Glossed reddish-brown above, with darker brown or blackish edges of scales on back giving net-like reticulated pattern. Head and nape glossed black, with clearly defined red or orange patch on nape. Head slightly flattened, with white streak on upper lip. Belly cream or white. Similar juvenile Common Brown Snake (see p. 144) is mostly diurnal. **DISTRIBUTION** Broadly distributed in eastern Australia, from base of Cape York Peninsula Qld, to south-western SA, including eastern and central

Qld, northern NSW and far north-eastern Vic. **HABITAT AND HABITS** Occupies range of drier habitats, including woodland, forests, tussock grassland, shrubland, heaths and adjacent suburban gardens, and often in areas scattered with termite mounds. Terrestrial and diurnal, sheltering during the day under rocks, logs, leaf litter or abandoned sheets of iron, or in crevices, and emerging to forage for small skinks, which are killed by envenoming and constriction. Oviparous, laying up to 10 eggs (average 3) in a clutch, often with more than 1 clutch in a year. If threatened by a human intruder, raises head in the air and strikes repeatedly with a closed mouth, but seldom bites.

Dunmall's Snake ■ *Glyphodon dunmalli* TL 650mm

DESCRIPTION Uniform glossy dark brown to olive-grey above, with head broader than body and faint pale blotches on lips. Underparts white. **DISTRIBUTION** Primarily confined to Brigalow Belt of south-eastern Qld, but also extends into adjacent areas of Brigalow habitat in inland northern NSW. Areas of its range have been affected by habitat fragmentation. **HABITAT AND HABITS** Favours wooded areas (especially Brigalow) on

deep cracking soils, where it is generally secretive; most commonly seen in warm, humid weather. Nocturnal and terrestrial, sheltering during the day under logs and ground litter, and in deep soil crevices, and emerging to forage for lizards. Oviparous. Should be treated with caution, with envenoming capable of producing moderate symptoms in humans.

Moon Snake ■ *Furina ornata* TL 700mm (females larger than males)
(Orange-naped Snake)

DESCRIPTION Slender. Yellowish to reddish-brown or orange above, with glossed brownish to black head and neck, and cream lips. Broad yellowish orange-red band across nape. Body scales edged with darker brown to give reticulated pattern. Underparts cream coloured. Similar juvenile Common Brown Snake (see p. 144) is mostly diurnal. **DISTRIBUTION** Widespread across northern and central-western Australia, including

northern Qld, NT, northern SA and majority of WA, with the exception of southern and central-western coasts and associated inland areas. **HABITAT AND HABITS** Found in open forest, woodland, spinifex-clad sandy or rocky deserts, and shrubland. Nocturnal and terrestrial, sheltering during the day beneath rocks and logs, in deep soil crevices or buried in dense leaf litter, and emerging to feed exclusively on small reptiles. Oviparous, laying up to 6 eggs (average 4) in a single clutch. Not considered highly dangerous.

Grey Snake ■ *Hemiaspis damelii* TL 550mm

DESCRIPTION Uniformly grey or olive-grey above, with darker grey head (black in juveniles) and black bar across nape, which may be lost with age. Creamish-white below, usually flecked with dark grey. **DISTRIBUTION** Inland south-eastern Qld, reaching coast near Rockhampton, and central inland NSW. **HABITAT AND HABITS** Favours flood-

prone, deep cracking clays in drier forests and woodland, where it shelters during the day in deep soil cracks or disused animal burrows, or under logs. Nocturnal and terrestrial, feeding largely on frogs, but will also eat small lizards. Viviparous, with 6–16 (average 10) live young in a litter, generally born in January–March. Not generally aggressive, but capable of inflicting painful bite and should be treated with caution.

Black-bellied Swamp Snake ■ *Hemiaspis signata* TL 650mm
(Marsh Snake; Swamp Snake)

DESCRIPTION Slender, and olive to grey-brown or blackish above, with darker forms having paler head; dark grey to black underneath. Face has narrow pale yellowish-white lines from eyes to neck, and along upper lip from snout to corner of mouth; the latter is often spotted and flecked with darker brown. **DISTRIBUTION** Coast and near coastal areas of eastern Australia, from southern NSW to northern Qld, although more patchily distributed in north. **HABITAT AND HABITS** Occurs in marshy areas of wet and dry forests and woodland, including rainforests, coastal heaths and well-watered gardens. Mostly diurnal and crepuscular, sheltering at night under rocks, dense leaf litter, logs and sheets of iron, but may be active on warmer nights. Forages in thick vegetation for frogs, tadpoles and skinks. Viviparous, with up to 20 (average 10) live young in a litter. Not aggressive, but bites from a large individual have been known to cause severe symptoms, such as localized pain and swelling, headaches and nausea.

Dorsal colour can range from olive to grey-brown or blackish

Pale-headed Snake
▪ *Hoplocephalus bitorquatus* TL 800mm (females generally larger than males)

DESCRIPTION DANGEROUSLY VENOMOUS. Slender, with a broad head. Uniformly greyish-black to dark grey-brown above, with lighter grey head and distinct greyish-white nape. Series of dark blotches on head and neck, and lips strongly barred with dark grey and cream. Pale cream to grey below, occasionally with darker flecks, and with each scale keeled. **DISTRIBUTION** Discontinuous along coast, ranges and western slopes of eastern Australia, from central NSW to Cairns, Qld. **HABITAT AND HABITS** Found in wet

and dry forests and open woodland, often in vicinity of water, where it uses tree hollows and loose bark for shelter during the day, emerging at night to hunt. Feeds arboreally on range of vertebrates, including frogs, reptiles and small mammals, either by hunting in the open or by waiting for prey to come close to its refuge. Viviparous, giving birth biennially to 2–17 young in a litter. Considered potentially lethal, with severe envenoming capable of causing major internal haemorrhaging.

Broad-headed Snake ▪ *Hoplocephalus bungaroides* TL 900mm

DESCRIPTION DANGEROUSLY VENOMOUS. Black above, with numerous, scattered, bright yellowish-white scales, forming irregular narrow transverse bands and longitudinal lines linking them together. Head broad, and with irregular yellow-white spots, and barring on upper lip. Underparts pale to dark grey, occasionally with yellowish blotches.

DISTRIBUTION NSW coast and ranges, within Sydney Basin (a radius of around 200km of Sydney). **HABITAT AND HABITS** Mostly restricted to rocky sandstone outcrops adjacent to forests and woodland, where it shelters in rock crevices or under larger rocks. During cold periods, prefers to reside in tree hollows within woodland. Feeds on small lizards such as Lesueur's Velvet Gecko (see p. 40), snakes and small mammals. Viviparous, with about 6 live young in a litter.

Stephens' Banded Snake ▪ *Hoplocephalus stephensii* TL 1.2m
(Yellow Banded Snake; Stephens's, or Stephen's, Banded Snake)

DESCRIPTION DANGEROUSLY VENOMOUS. Variable. Brown, grey or blackish, usually with brown or cream cross-bands, but occasionally unbanded. Head broad and dark, blotched with cream, and with black-and-white vertical lines on lips. Underparts cream to grey, with each scale keeled. Unbanded individuals may resemble Pale-headed Snake (see p. 135). **DISTRIBUTION** Coast and ranges of southern Qld and northern

NSW. **HABITAT AND HABITS** Occurs in wetter forests, including rainforests and vine thickets, where it is largely arboreal and nocturnal, using hollows in larger trees for shelter during the day. Feeds mainly on frogs, reptiles and small mammals. Viviparous, giving birth to up to 9 young in a litter, generally in December–February.

Tiger Snake ▪ *Notechis scutatus* TL 2m (size varies greatly between populations)

DESCRIPTION DANGEROUSLY VENOMOUS. Robust, with large, flat head and squarish frontal shield. Highly variable in colour and size, but most commonly dark olive-brown to blackish with numerous yellowish cross-bands above, and cream to grey

Melanism allows better heat absorption

Typical banded pattern that gives the species its common name

underparts. Unbanded individuals can be yellowish-brown to black. **DISTRIBUTION** Southern Australia from south-west mainland and islands of WA, through southern mainland and islands of SA, Vic, islands of Bass Strait and mainland Tas, eastern NSW and south-eastern Qld. **HABITAT AND HABITS** Favours well-watered areas, including wetlands, swamps, dams, creeks and lagoons, within a wide range of habitat types, from rainforests, open forests and woodland, to tussock grassland and grazing pasture. Mainly diurnal, but also nocturnal in warm weather. Shelters under ground debris, in dense vegetation or disused animal burrows. Predominantly terrestrial, foraging mainly for frogs, but also other small vertebrates, including mammals, lizards, fish and birds, and some carrion. Ovoviviparous, giving birth to around 20 young in a litter. When threatened, flattens the neck and upper body, exposing black skin between the scales.

Fierce Snake ▪ *Oxyuranus microplepidotus* TL 2.5m
(Inland Taipan; Western Taipan; Small-scaled Snake; Lignum Snake)

DESCRIPTION DANGEROUSLY VENOMOUS. Large, robust snake with rectangular-shaped head. Generally pale to dark brown, often richly coloured, or yellowish-olive above; many scales with darker edges, forming scattered speckled pattern. Head darker, either entirely blackish or with numerous darker flecks. Colour changes seasonally, becoming darker in winter and fading in summer. Belly yellowish with orange flecks.
DISTRIBUTION Inland Australia, including Channel country of south-western Qld, south-western NT, north-eastern SA and north-western NSW. A few isolated older records further south in NSW and near Vic border. **HABITAT AND HABITS** Occupies arid, sparsely vegetated floodplains with deeply cracking soils; also nearby gibber plains,

dunes and rocky outcrops. Diurnal and terrestrial; most active early in the day and late afternoon, sheltering at other times deep in soil cracks, crevices or holes. Feeds on small to medium-sized mammals, which are bitten repeatedly, with venom acting rapidly. Oviparous, laying 9–20 (average 16) eggs in a clutch. Extremely venomous, possessing the most potent venom of any snake. When provoked, raises forebody in an 'S' shape.

Taipan ▪ *Oxyuranus scutellatus* TL 2.5m
(Coastal Taipan; Eastern Taipan)

DESCRIPTION DANGEROUSLY VENOMOUS. Large, robust snake with rectangular-shaped head. Generally yellowish-olive to dark russet-brown above, occasionally dark grey to black, with paler head and reddish-orange eye. Underparts cream with irregular orange flecks. Colour changes seasonally, becoming darker in winter and fading in summer.
DISTRIBUTION Northern and eastern Australia, from Kimberley region WA, through

northern NT, eastern Qld and north-eastern NSW. **HABITAT AND HABITS** Occurs in wet and dry forests and woodland, coastal heaths, grassland and cultivated pastures. Primarily diurnal, becoming crepuscular and nocturnal in hot weather. Hunts terrestrially for small mammals, including rodents and bandicoots, and some birds. Oviparous, laying up to 20 eggs in a clutch. Possesses large quantities of highly toxic venom, and has the longest fangs of any Australian land snake.

Dwyer's Snake ■ *Parasuta dwyeri* TL 500mm
(Dwyer's Black-headed Snake)

DESCRIPTION Glossy pale brown to reddish-brown, with darker black head and neck. Each body scale has blackish base, paler on flanks, giving it a reticulated pattern. Head

short, somewhat widened and flattened, with pale cream-brown snout and lips. Belly white. **DISTRIBUTION** South-eastern inland Australia, including south central Qld, central NSW and northern Vic. **HABITAT AND HABITS** Occupies open woodland, grassland and rocky outcrops. Nocturnal and generally secretive, sheltering during the day under rocks, timber and leaf litter, and in disused animal burrows, and emerging to forage mainly for small lizards, including geckoes and skinks. Viviparous, with average of 3 young in a litter. Generally inoffensive and not considered dangerous to humans.

Little Whip Snake ■ *Parasuta flagellum* TL 400mm

DESCRIPTION Pale grey-brown to reddish-brown above, with each scale having darker base, giving it a reticulated pattern. Head relatively short, with black crown and snout, separated by pale brown cross-bar, and paler cream sides. Underparts pale to dark cream and unpatterned. **DISTRIBUTION** Coast, inland and ranges of south-eastern Australia, from south-east NSW, through Vic, to south-eastern SA. **HABITAT AND HABITS** Found

in eucalypt woodland, shrubland and grassland, typically on stony hills with large quantities of surface rocks. Nocturnal and terrestrial, sheltering during the day under rocks or logs, or in rock crevices, often repeatedly using the same shelter sites. Feeds mainly on small lizards and frogs. Viviparous, with up to 7 (average 4) live young in a litter. Secretive and generally inoffensive, but should be regarded as potentially dangerous, as bites can produce severe reactions.

Mitchell's Short-tailed Snake ■ *Parasuta nigriceps* TL 550mm
(Short-tailed Snake; Mallee Black-backed Snake, Black-backed Snake)

DESCRIPTION Generally brownish above, with wide purplish-black vertebral stripe, bordered on either side with reddish-brown, becoming paler reddish-orange on flanks. Black on top of head and neck, and whitish on lips and underside of body. **DISTRIBUTION** Southern mainland Australia from central-western NSW and north-western Vic, through southern SA, and south and south-western WA. **HABITAT AND**

HABITS Found in mallee woodland and semi-arid, open shrubland, grassland and plains. Nocturnal and terrestrial, sheltering during the day under rocks, logs or leaf litter, and in deep soil cracks and disused animal burrows. Emerges at night to feed on small lizards and snakes, including its own species. Viviparous, giving birth to up to 7 (average 4) live young in a litter. Venomous, but generally inoffensive and not considered dangerous to adult humans.

Mallee Black-headed Snake ■ *Parasuta spectabilis* TL 500mm
(Port Lincoln Snake; Spectacled Hooded Snake; Nullabor Hooded Snake; Bush's Hooded Snake)

DESCRIPTION Generally reddish-brown to grey-brown above, with black head and nape that, in some individuals, is split with cream cross-band in front of eyes. Three subspecies within range, varying mainly in shape and extent of black hood. Upper body scales have darker bases and edging. Underparts and lips whitish. **DISTRIBUTION** Southern mainland Australia from far western NSW and Vic, through southern SA, to Esperance in south-eastern WA. **HABITAT AND**

HABITS Occurs in wet (eastern) and drier (western) open woodland, mallee, acacia scrub and open shrubland. Terrestrial and nocturnal, sheltering during the day under rocks or logs, or in disused animal burrows, and emerging at night to feed on small lizards, including skinks and geckoes. Viviparous, with up to 7 (average 3) live young in a litter. Although venomous, generally inoffensive and not considered dangerous to adult humans.

King Brown Snake ■ *Pseudechis australis*
TL 2.5m (males larger than females)
(Mulga Snake)

DESCRIPTION DANGEROUSLY VENOMOUS. Australia's largest venomous snake, with broad head, prominent cheeks and pale reddish-brown iris. Pale brown, reddish-brown, coppery-brown or brownish-black above, with darker edges and greenish-yellow bases to scales, giving reticulated pattern. Belly white to pinkish-cream, occasionally with irregular orange blotches. **DISTRIBUTION** Broadly distributed across Australian mainland, with the exception of south-east and southern coastline. **HABITAT AND HABITS** Occurs in variety of habitats, including forests, grassland, shrubland and deserts. Mainly diurnal and crepuscular, but active at night during hotter weather. Shelters in rock cavities, deep soil cracks and disused animal burrows, and under logs and large rocks.

Hunts reptiles (including other snakes), frogs, birds and mammals, and also eats reptile and birds' eggs, and carrion. Oviparous, with up to 19 (average 9) eggs in a clutch. When threatened, inflates body and flattens neck. A single bite is capable of injecting large amounts of venom. Despite being called the King Brown Snake, it is actually a member of the black snakes.

Collett's Snake ■ *Pseudechis colletti* TL 1.5m (males larger than females)
(Down's Tiger Snake)

DESCRIPTION DANGEROUSLY VENOMOUS. Reddish-brown to black above, with large cream, pink or reddish blotches and irregular bands. Top of head uniformly dark, with paler snout. Belly and flanks salmon-pink to cream. **DISTRIBUTION** Central Qld.

HABITAT AND HABITS Found in open grassland, shrubland and woodland on cracking clay and black soil plains, and shelters in deep soil cracks and under logs. Diurnal, but may be active on warmer nights, and actively hunts mammals, frogs, lizards and other snakes. Oviparous, laying up to 14 eggs in a clutch. Relatively placid, but if provoked raises forebody in low, flattened curve and hisses.

Blue-bellied Black Snake ■ *Pseudechis guttatus*
TL 1.5m (males larger than females)
(Spotted Black Snake)

DESCRIPTION DANGEROUSLY VENOMOUS. Highly variable; generally bluish-black, grey or brownish above, with or without varying amounts of grey or cream spotting, and uniformly dark head. May also, rarely, have some pink colouration. Underparts dark bluish-grey. **DISTRIBUTION** Western slopes and ranges of north-eastern NSW and south-western Qld. **HABITAT AND HABITS** Occupies dry forests and woodland, open grassland, wetlands and cropped pasture. Generally diurnal, sheltering on most nights under logs or dense vegetation, or in deep soil cracks or disused animal burrows. Hunts terrestrially, predominantly for vertebrates, including frogs, lizards, snakes and small mammals. Oviparous, with up to 17 eggs in a clutch. If threatened, hisses loudly and raises and flattens forebody in low 'S' shape.

Bluish-black individual

Flattens neck and hisses when threatened

Red-bellied Black Snake ■ *Pseudechis porphyriacus* TL 2m
(Common Black Snake; Red-belly)

DESCRIPTION DANGEROUSLY VENOMOUS. Uniformly glossed black above, often with paler brownish snout. Crimson on lower flanks, fading to duller red, orange-pink or pale pinkish-cream on middle of belly, and black under tail. Eye is dark. **DISTRIBUTION** Eastern and south-eastern Australian mainland from Adelaide SA, through central and south-eastern Vic, central and eastern NSW, and eastern Qld. Populations becoming more isolated in north. **HABITAT AND HABITS** Favours moist areas, normally near watercourses, lagoons, swamps, drainage ditches and farm dams, but also occurs in forests, woodland, heaths and grassland. Predominantly diurnal, sheltering during the day in thick

grass tussocks or disused animal burrows, or under logs or large rocks. Forages on land or in water for frogs, tadpoles, fish, small mammals, lizards and snakes (including its own species), and can stay underwater for up to 20 minutes. Around 20 live young are laid in thin sacs (ovoviviparous) and emerge soon afterwards. Although capable of inflicting a fatal bite, when approached it normally remains motionless or tries to flee.

Strap-snouted Brown Snake ■ *Pseudonaja aspidorhyncha* TL 1.5m
(Shield-snouted Brown Snake)

DESCRIPTION DANGEROUSLY VENOMOUS. Glossy pale brown to blackish-brown above, with dark cross-band on neck, or with scattered dark brown or black spots on head and neck. May be uniformly coloured, but more often has varied irregular dark and pale banding, generally most visible on sides and posterior. Inside of mouth pale pinkish-grey, and when viewed from above, snout is chisel shaped. Cream, yellowish or brown on belly, paler on throat. **DISTRIBUTION** Southern-central Australia, including south-western Qld, western NSW, far north-western Vic, western SA and far south-eastern NT. **HABITAT AND HABITS** Wide range of arid or semi-arid habitats, including open

woodland, grassland, shrubland and deserts, where it can be active at any time of the day or night. Shelters under logs, rocks or other ground litter, or in crevices or disused animal burrows, emerging to feed on range of vertebrates, including small mammals, lizards and birds, which it kills by both envenoming and constriction. Oviparous, with around 12–16 eggs in a clutch, and 1–2 clutches laid in a season.

Speckled Brown Snake ■ *Pseudonaja guttata* TL 1.4m

DESCRIPTION DANGEROUSLY VENOMOUS. Pale brown to orange-yellow above, normally with dark black edges on body scales or, less commonly, with regular, transverse broad dark bands or blackish blotches. Belly cream or orange, with irregular darker orange-pink blotches. Throat whitish and inside of mouth bluish-black. **DISTRIBUTION** From central Qld to eastern NT, including far north-western SA. **HABITAT AND HABITS**

Found in arid tussock grassland on deeply cracking black soil plains and floodplains. Mainly diurnal and terrestrial, sheltering at night in deep soil cracks and under logs, and emerging during the day to hunt mainly for reptiles and small mammals, and occasionally frogs. Oviparous, with up to 6 eggs laid in a clutch; usually 1 clutch in a season, but 2 clutches in peak seasons. Venom contains neurotoxins.

Gwardar ▪ *Pseudonaja mengdeni* TL 1.6m
(Western Brown Snake; Mengden's Brown Snake)

DESCRIPTION DANGEROUSLY VENOMOUS. Two distinct forms: 1. pale to yellow-orange, with dark brown or black head and neck, dark reticulated pattern on posterior part of body, and occasionally broad dark transverse band; 2. brown to yellowish-brown, with pale brown head and grey band on neck, and dark reticulated pattern on posterior part of body. Transverse grey-brown or dark brown bands, either thin and indistinct, or alternating broad and narrow. In both forms belly is yellow or cream, blotched with orange or pink, inside of mouth is blackish and, when viewed from above, snout has rounded appearance. **DISTRIBUTION** Throughout most of mainland Australia, from western WA, to eastern Qld. Absent from tropical north, southern coastline and south-east. **HABITAT AND HABITS** Found in wide range of arid and semi-arid areas, including open woodland, grassland shrubland and deserts. Can be active at any time of the day or night. Shelters under logs, rocks or other ground litter, or in crevices or disused animal burrows, emerging to feed on range of vertebrates, including small mammals, lizards and birds, which it kills by both envenoming and constriction. Oviparous, with around 12–16 eggs in a clutch, and 1–2 clutches laid in a season.

Yellow-orange form *Brownish form*

Northern Brown Snake ▪ *Pseudonaja nuchalis* TL 1.6m

DESCRIPTION DANGEROUSLY VENOMOUS. Long and slender. Light to medium brown above, with or without dark brown bands, and occasionally darker brown or black on head and neck. Scattered dark brown or black scales on neck. Underparts yellowish-cream, often with salmon blotches (particularly on anterior section). Eye large with dark iris and orange ring around pupil. Snout squarish and inside of mouth is blackish. **DISTRIBUTION** Northern Australia, from Kimberley WA, through northern NT and northern Qld. **HABITAT AND HABITS** Favours dry, open forests, grassland and scrubland, where it shelters under logs, rocks or other ground litter, or in crevices or disused animal burrows. Largely diurnal, but active during warmer nights, preying mainly on small mammals and reptiles, as well as frogs and reptiles' eggs. Oviparous, laying 12–16 eggs per clutch, with 1–2 clutches produced in a season.

Common Brown Snake ■ *Pseudonaja textilis* TL 1.8m
(Eastern Brown Snake)

DESCRIPTION DANGEROUSLY VENOMOUS. Adults typically pale to dark brown and unpatterned; darker forms may have paler head. Underparts yellowish-cream or pinkish-orange, blotched with brown or grey. Eyes typically orange with dark surround and distinct brow. Juveniles have black head and black nape; occasionally banded on body. **DISTRIBUTION** Eastern Australia, from central and eastern NT, Qld (except Cape York Peninsula), to NSW, Vic and eastern SA. Central NT populations seem isolated from main range. **HABITAT AND HABITS** Found in dry, open habitats, including woodland, scrubland,

grassland and adjacent semi-urban areas, often in vicinity of water. Shelters under logs, rocks and sheets of iron, and in crevices, emerging to hunt during the day and warm nights on wide variety of vertebrates, including lizards, frogs, birds, small mammals and other snakes. Oviparous, laying up to 25 eggs in deep cracks in soil or disused animal burrows, with several clutches laid in a season when conditions are favourable. Usual threat display includes flattening of neck, then raising head and

Adult in striking posture

anterior part of body off the ground in 'S' shape.

Curl Snake ■ *Suta suta* TL 600mm
(Myall Snake)

DESCRIPTION Robust, with dark line, edged below with creamish-white, running from snout and through each eye. Iris golden-yellow to orange. Generally light brown to reddish-brown above, with darker head and variable blackish hood on nape. Underparts white. **DISTRIBUTION** Central and eastern Australia, from far western WA and in majority of NT, Qld, NSW, Vic and SA. Absent from coast and near coastal regions of most parts of its range. **HABITAT AND HABITS** Occurs in drier open habitats, including woodland, shrubland, grassland, and stony or clay deserts. Nocturnal and terrestrial,

sheltering during the day under logs and other groundcover, or in disused animal burrows, and emerging to feed on range of small vertebrates, including lizards and frogs. Viviparous, producing up to 7 live young in a litter. Although venomous, not known to cause fatalities, but should still be regarded as dangerous. When threatened, contorts body in series of exaggerated curling and uncurling actions.

Rough-scaled Snake ■ *Tropidechis carinatus* TL 900mm
(Clarence River Snake)

DESCRIPTION DANGEROUSLY VENOMOUS. Dull brown to olive-brown above, with irregular dark transverse bands or blotches, starting at neck and becoming paler and more obscure towards posterior half of body, and occasionally disappearing completely on tail. Scales of back and sides have raised lengthways central keel. Underparts yellowish-cream to olive-green, generally with darker blotches. **DISTRIBUTION** Patchily distributed on east coast of Australia, with isolated populations in northern Qld, and southern Qld to central NSW. **HABITAT AND HABITS** Found in rainforests, wet sclerophyll forests,

shrubland and pastures. Although terrestrial, it is a skilled climber and can be seen sheltering in tree hollows, basking on tree branches or actively hunting within foliage; also sits and waits for prey to come within striking distance. Feeds primarily on mammals and frogs. Viviparous, with average of 5–10 live young in a litter. Highly toxic venom and aggressive when threatened.

Bandy-bandy ■ *Vermicella annulata* TL 800mm
(Eastern Bandy-Bandy)

DESCRIPTION Alternating black-and-white cross-bands wrapping completely around body, with up to 75 black rings evident. Snout black, eyes small, and tail short and blunt. Does not overlap with any other members of the genus, all of which have similar colour patterns. **DISTRIBUTION** Widespread through eastern and far northern Australia, from central northern NT, northern and eastern Qld, NSW, northern Vic and south-eastern SA. **HABITAT AND HABITS** Occurs in range of habitats from wet coastal rainforest to

sandy spinifex desert, where it can be found sheltering under rocks and logs. Nocturnal and fossorial. Presumed to feed exclusively on blind snakes, some as large as itself, and able to go for extended periods without food or water. Oviparous, laying 2–13 eggs in a clutch. Venomous, but not considered dangerous. When threatened, loops parts of body high off the ground.

Reef Shallows Seasnake ▪ *Aipysurus duboisii* TL 1.1m
(Dubois's Sea Snake; Dubois' Sea Snake; Duboi's Seasnake)

DESCRIPTION Moderately built with small, broad head, slender neck and laterally compressed tail. Variable amounts of dark purplish-brown and cream, with paler edges of scales forming reticulated pattern. Lower flanks typically more whitish-cream, forming

variably distinct wedge-shaped areas that extend up sides. **DISTRIBUTION** Seas off northern Australia, from central WA, through NT, to southern Qld. **HABITAT AND HABITS** Marine. Most commonly seen in shallow water near coral reefs at depths of 3–4m, but known to descend to 50m, where it feeds on various fish species, including eels, which are caught near the sea floor, generally in the early evening. Can stay submerged for up to 2 hours, but generally comes to the surface more regularly to breathe. Viviparous, giving birth to 4–6 live young.

Olive-headed Seasnake ▪ *Hydrophis major* TL 1.6m
(Oliveheaded Sea Snake; Greater Sea Snake)

DESCRIPTION DANGEROUSLY VENOMOUS. Robust, with long, slender neck, moderately sized head and laterally compressed tail. Olive or pale brownish-grey above, with alternating large, elongated, oval and narrower darker brown or blackish cross-bars. Sides and belly generally yellowish-cream with dark brown spots on flanks. Patterning more contrasting in juveniles. **DISTRIBUTION** Seas off northern and eastern Australia, from central WA, through NT and Qld, to southern NSW. **HABITAT AND HABITS** Generally found in deeper marine waters at more than 20m, but also in tidal estuaries and creeks with soft sandy or muddy floors, where it feeds on bottom-dwelling fish, including catfish and gobies. Can stay submerged for up to 2 hours, but usually comes to the surface more regularly to breathe. Viviparous, giving birth to 6–12 live young in a litter.

Adult

Juvenile

Spotted Seasnake ▪ *Hydrophis ornatus* TL 1.4m
(Spotted Sea Snake; Ocellated Seasnake)

DESCRIPTION DANGEROUSLY VENOMOUS. Stout, with uniformly thick head and neck, and laterally compressed tail. Grey or blue-grey above, with series of large, elongated, blackish oval cross-bars, and paler, often dark-edged, eye-like spots on sides. Pattern becomes less distinct with age. Creamish-white belly and flanks. **DISTRIBUTION** Seas

off northern and eastern Australia, from northern WA, through NT, to southern Qld. Further south to southern WA and Vic in warmer months. **HABITAT AND HABITS** Generally found in deeper marine waters, to 50m, but also in tidal estuaries and creeks with soft sandy or muddy floors, where it feeds on fish that live near or on the bottom, including wrasse, slimies and parrotfish. Can stay submerged for up to 2 hours, but usually comes to the surface more regularly to breathe. Viviparous, averaging 6 live young in a litter.

Yellow-bellied Seasnake ▪ *Hydrophis platurus* TL 1m
(Yellowbelly Sea Snake; Pelagic Sea Snake)

DESCRIPTION DANGEROUSLY VENOMOUS. Distinctively dark brown or black on upper back, with sharply contrasting yellow flanks and undersurface. Tail laterally compressed, predominantly yellow, with numerous dark markings. Head distinct and elongated, with large dark eye. **DISTRIBUTION** Seas off western, northern and eastern Australia, from south-west WA, through NT, Qld, NSW and Vic, to Tas. **HABITAT AND**

HABITS Marine. Favours warmer open ocean waters, typically above 18 °C, but also enters cooler waters and possibly tidal estuaries, perhaps as the result of storms and rough seas. Lives and feeds in surface layers of open ocean, feeding exclusively on small fish, which are ambushed as they approach a floating snake for shelter, or actively chased as the snake drifts through the ocean on warm currents. Ovoviviparous, giving birth to 2–6 fully formed young, after gestation period of around 6 months.

Stokes' Seasnake ■ *Hydrophis stokesii* TL 2m

DESCRIPTION DANGEROUSLY VENOMOUS. Heavily built and stout, with large head and long fangs. Highly variable in colour, including cream, brown, bluish-grey or black, generally with alternating large, elongated oval and narrower dark cross-bars on back. May also have dark, eye-like spots on sides. Pattern more contrasting on juveniles, and may be absent on adults. **DISTRIBUTION** Seas off northern and eastern Australia, from central WA, through NT and southern Qld, to southern NSW. **HABITAT AND HABITS** Found in marine waters to around 20m, but also in tidal estuaries and creeks with soft

sandy or muddy floors. Feeds on fish, including toadfish, jawfish and other slow-moving types, which are found by foraging in reef crevices and across the sea floor. Can stay submerged for up to 2 hours, but generally comes to the surface more regularly to breathe. Viviparous, with up to 20 (average 10) live young in a litter. Aggressive and known to bite repeatedly.

Wide-faced Sea Krait ■ *Laticauda colubrina* TL 1.35m
(White-lipped Sea Krait; Yellow-lipped Sea Krait)

DESCRIPTION DANGEROUSLY VENOMOUS. Cylindrical, with shallow, laterally compressed tail. Top of head black, and snout and upper lip above eye yellow. Body has alternating black-and-blue or blue-grey rings. Paler rings have reticulated pattern. Underparts yellowish. **DISTRIBUTION** Occasionally sighted along east coast of Australia. More widely distributed from India to islands of west Pacific. **HABITAT AND HABITS** Amphibious, inhabiting coral and rocky reefs, where it feeds almost exclusively on eels, which are envenomed and swallowed whole. After feeding, it needs to return to land to digest its food, and shelters in rocky crevices or hollows in fallen logs for protection. Oviparous, laying 5–10 eggs on land, in caves or crevices.

Alternating rings can be blue-grey or bright blue in different individuals

Macleay's Water Snake ■ *Pseudoferania polylepis* TL 800mm
(Macleay's Mud Snake; Smooth Watersnake)

DESCRIPTION Brown to dark olive-grey above, often with orange, dark brown or blackish longitudinal stripes along back or upper sides and, at times, whitish cream line along lower flanks. Underparts cream or yellowish with darker greyish-black stripe on underside of tail, which usually extends along length of belly. Often has darker eye-stripe that extends from snout to rear of mouth. **DISTRIBUTION** Coastal plains of northern Australia, from western Arnhem Land NT, to southern Cape York Peninsula Qld. **HABITAT AND HABITS** Aquatic, favouring freshwater billabongs, lagoons, marshes, creeks, rivers and floodwaters, and can also be seen on riverbanks and overhanging vegetation. Hunts either by ambush, lying hidden on the bottoms of pools with just the tip of the snout protruding, or by actively seeking fish, frogs and crustaceans. Ovoviviparous, with 4–27 (average 12) live young in a litter. Weakly venomous and not considered dangerous to humans.

Dark-spined Blind Snake ■ *Anilios bicolor* TL 375mm

DESCRIPTION Small, moderately stout and worm-like, with glossy scales that are generally uniform in size around body, and small, dark eye-spots. Body thickness uniform along length, and tail bluntly rounded with horn-like scale at extremity. Dark brown to purplish-brown above and whitish below, with tail all or partially black. Snout rounded when viewed from overhead, and angular when viewed from side. **DISTRIBUTION** Drier parts of southern mainland, from central-western WA, through SA, to central Vic and NSW. **HABITAT AND HABITS** Fossorial in soft, loamy soils, but can be seen on the surface following rain or on humid nights. Nocturnal, often sheltering during the day in underground burrows, or under rocks or logs, feeding at night on invertebrates, mostly on eggs and young of ants and termites. Oviparous. Non-venomous, with small jaws that are incapable of biting humans, but secretes strong smell when disturbed.

Prong-snouted Blind Snake ■ *Anilios bituberculatus* TL 375mm
(Beaked Blind Snake; Peters's Blind Snake)

DESCRIPTION Small, slender and worm-like, with glossy scales that are generally uniform in size around body and small, dark eye-spots. Body thickness uniform along length, and tail bluntly rounded, with horn-like scale at extremity. Pale pinkish-brown above and pinkish-white below. Nostril area distinctly angular and projecting, giving snout trilobed appearance when viewed from above. **DISTRIBUTION** Southern mainland, from coastal

WA. through SA, Vic and NSW, to southern Qld. Absent from far south-west WA and coastal Vic and NSW. **HABITAT AND HABITS** Fossorial in soft, loamy soils in open woodland, but can be seen on the surface following rain or on humid nights. Nocturnal, often sheltering during the day in underground burrows, or under rocks or logs. Feeds entirely on invertebrates, mostly on eggs and young of ants and termites. Oviparous, laying 2–9 (average 6) eggs in a clutch. Non-venomous, with small jaws that are incapable of biting humans, but secretes strong smell when disturbed.

Northern Blind Snake ■ *Anilios diversus* TL 300mm

DESCRIPTION Small, moderately slender and worm-like, with glossy scales that are generally uniform in size around body, and small, dark eye-spots. Body thickness uniform along length, and tail bluntly rounded, with horn-like scale at extremity. Brown to purplish-brown above and pinkish-white below. Snout rounded when viewed from above and from side. **DISTRIBUTION** Northern Australia, from inland south-eastern Qld, through central and northern NT, to north-eastern WA. **HABITAT AND HABITS**

Fossorial in soft, loamy soils, but can be seen on the surface following rain or on humid nights. Nocturnal, often sheltering during the day in underground burrows, or under rocks or logs, feeding at night on invertebrates, mostly on eggs and young of ants and termites. Oviparous. Non-venomous, with small jaws that are incapable of biting humans, but secretes strong smell when disturbed.

Beaked Blind Snake ■ *Anilios grypus* TL 400mm
(Long-beaked Blind Snake)

DESCRIPTION Small and worm-like, with glossy scales that are generally uniform in size around body and small, dark eye-spots. Body thickness uniform along length, and tail bluntly rounded, with horn-like scale at extremity. Pale brown above and whitish below, with blackish tail. Snout elongated, with distinct downwards hook when viewed from side. **DISTRIBUTION** Central and northern Australia, from north-western WA coast, through central and southern NT and northern SA, to central Qld. Reaches coast in Gulf of Carpenteria. **HABITAT AND HABITS**

Fossorial in soft, loamy soils, but can be seen on the surface following rain or on humid nights. Nocturnal, often sheltering during the day in underground burrows, or under rocks or logs, and feeds entirely on invertebrates, mostly on eggs and young of ants and termites. Oviparous, with average of 3 soft-shelled, oval eggs in clutch. Non-venomous, with small jaws that are incapable of biting humans, but secretes strong smell when disturbed.

Robust Blind Snake ■ *Anilios ligatus* TL 400mm

DESCRIPTION Stout and worm-like, with glossy scales that are generally uniform in size around body and small, dark eye-spots. Head and neck narrower than body thickness and tail bluntly rounded, with horn-like scale at extremity. Dark brown to purplish above and whitish below. Rostral scale almost twice as long as it is wide. **DISTRIBUTION** Northern and eastern Australia, from Kimberley region WA to Gulf of Carpentaria Qld, and from coastal southern Cape York Peninsula Qld to northern-central NSW. **HABITAT AND HABITS** Fossorial in soft, loamy soils, but can be seen on the surface following rain or on humid nights. Nocturnal, often sheltering during the day in underground burrows, or under

rocks or logs, feeding at night on invertebrates, mostly on eggs and young of ants and termites. Oviparous, laying 4–13 (average 8) soft-shelled eggs in clutch. Non-venomous, with small jaws that are incapable of biting humans, but secretes strong smell when disturbed.

Blackish Blind Snake ■ *Anilios nigrescens* TL 550mm

DESCRIPTION Moderately stout and worm-like, with glossy scales that are generally uniform in size around body and small, dark eye-spots. Body thickness generally uniform along length and tail bluntly rounded, with horn-like scale at extremity. Pinkish-brown to purplish-black above, and white or pinkish below. **DISTRIBUTION** South-eastern Australian mainland, from south-eastern Qld, through eastern NSW, to central and south-western Vic. **HABITAT AND HABITS** Fossorial in soft, loamy soils, but can be seen on

the surface following rain or on humid nights. Nocturnal, often sheltering during the day in underground burrows, under rocks or logs, or in rotting logs above the ground, sometimes communally with members of the same species. Feeds entirely on invertebrates, mostly on eggs and young of ants and termites. Oviparous, producing up to 34 soft-shelled eggs in a clutch. Non-venomous, with small jaws that are incapable of biting humans, but secretes a strong smell when disturbed.

Proximus Blind Snake ■ *Anilios proximus* TL 600mm

DESCRIPTION Heavily built and worm-like, with glossy scales that are generally uniform in size around body and small, dark eye-spots. Body thickness uniform along length and tail bluntly rounded, with horn-like scale at extremity. Dark brown to dark purplish-grey above and yellowish-cream below. Snout rounded when viewed from above and from side. **DISTRIBUTION** Eastern Australia from Cape York Peninsula, through central and southern NSW, to central Vic. **HABITAT AND HABITS** Fossorial in soft, loamy soils in

wide variety of habitats, but can be seen on the surface following rain or on humid nights. Nocturnal, often sheltering during the day in underground burrows, or under rocks or logs, feeding at night on invertebrates, mostly on eggs and young of ants, including bulldog ants, and termites. Oviparous, laying up to 35 (average 13) soft-shelled eggs in a clutch. Non-venomous, with small jaws that are incapable of biting humans, but secretes strong smell when disturbed.

Brown-snouted Blind Snake ■ *Anilios wiedii* TL 300mm

DESCRIPTION Small and worm-like, with glossy scales that are generally uniform in size around body and small, dark eye-spots. Body thickness uniform along length and tail bluntly rounded, with horn-like scale at extremity. Pinkish to reddish-brown above and pinkish-cream below. Snout rounded when viewed from above and from side.
DISTRIBUTION Eastern Australia from Central Qld coast to inland NSW. **HABITAT AND HABITS** Fossorial in soft, loamy soils in open woodland and shrubland, but can be seen on the surface following rain or on humid nights. Nocturnal, often sheltering during the day in underground burrows, or under rocks or logs, sometimes communally. Feeds entirely on invertebrates, mostly on eggs and young of ants and termites. Oviparous, laying 1–8 (average 4) soft-shelled eggs in a clutch. Non-venomous, with small jaws that are incapable of biting humans, but secretes a strong smell when disturbed.

CROCODILES (CROCODILIA)

The order Crocodilia groups together the world's 25 currently described species of crocodylians, alligators, caimans and gharials. Australia is home to two crocodylians, the 'true' crocodiles, one of which, the Saltwater Crocodile, is the largest known living reptile in the world.

Freshwater Crocodile ▪ *Crocodylus johnsoni* TL 3m

(Johnston's Crocodile; Johnson's Crocodile; Freshie; Johnstone's River Crocodile; Johnstone's Crocodile; Fish Crocodile)

DESCRIPTION Grey to greenish-brown in colour, with irregular darker patches along sides, flanks and top of body. Smooth, slender snout compared to Saltwater Crocodile's (see opposite), and large, triangular scutes (thickened scales) along top of tail.

DISTRIBUTION Found in near coastal and adjacent inland areas of northern Australia from Kimberleys, WA, to Gulf of Carpentaria and southern Cape York Peninsula, Qld.

HABITAT AND HABITS Occupies freshwater rivers, lagoons and swamps, floodplains during wet season, and occasionally found in more saline, brackish waters. Walks with elevated body. Not regarded as dangerous to people, but swimmers have been bitten,

Juvenile

either by accident or for defensive reasons, and bites cause deep lacerations and infection. When threatened, inflates and vibrates body, creating large ripples in the water. Feeds mostly on insects and fish, but spiders, amphibians, crustaceans and small reptiles (including young crocodiles), birds and mammals are also consumed. Oviparous, with clutches of 4–20 hard-shelled eggs, laid in hole dug in sandbank. Females do not guard nest, but assist hatched young to reach water.

Adult

Saltwater Crocodile ■ *Crocodylus porosus* TL 5m (rarely to 7m)
(Estuarine Crocodile; Salty)

DESCRIPTION DANGEROUS. Unmistakable. Long, broad snout, heavily built body and long, powerful tail. Back and limbs mottled grey-brown to blackish, with numerous osteoderms (bony plates) visible on neck, back and flanks. Underside pale cream. Males typically larger than females. **DISTRIBUTION** Coastal regions and drainage systems of northern and north-eastern Australia, from Broome, WA to around Gladstone, Qld, but also in deeper oceans and on islands up to 100km from mainland. **HABITAT AND HABITS** Occurs in various coastal habitats, including fresh and brackish rivers, estuaries, creeks, swamps, lagoons and billabongs, and readily enters the open sea. Active year round, and individuals often seen basking on open mud banks. If threatened, emits low, rumbling growl. Young eat insects, fish, crustaceans and reptiles; adults eat mammals, fish, birds, reptiles (including turtles and smaller crocodiles) and, on rare occasions, people. There are normally warning signs in place in areas where people are at risk from attacks. Oviparous, laying up to 70 hard-shelled eggs in mound of vegetation, which is protected by female; she assists hatched young by digging them out and carrying them in her mouth to water.

Adult

Juvenile

AUSTRALIAN REPTILE LIST

Common and scientific names follow The Reptile Database and Cogger (see further information p. 172).

For each species, an 'x' indicates presence in a particular state or confined to offshore islands. An asterisk (*) denotes that the species has been included in the species accounts section of the book. State abbreviations are as follows (Australian Capital Territory distributions are incorporated within New South Wales):

Q	Queensland
NS	New South Wales
V	Victoria
T	Tasmania
S	South Australia
W	Western Australia
NT	Northern Territory
O	Offshore Islands (only)

Abbreviations of IUCN Red List status:

CR	Critically Endangered
EN	Endangered
VU	Vulnerable
NT	Near Threatened
LC	Least Concern
DD	Data Deficient
NE	Not Evaluated

COMMON NAME	SCIENTIFIC NAME	Q	NS	V	T	S	W	NT	O	IUCN
Emydidae (Pond Turtles)										
Common Slider	Trachemys scripta	x	x				x			NE
Carettochelyidae (Pignose Turtles)										
Pig-nosed Turtle	Carettochelys insculpta							x		VU
Cheloniidae (Sea Turtles)										
Loggerhead Turtle*	Caretta caretta	x	x	x	x	x	x	x		VU
Green Turtle*	Chelonia mydas	x	x	x		x	x	x		EN
Hawksbill Turtle*	Eretmochelys imbricata	x	x	x	x		x	x		CR
Pacific Ridley Turtle	Lepidochelys olivacea	x	x	x	x	x	x	x		VU
Flatback Turtle*	Natator depressus	x				x	x	x		DD
Dermochelyidae (Leatherback Turtles)										
Leathery Turtle*	Dermochelys coriacea	x	x	x	x	x	x	x		VU
Chelidae (Austro-American Sideneck Turtles)										
Sandstone Snake-necked Turtle	Chelodina burrungandjii						x	x		NE
Cann's Long-necked Turtle*	Chelodina canni	x						x		NE
Collie's Snake-necked Turtle	Chelodina colliei						x			NT
Broad-shelled Turtle*	Chelodina expansa	x	x	x		x				NE
Eastern Snake-necked Turtle*	Chelodina longicollis	x	x	x	x	x				NE
Northern Snake-necked Turtle*	Chelodina oblonga	x					x	x		NE
Flat-shelled Turtle	Chelodina steindachneri						x			NE
White-throated Snapping Turtle*	Elseya albagula	x								NE
Northern Snapping Turtle	Elseya dentata						x	x		NE
Yellow-bellied Snapping Turtle	Elseya flaviventralis							x		NE
Irwin's Snapping Turtle*	Elseya irwini	x								NE
Gulf Snapping Turtle	Elseya lavarackorum	x						x		NE
Mary River Turtle	Elusor macrurus	x								EN
Macquarie Turtle*	Emydura macquarii	x	x	x	x	x				NE
Jardine River Turtle	Emydura subglobosa	x						x		LC
Northern Yellow-faced Turtle*	Emydura tanybaraga	x						x		NE
North-west Red-faced Turtle	Emydura victoriae						x	x		NE
Manning River Helmeted Turtle	Flaviemys purvisi		x							DD
Western Swamp Turtle	Pseudemydura umbrina						x			CR
Fitzroy River Turtle	Rheodytes leukops	x								VU
Western Sawshelled Turtle	Wollumbinia belli	x	x							EN
George's Helmeted Turtle	Wollumbinia georgesi		x							DD
Common Sawshell Turtle*	Wollumbinia latisternum	x	x					x		NE
Agamidae (Dragon Lizards)										
Jacky Lizard*	Amphibolurus muricatus	x	x	x		x				NE

COMMON NAME	SCIENTIFIC NAME	Q	NS	V	T	S	W	NT	O	IUCN
Mallee Tree Dragon	Amphibolurus norrisi			x		x	x			LC
Chameleon Dragon	Chelosania brunnea	x					x	x		NE
Frilled Lizard*	Chlamydosaurus kingii	x	x				x	x		LC
Gravel Dragon	Cryptagama aurita						x	x		NE
Western Heath Dragon	Ctenophorus adelaidensis					x	x			NE
Shark Bay Heath Dragon	Ctenophorus butleri						x			NE
Ring-tailed Dragon	Ctenophorus caudicinctus	x				x	x	x		NE
Southern Heath Dragon	Ctenophorus chapmani					x	x			NE
Black-collared Dragon	Ctenophorus clayi					x	x	x		NE
Bicycle Lizard	Ctenophorus cristatus					x	x			NE
Tawny Dragon	Ctenophorus decresii		x			x				NE
Long-tailed Sand-dragon	Ctenophorus femoralis						x			NE
Peninsula Dragon	Ctenophorus fionni					x				NE
Mallee Military Dragon*	Ctenophorus fordi	x	x	x		x	x			NE
Gibber Dragon	Ctenophorus gibba					x				NE
Central Military Dragon	Ctenophorus isolepis	x				x	x	x		NE
Spotted Military Dragon	Ctenophorus maculatus						x			NE
Lake Eyre Dragon	Ctenophorus maculosus					x				LC
Mckenzie's Dragon	Ctenophorus mckenziei					x	x			NE
Barrier Range Dragon	Ctenophorus mirrityana		x			x				NE
Central Netted Dragon*	Ctenophorus nuchalis	x	x			x	x	x		LC
Ornate Dragon	Ctenophorus ornatus						x			LC
Gnaraloo Heath Dragon	Ctenophorus parviceps						x			NE
Painted Dragon*	Ctenophorus pictus	x	x	x		x	x	x		NE
Western Netted Dragon	Ctenophorus reticulatus					x	x	x		NE
Reddening Sand-dragon	Ctenophorus rubens						x			NE
Rusty Dragon	Ctenophorus rufescens					x	x			NE
Claypan Dragon	Ctenophorus salinarum						x			NE
Lozenge-marked Dragon	Ctenophorus scutulatus						x			NE
Ochre Dragon	Ctenophorus tjantjalka					x				LC
Red-barred Dragon	Ctenophorus vadnappa					x				NE
Yinnietharra Rock Dragon	Ctenophorus yinnietharra						x			VU
Carnarvon Dragon	Diporiphora adducta						x			NE
White-lipped Two-line Dragon	Diporiphora albilabris						x	x		LC
Mulga Dragon	Diporiphora amphiboluroides						x			NE
Arnhem Dragon	Diporiphora arnhemica						x	x		NE
Tommy Roundhead*	Diporiphora australis	x	x							NE
Robust Two-line Dragon	Diporiphora bennettii						x	x		NE
Two-lined Dragon*	Diporiphora bilineata	x						x		NE
Crystal Creek Two-line Dragon	Diporiphora convergens						x			DD
Lally's Two-line Dragon	Diporiphora lalliae						x	x		LC
Pink Two-line Dragon	Diporiphora linga					x	x			LC
Yellow-sided Two-line Dragon	Diporiphora magna	x					x	x		NE
Two-pored Dragon	Diporiphora margaretae						x			NE
Nobbi Dragon*	Diporiphora nobbi	x	x	x		x				NE
Grey-striped Western Desert Dragon	Diporiphora paraconvergens						x			NE
Brigalow Nobbi	Diporiphora phaeospinosa	x								NE
Pindan Two-line Dragon	Diporiphora pindan						x			NE
Plain-backed Two-line Dragon	Diporiphora reginae					x	x			NE
Superb Two-line Dragon	Diporiphora superba						x	x		NE
Pilbara Two-line Dragon	Diporiphora valens						x			NE
Northern Pilbara Tree Dragon	Diporiphora vescus						x			NE
Blue-lined Dragon	Diporiphora winneckei	x	x			x	x	x		NE
Long-nosed Dragon	Gowidon longirostris					x	x	x		NE
Water Dragon*	Intellagama lesueurii	x	x	x						NE
Burns' Dragon*	Lophognathus burnsi	x	x							NE
Gilbert's Dragon*	Lophognathus gilberti	x					x	x		LC
Swamplands Lashtail	Lophognathus temporalis	x					x	x		NE
Boyd's Forest Dragon*	Lophosaurus boydii	x								NE
Southern Angle-headed Dragon*	Lophosaurus spinipes	x	x							NE
Thorny Devil	Moloch horridus	x				x	x	x		NE
Bearded Dragon*	Pogona barbata	x	x	x	x	x				LC
Downs Bearded Dragon*	Pogona henrylawsoni	x								NE
Kimberley Bearded Dragon	Pogona microlepidota						x			NE
Dwarf Bearded Dragon	Pogona minor					x	x	x		NE
Nullarbor Bearded Dragon	Pogona nullarbor					x	x			NE
Central Bearded Dragon*	Pogona vitticeps	x	x	x		x		x		NE
Mountain Dragon*	Rankinia diemensis		x	x	x					LC
Centralian Earless Dragon	Tympanocryptis centralis	x				x	x	x		NE
Pebble Dragon	Tympanocryptis cephalus	x				x	x	x		NE

COMMON NAME	SCIENTIFIC NAME	Q	NS	V	T	S	W	NT	O	IUCN
Condamine Earless Dragon	Tympanocryptis condaminensis	x								NE
Hammersley Pebble-mimic Dragon	Tympanocryptis diabolicus									NE
Fortescue Pebble-mimic Dragon	Tympanocryptis fortescuensis									NE
Gascoyne Pebble-mimic Dragon	Tympanocryptis gigas						x			NE
Nullarbor Earless Dragon	Tympanocryptis houstoni					x	x			NE
Gibber Earless Dragon	Tympanocryptis intima	x	x			x		x		NE
Lined Earless Dragon*	Tympanocryptis lineata	x	x	x		x	x	x		NE
Five-lined Earless Dragon	Tympanocryptis pentalineata	x								NE
Grassland Earless Dragon*	Tympanocryptis pinguicolla	x	x	x				x		VU
Goldfields Pebble-mimic Dragon	Tympanocryptis pseudopsephos						x			NE
Eyrean Earless Dragon*	Tympanocryptis tetraporophora	x	x			x		x		NE
Even-scaled Earless Dragon	Tympanocryptis uniformis							x		DD
Roma Earless Dragon	Tympanocryptis wilsoni	x								NE
Gekkonidae (Typical Geckoes)										
Alexander's Gecko	Christinus alexanderi					x	x			NE
Lord Howe Island Gecko	Christinus guentheri								x	VU
Marbled Gecko*	Christinus marmoratus			x	x	x	x			NE
Pascoe River Ring-tailed Gecko	Cyrtodactylus adorus	x								NE
Hoskin's Ring-tailed Gecko	Cyrtodactylus hoskini	x								NE
McDonald's Ring-tailed Gecko	Cyrtodactylus mcdonaldi	x								NE
McIlwraith Ring-tailed Gecko	Cyrtodactylus pronarus	x								NE
Christmas Island Forest Gecko	Cyrtodactylus sadleiri								x	NE
Ring-tailed Gecko*	Cyrtodactylus tuberculatus	x								NE
Northern Dtella	Gehyra australis	x					x	x		LC
Short-tailed Dtella	Gehyra baliola	x								NE
Borroloola Dtella	Gehyra borroloola	x						x		LC
Chain-backed Dtella	Gehyra catenata	x								NE
Dubious Dtella*	Gehyra dubia	x	x					x		LC
Einasleigh Rock Dtella	Gehyra einasleighensis	x								NE
Kimberley Karst gecko	Gehyra girloorloo						x			NE
Koira Dtella	Gehyra koira						x	x		NE
Southern Rock Dtella*	Gehyra lazelli		x			x				NE
Dwarf Dtella	Gehyra minuta							x		NE
Centralian Dtella	Gehyra montium					x	x	x		NE
Moritz's Dtella	Gehyra moritzi							x		NE
Multi-pored Gecko	Gehyra multiporosa						x			NE
Skin-shedding Dtella	Gehyra mutilata	x								NE
Northern Spotted Rock Dtella*	Gehyra nana	x					x	x		NE
Kimberley Plateau Dtella	Gehyra occidentalis						x	x		NE
Oceanic Gecko	Gehyra oceanica	x						x		NE
Arnhemland Watercourse Dtella	Gehyra pamela							x		NE
Pilbara Dtella	Gehyra pilbara						x	x		LC
Rock-dwelling Dtella	Gehyra pulingka					x		x		NE
Spotted Dtella	Gehyra punctata					x	x	x		NE
Purplish Dtella	Gehyra purpurascens	x				x	x	x		NE
Robust Dtella	Gehyra robusta	x						x		NE
Small Wedge-toed Gecko	Gehyra spheniscus						x			NE
Tree Dtella	Gehyra variegata						x			NE
Eastern Tree Dtella*	Gehyra versicolor	x	x	x	x	x		x		NE
Crocodile-faced Dtella	Gehyra xenopus						x			NE
House Gecko*	Hemidactylus frenatus	x	x				x	x		NE
Black Pilbara Gecko	Heteronotia atra						x			NE
Bynoe's Gecko*	Heteronotia binoei	x	x	x		x	x	x		NE
Pale-headed Gecko	Heteronotia fasciolatus							x		NE
Bynoe's Prickly Gecko	Heteronotia planiceps						x	x		NE
Desert Cave Gecko	Heteronotia spelea						x	x		NE
Christmas Island Gecko	Lepidodactylus listeri								x	VU
Mourning Gecko	Lepidodactylus lugubris	x						x		NE
Slender Chained Gecko	Lepidodactylus pumilus	x								NE
Chevert's Gecko*	Nactus cheverti	x								NE
Eborac Island Gecko	Nactus eboracensis	x								NE
Black Mountain Gecko	Nactus galgajuga	x								NE
Pelagic Gecko	Nactus pelagicus	x								NE
Carphodactylidae (Southern Padless Geckoes)										
Chameleon Gecko	Carphodactylus laevis	x								NE
Centralian Knob-tailed Gecko	Nephrurus amyae					x		x		NE
Prickly Knob-tailed Gecko*	Nephrurus asper	x						x		NE

COMMON NAME	SCIENTIFIC NAME	Q	NS	V	T	S	W	NT	O	IUCN
Pernatty Knob-tail	Nephrurus deleani					x				EN
Pale Knob-tailed Gecko	Nephrurus laevissimus					x	x	x		NE
Smooth Knob-tailed Gecko*	Nephrurus levis	x	x			x	x	x		LC
Northern Knob-tailed Gecko	Nephrurus sheai						x	x		NE
Starred Knob-tailed Gecko	Nephrurus stellatus					x	x			LC
Midline Knob-tail	Nephrurus vertebralis						x			NE
Banded Knob-tail	Nephrurus wheeleri						x			LC
Long-tailed Northern Leaf-tailed Gecko	Orraya occultus	x								DD
Mount Elliot Broad-tailed Gecko	Phyllurus amnicola	x								NE
Ringed Thin-tail Gecko	Phyllurus caudiannulatus	x								NE
Connor's Range Broad-tailed Gecko	Phyllurus championae	x								NE
Gulbaru Gecko	Phyllurus gulbaru	x								CR
Mount Jukes Broad-tailed Gecko	Phyllurus isis	x								NE
Gympie Broad-tailed Gecko	Phyllurus kabikabi	x								NE
Peppered-belly Broad-tailed Gecko	Phyllurus nepthys	x								NE
Mount Ossa Broad-tailed Gecko	Phyllurus ossa	x								LC
Broad-tailed Gecko*	Phyllurus platurus		x							NE
Northern Leaf-tailed Gecko	Saltuarius cornutus	x	x							LC
Cape York Leaf-tailed Gecko	Saltuarius eximius	x								NE
Upper Clarence Leaf-tailed Gecko	Saltuarius kateae	x								NE
Mort's Leaf-tailed Gecko	Saltuarius moritzi		x							NE
Rough-throated Leaf-tail Gecko*	Saltuarius salebrosus	x								NE
Southern Leaf-tailed Gecko*	Saltuarius swaini	x	x							NE
Granite-belt Leaf-tailed Gecko	Saltuarius wyberba	x	x							NE
Barking Gecko*	Underwoodisaurus milii	x	x	x		x	x	x		NE
Pilbara Barking Gecko	Underwoodisaurus seorsus						x			NE
Border Thick-tailed Gecko*	Uvidicolus sphyrurus	x	x							NT
Diplodactylidae (Austral Geckoes)										
Clouded Gecko*	Amalosia jacovae	x	x							NE
Lesueur's Velvet Gecko*	Amalosia lesueurii	x	x							NE
Slim Velvet Gecko	Amalosia obscura						x			NE
Zigzag Velvet Gecko*	Amalosia rhombifer	x	x				x	x		NE
Central Uplands Clawless Gecko	Crenadactylus horni					x		x		NE
Kimberley Clawless Gecko	Crenadactylus naso	x					x	x		NE
Western Clawless Gecko	Crenadactylus occidentalis						x			NE
Clawless Gecko	Crenadactylus ocellatus					x	x	x		NE
Pilbara Clawless Gecko	Crenadactylus pilbarensis						x			NE
South-west Kimberley Clawless Gecko	Crenadactylus rostralis						x			NE
Cape Range Clawless Gecko	Crenadactylus tuberculatus						x			NE
Eastern Deserts Fat-tailed Gecko	Diplodactylus ameyi	x	x							NE
Gulf Fat-tailed Gecko	Diplodactylus barraganae	x								NE
Western Fat-tailed Gecko	Diplodactylus bilybara						x			NE
South Coast Gecko	Diplodactylus calcicolus					x	x			NE
Cape Range Stone Gecko	Diplodactylus capensis						x			NE
Fat-tailed Diplodactylus*	Diplodactylus conspicillatus	x				x	x	x		NE
Kimberley Fat-tailed Gecko	Diplodactylus custos						x			NE
Lake Disappointment Ground Gecko	Diplodactylus fulleri						x			NE
Ranges Stone Gecko	Diplodactylus furcosus					x				NE
Northern Pilbara Beak-faced Gecko	Diplodactylus galaxias						x			NE
Helmeted Gecko	Diplodactylus galeatus					x		x		NE
Wheat-belt Stone Gecko	Diplodactylus granariensis					x	x			LC
Northern Fat-tailed Gecko	Diplodactylus hillii							x		NE
Kenneally's Gecko	Diplodactylus kenneallyi						x			NE
Kluge's Gecko	Diplodactylus klugei						x			NE
Desert Fat-tailed Gecko	Diplodactylus laevis	x	x			x	x	x		NE
Speckled Stone Gecko	Diplodactylus lateroides						x			NE
Pilbara Stone Gecko	Diplodactylus mitchelli						x			NE
Cloudy Stone Gecko	Diplodactylus nebulosus						x			NE
Ornate Stone Gecko	Diplodactylus ornatus						x			LC
Eastern Fat-tailed Gecko*	Diplodactylus platyurus	x	x							NE
Spotted Sandplain Gecko	Diplodactylus polyophthalmus						x			NE
Fine-faced Gecko	Diplodactylus pulcher					x	x			NE
Southern Pilbara Beak-faced Gecko	Diplodactylus savagei						x			NE
Tessellated Gecko*	Diplodactylus tessellatus	x	x	x		x			x	NE
Eastern Stone Gecko*	Diplodactylus vittatus	x	x	x		x				NE
Desert Wood Gecko	Diplodactylus wiru					x	x			NE
Reticulated Velvet Gecko	Hesperoedura reticulata						x			NE

COMMON NAME	SCIENTIFIC NAME	Q	NS	V	T	S	W	NT	O	IUCN
White-spotted Ground Gecko	Lucasium alboguttatum						x			NE
Southern Sandplain Gecko	Lucasium bungabinna					x	x			NE
Gibber Gecko*	Lucasium byrnei	x	x			x		x		LC
Beaded Gecko*	Lucasium damaeum	x	x	x		x	x	x		NE
Pale-striped Ground Gecko	Lucasium immaculatum	x						x		NE
Main's Ground Gecko	Lucasium maini						x	x		NE
Yellow-snouted Ground Gecko	Lucasium occultum							x		NE
Mottled Ground Gecko	Lucasium squarrosum						x			NE
Box-patterned Gecko*	Lucasium steindachneri	x	x			x				NE
Crowned Gecko	Lucasium stenodactylum	x	x			x	x	x		NE
Pilbara Ground Gecko	Lucasium wombeyi						x			NE
Robust Velvet Gecko*	Nebulifera robusta	x	x							NE
Gulf Marbled Velvet Gecko	Oedura bella	x						x		NE
Northern Velvet Gecko*	Oedura castelnaui	x								NE
Northern Spotted Velvet Gecko*	Oedura coggeri	x								NE
Fringe-toed Velvet Gecko	Oedura filicipoda						x			NE
Western Marbled Velvet Gecko	Oedura fimbria						x			NE
Dotted Velvet Gecko	Oedura gemmata							x		NE
Gracile Velvet Gecko	Oedura gracilis						x	x		NE
Quinkan Velvet Gecko	Oedura jowalbinna	x								NE
Mereenie velvet gecko	Oedura luritja							x		NE
Marbled Velvet Gecko*	Oedura marmorata	x	x			x	x	x		NE
Ocellated Velvet Gecko*	Oedura monilis	x	x							NE
Limestone Range Velvet Gecko	Oedura murrumanu						x			NE
Southern Spotted Velvet Gecko*	Oedura tryoni	x	x							NE
Giant Tree Gecko*	Pseudothecadactylus australis	x								NE
Western Giant Cave Gecko	Pseudothecadactylus cavaticus						x			NE
Giant Cave Gecko	Pseudothecadactylus lindneri							x		NE
Border Beaked Gecko	Rhynchoedura angusta	x	x			x				NE
Eyre Basin Beaked Gecko	Rhynchoedura eyrensis					x				NE
Brigalow Beaked Gecko*	Rhynchoedura mentalis	x								NE
Eastern Beaked Gecko*	Rhynchoedura ornsbyi	x	x							NE
Western Beaked Gecko	Rhynchoedura ornata	x	x			x	x	x		NE
Northern Beaked Gecko	Rhynchoedura sexapora						x	x		NE
Goldfields Spiny-tailed Gecko	Strophurus assimilis					x	x			NE
Northern Spiny-tailed Gecko	Strophurus ciliaris	x	x			x	x	x		LC
Congoo Gecko	Strophurus congoo	x								NE
Jewelled Gecko	Strophurus elderi	x	x			x	x	x		NE
Arnhem Phasmid Gecko	Strophurus horneri							x		NE
Southern Spiny-tailed Gecko*	Strophurus intermedius	x	x			x	x	x		NE
Southern Phasmid Gecko	Strophurus jeanae						x	x		LC
Kristin's Spiny-tailed Gecko*	Strophurus krisalys	x								NE
Short-tailed Striped Gecko	Strophurus mcmillani						x			NE
Robust Striped Gecko	Strophurus michaelseni						x	x		LC
Exmouth Spiny-tailed Gecko	Strophurus rankini						x			NE
Robinson's Spiny-tailed Gecko	Strophurus robinsoni						x	x		NE
Soft Spiny-tailed Gecko	Strophurus spinigerus						x			NE
Western Spiny-tailed Gecko	Strophurus strophurus						x			NE
Phasmid Striped Gecko*	Strophurus taeniatus	x					x	x		NE
Golden-tailed Gecko*	Strophurus taenicauda	x								NT
Western Shield Spiny-tailed Gecko	Strophurus wellingtonae						x			NE
Eastern Spiny-tailed Gecko*	Strophurus williamsi	x	x	x		x				NE
Mount Augustus Spiny-tailed Gecko	Strophurus wilsoni						x			NE
Pygopodidae (Legless Lizards)										
Eared Worm-lizard	Aprasia aurita			x		x				CR
Batavia Coast Worm-lizard	Aprasia clairae						x			NE
Shark Bay Worm-lizard	Aprasia haroldi						x			NE
Mallee Worm-lizard*	Aprasia inaurita		x	x		x	x			NE
Gnaraloo Worm Lizard	Aprasia litorea						x			NE
Pink-tailed Legless Lizard*	Aprasia parapulchella		x	x						NE
Black-headed Worm-lizard	Aprasia picturata						x			NE
Flinders Ranges Worm-lizard	Aprasia pseudopulchella					x				NT
Granite Worm-lizard	Aprasia pulchella					x	x			NE
Sand-plain Worm-lizard	Aprasia repens						x			NE
Ningaloo Worm Lizard	Aprasia rostrata						x			VU
Black-tipped Worm-lizard	Aprasia smithi						x			NE
Lined Worm-lizard	Aprasia striolata					x	x			NE
Wicherina Worm Lizard	Aprasia wicherina						x			NE
Marble-faced Delma*	Delma australis		x	x		x	x	x		NE

COMMON NAME	SCIENTIFIC NAME	Q	NS	V	T	S	W	NT	O	IUCN
Rusty-topped Delma	Delma borea	x				x	x	x		NE
Unbanded Delma*	Delma butleri	x	x	x		x	x	x		NE
Javelin Lizard	Delma concinna						x			NE
Banded Delma	Delma desmosa					x	x	x		NE
Pilbara Delma	Delma elegans						x			NE
Fraser's Delma	Delma fraseri						x			LC
Side-barred Delma	Delma grayii						x			NE
Neck-barred Delma	Delma haroldi					x	x	x		NE
Heath Delma	Delma hebesa		x	x	x					NE
Many-lined Delma*	Delma impar		x	x		x				VU
Patternless Delma*	Delma inornata	x	x	x		x				NE
Single-striped Delma	Delma labialis	x								VU
Atherton Delma	Delma mitella	x								NE
Gulfs Delma	Delma molleri					x				NE
Sharp-snouted Delma	Delma nasuta	x				x	x	x		NE
Peace Delma	Delma pax						x			NE
Peterson's Delma	Delma petersoni					x	x			NE
Leaden Delma*	Delma plebeia	x	x							NE
Teale's Delma	Delma tealei						x			NE
Excitable Delma*	Delma tincta	x	x			x	x	x		NE
Adorned Delma	Delma torquata	x	x							VU
Burton's Snake-lizard*	Lialis burtonis	x	x	x		x	x	x		NE
Bronzeback	Ophidiocephalus taeniatus					x		x		VU
Brigalow Scaly-foot*	Paradelma orientalis	x								VU
Keeled Legless Lizard	Pletholax gracilis						x			NE
Common Scaly-foot*	Pygopus lepidopodus	x	x	x		x	x			NE
Hooded Scaly-foot	Pygopus nigriceps	x	x	x		x	x	x		NE
Cape York Scaly-foot	Pygopus robertsi	x								NE
Eastern Hooded Scaly-foot*	Pygopus schraderi	x	x	x		x		x		NE
Northern Hooded Scaly-foot	Pygopus steelescotti	x					x	x		NE
Scincidae (Skinks)										
Eastern Three-lined Skink*	Acritoscincus duperreyi		x	x	x	x				NE
Red-throated Skink*	Acritoscincus platynotus	x	x	x						NE
Western Three-lined Skink	Acritoscincus trilineatus						x			LC
Highlands Forest-skink*	Anepischetosia maccoyi		x	x						NE
Short-necked Worm-skink*	Anomalopus brevicollis	x								LC
Speckled Worm-skink*	Anomalopus gowi	x								LC
Two-clawed Worm-skink*	Anomalopus leuckartii	x	x							NE
Five-clawed Worm-skink*	Anomalopus mackayi	x	x							VU
Cape York Worm-skink	Anomalopus pluto	x								NE
Punctate Worm-skink	Anomalopus swansoni		x							NE
Three-clawed Worm-skink*	Anomalopus verreauxii	x	x							NE
Major Skink*	Bellatorias frerei	x	x							NE
Land Mullet*	Bellatorias major	x	x							NE
Arnhem Land Gorges Skink	Bellatorias obiri							x		NE
Cone-eared Calyptotis*	Calyptotis lepidorostrum	x								NE
Red-tailed Calyptotis*	Calyptotis ruficauda	x	x							NE
Scute-snouted Calyptotis*	Calyptotis scutirostrum	x	x							NE
Broad-templed Calyptotis*	Calyptotis temporalis	x								NE
Thornton Peak Calyptotis	Calyptotis thorntonensis	x								NE
Southern Forest Cool-skink*	Carinascincus coventryi		x	x						NE
Alpine Cool-skink	Carinascincus greeni				x					NE
Metallic Cool-skink*	Carinascincus metallicus		x	x						NE
Boulder Cool-skink	Carinascincus microlepidotus			x						NE
Ocellated Skink*	Carinascincus ocellatus			x						NE
Heath Cool-skink	Carinascincus orocryptus			x						NE
Pedra Branca Cool-skink	Carinascincus palfreymani			x						VU
Agile Cool-skink	Carinascincus pretiosus			x						NE
Bauxite Rainbow-skink	Carlia amax	x					x	x		NE
Sandy Rainbow-skink	Carlia dogare	x								LC
Slender Rainbow-skink	Carlia gracilis						x	x		LC
Lined Rainbow-skink*	Carlia jarnoldae	x								NE
Rough Brown Rainbow-skink	Carlia johnstonei						x			NE
Closed-litter Rainbow-skink*	Carlia longipes	x						x		NE
Shaded-litter Rainbow-skink*	Carlia munda	x	x				x	x		NE
Open-litter Rainbow-skink*	Carlia pectoralis	x	x							NE
Eastern Torres Rainbow-skink	Carlia quinquecarinata	x								NE
Blue-throated Rainbow-skink	Carlia rhomboidalis	x								NE
Crevice Rainbow-skink	Carlia rimula	x								NE
Black-throated Rainbow-skink*	Carlia rostralis	x								NE

COMMON NAME	SCIENTIFIC NAME	Q	NS	V	T	S	W	NT	O	IUCN
Orange-flanked Rainbow Skink*	Carlia rubigo	x								NE
Red-throated Rainbow-skink	Carlia rubrigularis	x								LC
Red-sided Rainbow-skink	Carlia rufilatus						x	x		NE
Robust Rainbow-skink*	Carlia schmeltzii	x	x							NE
Macleay's Rainbow-skink	Carlia sexdentata	x						x		NE
Brown Bicarinate Rainbow-skink*	Carlia storri	x								NE
Southern Rainbow-skink*	Carlia tetradactyla	x	x	x						LC
Desert Rainbow-skink	Carlia triacantha					x	x	x		NE
Lively Rainbow Skink*	Carlia vivax	x	x							NE
Cape Melville Rainbow Skink	Carlia wundalthini	x								NE
Lemon-barred Forest-skink	Concinnia amplus	x								NE
Northern Barsided Skink*	Concinnia brachysoma	x								NE
Bartle Frere Barsided Skink	Concinnia frerei	x								NE
Dark Barsided Skink*	Concinnia martini	x	x							NE
Prickly Forest Skink*	Concinnia queenslandiae	x								NE
Stout Barsided Skink	Concinnia sokosoma	x								LC
Barred-sided Skink*	Concinnia tenuis	x	x	x						NE
Yellow-blotched Forest-skink	Concinnia tigrinus	x								NE
Adams' Snake-eyed Skink	Cryptoblepharus adamsi	x								NE
Inland Snake-eyed Skink*	Cryptoblepharus australis	x	x	x		x	x	x		NE
Buchanan's Snake-eyed Skink	Cryptoblepharus buchananii						x			NE
Swanson's Snake-eyed Skink	Cryptoblepharus cygnatus							x		NE
Dappled Snake-eyed Skink	Cryptoblepharus daedalos							x		NE
Blue-tailed Snake-eyed Skink	Cryptoblepharus egeriae								x	NE
Noble Snake-eyed Skink	Cryptoblepharus exochus							x		NE
Black-boulder Shinning-skink	Cryptoblepharus fuhni	x								NE
Arafura Snake-eyed Skink	Cryptoblepharus gurrmul							x		NE
Juno's Snake-eyed Skink	Cryptoblepharus juno						x	x		NE
Coastal Snake-eyed Skink	Cryptoblepharus litoralis	x						x		NE
Blotched Shinning-skink	Cryptoblepharus megastictus						x	x		NE
Merten's Snake-eyed Skink	Cryptoblepharus mertensi							x		NE
Metallic Snake-eyed Skink*	Cryptoblepharus metallicus	x					x	x		NE
Pale Snake-eyed Skink	Cryptoblepharus ochrus					x				NE
Ragged Snake-eyed Skink*	Cryptoblepharus pannosus	x	x	x		x		x		NE
Péron's Snake-eyed Skink	Cryptoblepharus plagiocephalus						x			NE
Elegant Snake-eyed Skink*	Cryptoblepharus pulcher	x	x			x	x			NE
Tawny Snake-eyed Skink	Cryptoblepharus ruber	x	x			x	x	x		NE
Pygmy Snake-eyed Skink	Cryptoblepharus tytthos						x	x		NE
Russet Snake-eyed Skink	Cryptoblepharus ustulatus						x			NE
Cream-striped Shining-skink*	Cryptoblepharus virgatus	x	x	x		x	x			NE
Spangled Snake-eyed Skink	Cryptoblepharus wulbu							x		NE
Agile Snake-eyed Skink	Cryptoblepharus zoticus	x						x		NE
Grassplains Ctenotus	Ctenotus agrestis	x								NE
Lively Ctenotus	Ctenotus alacer	x					x	x		NE
Ajana Ctenotus	Ctenotus alleni						x			NE
Brown-blazed Wedgesnout Ctenotus*	Ctenotus allotropis	x	x							LC
Airlie Island Ctenotus	Ctenotus angusticeps						x			NE
Oorida Ctenotus	Ctenotus aphrodite	x								NE
Arcane Ctenotus	Ctenotus arcanus	x	x							NE
Ariadna's Ctenotus	Ctenotus ariadnae	x				x	x	x		NE
Arnhem Land Ctenotus	Ctenotus arnhemensis							x		NE
Stony Downs Ctenotus	Ctenotus astarte	x						x		NE
Elegant Ctenotus	Ctenotus astictus							x		NE
Southern Mallee Ctenotus	Ctenotus atlas			x	x	x	x			NE
Western Limestone Ctenotus	Ctenotus australis						x			NE
White-faced Ctenotus	Ctenotus borealis							x		NE
Short-footed Ctenotus	Ctenotus brevipes	x						x		NE
Brooks Ctenotus	Ctenotus brooksi					x	x	x		NE
Plain-backed Kimberley Ctenotus	Ctenotus burbidgei						x			LC
Blue-tailed Ctenotus	Ctenotus calurus	x				x	x	x		NE
Capricorn Ctenotus	Ctenotus capricorni	x								NE
Chain-striped South-west Ctenotus	Ctenotus catenifer						x			NE
Brown-backed Ctenotus	Ctenotus coggeri							x		NE
Buff-tailed Finesnout Ctenotus	Ctenotus colletti						x			NE
Ten-lined Ctenotus	Ctenotus decaneurus	x					x	x		NE
Darling Range South-west Ctenotus	Ctenotus delli						x			NE
Pilbara Ctenotus	Ctenotus duricola						x			NE
Fine Side-lined Ctenotus	Ctenotus dux					x	x	x		NE

COMMON NAME	SCIENTIFIC NAME	Q	NS	V	T	S	W	NT	O	IUCN
Brown-tailed Finesnout Ctenotus	Ctenotus ehmanni						x			NE
Port Essington Ctenotus	Ctenotus essingtonii	x						x		NE
Nullabor Ctenotus	Ctenotus euclae					x	x			NE
Brown-backed Yellow-lined Ctenotus	Ctenotus eurydice	x	x							NE
Black-backed Yellow-lined Ctenotus	Ctenotus eutaenius	x						x		NE
Kakadu Ctenotus	Ctenotus gagudju							x		LC
Jewelled Sandplain Ctenotus	Ctenotus gemmula						x			LC
Grand Ctenotus	Ctenotus grandis					x	x	x		NE
Greer's Ctenotus	Ctenotus greeri					x	x	x		NE
Chained Ctenotus	Ctenotus halysis						x			NE
Nimble Ctenotus	Ctenotus hanloni					x	x	x		NE
Stout Ctenotus	Ctenotus hebetior	x						x		NE
Clay-soil Ctenotus	Ctenotus helenae	x				x	x	x		LC
Hill's Ctenotus	Ctenotus hilli							x		NE
North West Cape Ctenotus	Ctenotus iapetus						x			NE
Odd-striped Ctenotus	Ctenotus impar						x			NE
Unspotted Yellow-sided Ctenotus*	Ctenotus ingrami	x	x				x			NE
Bar-shouldered Ctenotus*	Ctenotus inornatus	x	x	x		x	x	x		LC
Black-soil Ctenotus	Ctenotus joanae	x				x		x		NE
Alligator Rivers Ctenotus	Ctenotus kurmbudj							x		NE
Common South-west Ctenotus	Ctenotus labillardieri						x			NE
Lancelin Ctenotus	Ctenotus lancelini								x	VU
Gravelly-soil Ctenotus*	Ctenotus lateralis	x						x		NE
Orange-tailed Finesnout Ctenotus	Ctenotus leae	x	x			x	x	x		NE
Leonhardi's Ctenotus*	Ctenotus leonhardii	x	x			x	x	x		LC
Maryan's Ctenotus	Ctenotus maryani						x			NE
Whiptail Ctenotus	Ctenotus mastigura						x			NE
Median-striped Ctenotus	Ctenotus mesotes						x			NE
Military Ctenotus	Ctenotus militaris						x	x		NE
Checker-sided Ctenotus	Ctenotus mimetes						x			NE
Atherton Ctenotus	Ctenotus monticola	x								NE
Long-snouted Ctenotus	Ctenotus nasutus					x	x	x		NE
Pin-striped Finesnout Ctenotus	Ctenotus nigrilineatus						x			NE
Nullum Ctenotus	Ctenotus nullum	x								NE
Olympic Ctenotus	Ctenotus olympicus	x	x			x		x		NE
Coastal Plains Skink	Ctenotus ora						x			NE
Eastern Ctenotus*	Ctenotus orientalis	x	x	x		x	x			NE
North-western Wedgesnout Ctenotus	Ctenotus pallescens						x	x		NE
Leopard Ctenotus*	Ctenotus pantherinus	x	x			x	x	x		NE
Coarse Sands Ctenotus	Ctenotus piankai	x				x	x	x		NE
Pretty Ctenotus	Ctenotus pulchellus	x						x		NE
Fourteen-lined Ctenotus	Ctenotus quattuordecimlineatus					x	x	x		NE
Quinkan Ctenotus	Ctenotus quinkan	x								NE
Arnhem Plain-backed Ctenotus	Ctenotus quirinus							x		NE
Cape Heath Ctenotus	Ctenotus rawlinsoni	x								NE
Pale-rumped Ctenotus*	Ctenotus regius	x	x	x		x	x	x		NE
Fissure Ctenotus	Ctenotus rimacolus						x	x		NE
Robust Ctenotus*	Ctenotus robustus	x	x	x		x	x	x		NE
Rosy Ctenotus	Ctenotus rosarium	x								NE
Ruddy Ctenotus	Ctenotus rubicundus						x			NE
Rufous Finesnout Ctenotus	Ctenotus rufescens						x			NE
Rusty-shouldered Ctenotus	Ctenotus rutilans						x			NE
Black-soil Rises Ctenotus	Ctenotus schevilli	x								NE
Barred Wedgesnout Ctenotus*	Ctenotus schomburgkii	x	x	x		x	x	x		NE
Massive-gibber Ctenotus	Ctenotus septenarius	x				x	x	x		NE
Gravel-downs Ctenotus	Ctenotus serotinus	x								NE
North-western Sandy-loam Ctenotus	Ctenotus serventyi						x			NE
Spalding's Ctenotus*	Ctenotus spaldingi	x	x	x		x		x		NE
Buff-striped Ctenotus	Ctenotus storri							x		NE
Eastern Barred Wedgesnout Ctenotus*	Ctenotus strauchii	x	x	x		x		x		NE
Carpentarian Ctenotus	Ctenotus striaticeps	x						x		NE
Stuart's Ctenotus	Ctenotus stuarti							x		NE
Sharp-browed Ctenotus	Ctenotus superciliaris						x	x		NE
Ribon Ctenotus	Ctenotus taeniatus	x	x	x		x		x		NE
Copper-tailed Skink*	Ctenotus taeniolatus	x	x	x						NE

COMMON NAME	SCIENTIFIC NAME	Q	NS	V	T	S	W	NT	O	IUCN
Tanami Ctenotus	Ctenotus tanamiensis						x	x		NE
Dwarf Ctenotus	Ctenotus tantillus						x	x		NE
Hinchinbrook Ctenotus	Ctenotus terrareginae	x								NE
Spotted Ctenotus	Ctenotus uber		x	x		x	x	x		NE
Uneven-striped Ctenotus	Ctenotus vagus						x			NE
Scant-striped Ctenotus	Ctenotus vertebralis							x		NE
Wide-striped Ctenotus	Ctenotus xenopleura						x			NE
Shark Bay South-west Ctenotus	Ctenotus youngsoni						x			NE
Hamelin Pool Ctenotus	Ctenotus zastictus						x			VU
Southern Cape York Finesnout Ctenotus	Ctenotus zebrilla	x								NE
Common Slender Blue-tongue	Cyclodomorphus branchialis					x	x	x		NE
Tasmanian She-oak Skink*	Cyclodomorphus casuarinae				x					NE
Western Slender Blue-tongue	Cyclodomorphus celatus						x			LC
Pink-tongued Lizard*	Cyclodomorphus gerrardii	x	x							NE
Giant Slender Blue-tongue	Cyclodomorphus maximus						x			NE
Spinifex Slender Blue-tongue	Cyclodomorphus melanops	x	x			x	x	x		NE
Mainland She-oak Skink*	Cyclodomorphus michaeli		x	x						NE
Alpine She-oak Skink	Cyclodomorphus praealtus		x	x						NE
Saltbush Slender Blue-tongue*	Cyclodomorphus venustus	x	x			x				NE
Cunningham's Skink*	Egernia cunninghami	x	x	x		x				NE
Western Pilbara Spiny-tailed Skink	Egernia cygnitos						x			NE
Pygmy Spiny-tailed Skink	Egernia depressa						x			NE
Kimberley Crevice-skink	Egernia douglasi						x			NE
Central Pygmy Spiny-tailed Skink	Egernia eos						x			NE
Eastern Pilbara Spiny-tailed Skink	Egernia epsisolus						x			NE
Goldfields Crevice-skink	Egernia formosa						x			NE
Hosmer's Skink*	Egernia hosmeri	x						x		NE
King's Skink	Egernia kingii						x			LC
Eastern Crevice Skink	Egernia mcpheei	x	x							NE
South-western Crevice-skink	Egernia napoleonis						x			NE
Pilbara Crevice-skink	Egernia pilbarensis						x			NE
Bright Crevice-skink	Egernia richardi					x	x			NE
Yakka Skink*	Egernia rugosa	x								LC
Black Rock Skink*	Egernia saxatilis	x	x	x						NE
Gidgee Skink*	Egernia stokesii	x	x			x	x	x		NE
Tree Skink*	Egernia striolata	x	x	x		x				NE
Littoral Whiptail-skink	Emoia atrocostata	x								NE
Shrub Whiptail-skink	Emoia longicauda	x								NE
Christmas Island Whiptail-skink	Emoia nativitatis								x	NE
Brown-sided Bar-lipped Skink	Eremiascincus brongersmai						x			LC
Douglas' Skink	Eremiascincus douglasi						x			NE
Narrow-banded Sand-swimmer*	Eremiascincus fasciolatus	x				x	x	x		NE
Northern Bar-lipped Skink	Eremiascincus isolepis	x					x	x		NE
Mosaic Desert Skink	Eremiascincus musivus						x			NE
Lowlands Bar-lipped Skink	Eremiascincus pardalis	x								NE
Ghost Skink	Eremiascincus phantasmus	x	x			x		x		NE
Broad-banded Sand-swimmer*	Eremiascincus richardsonii	x	x	x		x	x	x		NE
Elf Skink	Eroticoscincus graciloides	x								NE
Bar-lipped Sheen-skink	Eugongylus rufescens	x								NE
Yellow-bellied Water-skink*	Eulamprus heatwolei	x	x	x		x				LC
Alpine Water Skink	Eulamprus kosciuskoi	x	x	x						NE
Blue Mountains Swamp-skink	Eulamprus leuraensis		x							EN
Eastern Water-skink*	Eulamprus quoyii	x	x	x		x				NE
Southern Water-skink*	Eulamprus tympanum		x	x		x				NE
Mount Elliot Mulch-skink	Glaphyromorphus clandestinus	x								NE
Slender Mulch-skink	Glaphyromorphus cracens	x								NE
Cape York Mulch-skink	Glaphyromorphus crassicaudus	x						x		LC
Darwin Skink	Glaphyromorphus darwiniensis							x		NE
Brown-tailed Bar-lipped Skink	Glaphyromorphus fuscicaudis	x								NE
Atherton Tableland Mulch-skink	Glaphyromorphus mjobergi	x								NE
Black-tailed Bar-lipped Skink*	Glaphyromorphus nigricaudis	x						x		NE
McIlwraith Bar-lipped Skink	Glaphyromorphus nyanchupinta	x								NE
Cape Melville Bar-lipped Skink	Glaphyromorphus othelarrni	x								NE
Dwarf Mulch-skink	Glaphyromorphus pumilus	x								NE

COMMON NAME	SCIENTIFIC NAME	Q	NS	V	T	S	W	NT	O	IUCN
Fine-spotted Mulch-skink*	Glaphyromorphus punctulatus	x	x							NE
Rainforest Cool-skink*	Harrisoniascincus zia	x	x							NE
Three-toed Earless Skink	Hemiergis decresiensis					x				LC
South-western Mulch-skink	Hemiergis gracilipes						x			NE
Southwestern Earless Skink	Hemiergis initialis					x	x			NE
Triodia Earless Skink	Hemiergis millewae			x		x	x			NE
Lowlands Earless Skink*	Hemiergis peronii			x		x	x			NE
Two-toed Earless Skink*	Hemiergis quadrilineata						x			LC
Eastern Three-toed Earless Skink*	Hemiergis talbingoensis	x	x	x						NE
Murray's Skink*	Karma murrayi	x	x							NE
Tryon's Skink	Karma tryoni	x	x							LC
Diamond-shielded Sunskink	Lampropholis adonis	x								NE
Friendly Sunskink	Lampropholis amicula	x	x							NE
Montane Sunskink	Lampropholis caligula		x							NE
Rainforest Sunskink	Lampropholis coggeri	x								NE
Bunya Sunskink	Lampropholis colossus	x								NE
Plain-backed Sunskink	Lampropholis couperi	x								NE
Dark-flecked Garden Sunskink*	Lampropholis delicata	x	x	x	x	x				NE
Elongate Sunskink	Lampropholis elongata		x							NE
Pale-flecked Garden Sunskink*	Lampropholis guichenoti	x	x	x		x				NE
Saxicoline Sunskink	Lampropholis mirabilis	x								NE
Grey-bellied Sunskink	Lampropholis robertsi	x								NE
Desert Plain Slider	Lerista aericeps	x	x			s		s		NE
Greater Robust Fine-lined Slider	Lerista allanae	x								CR
Cape Range Slider	Lerista allochira						x			LC
Limbless Fine-lined Slider	Lerista ameles	x								NE
Fortescue Slider	Lerista amicorum						x			NE
Dampier Land Limbless Slider	Lerista apoda						x			NE
Bight Slider	Lerista arenicola					x	x			NE
Stripe-sided Robust Slider	Lerista axillaris						x			NE
Baynes's Slider	Lerista baynesi					x	x			NE
North-western Sandslider	Lerista bipes					x	x	x		NE
Inland Kimberley Slider	Lerista borealis						x			NE
South-eastern Slider*	Lerista bougainvillii			x	x	x	x			NE
Bungle Bungle Robust Slider	Lerista bunglebungle						x			NE
Carpentaria Fine-lined Slider	Lerista carpentariae							x		NE
Fine-lined Slider	Lerista chordae	x								NE
Bold-striped Slider	Lerista christinae						x			NE
Vine-thicket Fine-lined Slider	Lerista cinerea	x								NE
Sharp-blazed Three-toed Slider	Lerista clara						x			NE
Nubbined Fine-lined Slider	Lerista colliveri	x								NE
Blinking Broad-blazed Slider	Lerista connivens						x			LC
Central Deserts Robust Slider	Lerista desertorum					x	x	x		NE
South-western Orange-tailed Slider	Lerista distinguenda					x	x			NE
Southern Slider	Lerista dorsalis					x	x			NE
Edwards's Slider	Lerista edwardsae					x	x			NE
Elegant Slider	Lerista elegans						x			NE
Wide-striped Mulch Slider	Lerista elongata						x			LC
Noonbah Robust Slider	Lerista emmotti	x	x							NE
West Coast Mulga Slider	Lerista eupoda						x			NE
Pilbara Flame-tailed Slider	Lerista flammicauda						x			NE
Eastern Mulch-slider*	Lerista fragilis	x	x							NE
Centralian Slider	Lerista frosti					x		x		NE
Gascoyne Broad-blazed Slider	Lerista gascoynensis						x			NE
Bold-striped Robust Slider	Lerista gerrardii						x			NE
South-eastern Kimberley Sandslider	Lerista greeri						x			NE
Griffin's Lerista	Lerista griffini						x	x		NE
Gnaraloo Mulch-slider	Lerista haroldi						x			NE
Hobson's Fine-lined Slider	Lerista hobsoni	x								NE
Taper-tailed West-coast Slider	Lerista humphriesi						x			NE
Mcivor River Slider	Lerista ingrami	x								NE
Robust Duneslider	Lerista ips						x	x		NE
Jackson's Slider	Lerista jacksoni	x								NE
Kalumburu Kimberley Slider	Lerista kalumburu						x			NE
Karl Schmidt's Lerista	Lerista karlschmidti							x		NE
Dark Broad-blazed Slider	Lerista kendricki						x			NE
Kennedy Range Broad-blazed Slider	Lerista kennedyensis						x			LC
King's Slider	Lerista kingi						x			NE
Southern Sandslider*	Lerista labialis	x	x			x	x	x		NE

COMMON NAME	SCIENTIFIC NAME	Q	NS	V	T	S	W	NT	O	IUCN
Perth Slider	Lerista lineata						x			NE
Dotted-line Robust Slider	Lerista lineopunctulata						x			NE
Unpatterned Robust Slider	Lerista macropisthopus						x			NE
Little Slider	Lerista micra						x			NE
South-western Slider	Lerista microtis					x	x			NE
Wood Mulch-slider	Lerista muelleri						x			NE
Pilbara Robust Slider	Lerista neander						x			NE
Vevin's Slider	Lerista nevinae						x			NE
Inland Broad-blazed Slider	Lerista nichollsi						x			NE
Carnarvon Slider	Lerista occulta						x			NE
Onslow Broad-blazed Slider	Lerista onsloviana						x			LC
North-eastern Orange-tailed Slider	Lerista orientalis	x						x		NE
Pale Broad-blazed Slider	Lerista petersoni						x			NE
Southern Robust Slider	Lerista picturata					x	x			NE
Keeled Slider	Lerista planiventralis						x			NE
Yampi Sandslider	Lerista praefrontalis						x			NE
Blunt-tailed West-coast Slider	Lerista praepedita						x			NE
Eastern Robust Slider*	Lerista punctatovittata	x	x	x		x				NE
Dotty-tailed Robust Slider	Lerista puncticauda						x			NE
Four-lined Slider	Lerista quadrivincula						x			NE
Broad-eyed Slider	Lerista robusta						x			NE
Rochford Slider	Lerista rochfordensis	x								NE
Rolfe's Slider	Lerista rolfei						x			NE
Dampierland Plain Slider	Lerista separanda						x			NE
Fitzroy Sandslider	Lerista simillima						x			NE
Pale-striped Mulch Slider	Lerista speciosa					x				NE
Spotted Broad-blazed Slider	Lerista stictopleura						x			NE
Chillagoe Fine-lined Slider	Lerista storri	x								NE
Arnhem Coast Fine-lined Slider	Lerista stylis							x		LC
Ribbon Slider	Lerista taeniata					x	x	x		LC
Phantom Mole Slider	Lerista talpina						x			NE
Robust Mulch Slider	Lerista terdigitata					x				NE
Timid Slider*	Lerista timida	x	x	x		x	x	x		NE
Dark-backed Mulch Slider	Lerista tridactyla						x			NE
Slender Broad-blazed Slider	Lerista uniduo						x			NE
Leaden-bellied Fine-line Slider	Lerista vanderduysi	x								NE
Shark Bay Broad-blazed Slider	Lerista varia						x			NE
Powerful Lerista	Lerista verhmens						x			NE
Slender Duneslider	Lerista vermicularis						x			LC
Ravensthorpe Range Slider	Lerista viduata						x			NE
Side-striped Fine-lined Slider	Lerista vittata	x								EN
Coastal Kimberley Slider	Lerista walkeri						x			LC
Two-toed Fine-lined Slider	Lerista wilkinsi	x								NE
Yellow-tailed Plain Slider	Lerista xanthura		x			x	x	x		NE
Yuna Broad-blazed Slider	Lerista yuna						x			NE
Zietz's Slider	Lerista zietzi						x			NE
Wide-striped Four-toed Slider	Lerista zonulata	x								NE
Bamboo Range Rock Skink	Liburnascincus artemis	x								NE
Coen Rainbow-skink	Liburnascincus coensis	x								NE
Outcrop Rainbow-skink*	Liburnascincus mundivensis	x								NE
Black Mountain Rainbow-skink	Liburnascincus scirtetis	x								LC
Guthega Slider	Liopholis guthega		x	x						NE
Desert Skink*	Liopholis inornata		x	x		x	x	x		LC
Great Desert Skink	Liopholis kintorei					x	x	x		VU
Centralian Ranges Rock-skink	Liopholis margaretae					x		x		NE
Eastern Ranges Rock-skink*	Liopholis modesta	x	x							NE
Montane Rock-skink	Liopholis montana		x	x						NE
Bull Skink	Liopholis multiscutata			x		x	x			NE
South-western Rock-skink	Liopholis pulchra						x			NE
Slater's Egernia	Liopholis slateri					x		x		NE
Night Skink	Liopholis striata					x	x	x		LC
White's Skink*	Liopholis whitii	x	x	x	x	x				LC
Eastern Mourning Skink*	Lissolepis coventryi		x	x		x				NE
Western Mourning Skink	Lissolepis luctuosa						x			NE
Mt Surprise Litter-skink	Lygisaurus abscondita	x								NE
Large-disced Litter-skink	Lygisaurus aeratus	x								NE
Tree-base Litter-skink*	Lygisaurus foliorum	x	x							NE
Rainforest Edge Litter-skink	Lygisaurus laevis	x								NE
Translucent Litter-skink	Lygisaurus macfarlani	x						x		NE
Red-tailed Litter-skink	Lygisaurus malleolus	x								NE

COMMON NAME	SCIENTIFIC NAME	Q	NS	V	T	S	W	NT	O	IUCN
Fire-tailed Rainbow-skink	*Lygisaurus parrhasius*	x								NE
Chillagoe Litter-skink	*Lygisaurus rococo*	x								NE
Eastern Cape Litter-skink	*Lygisaurus sesbrauna*	x								LC
Endeavour River Litter-skink	*Lygisaurus tanneri*	x								NE
Sun-loving Litter-skink	*Lygisaurus zuma*	x								NE
Top End Dwarf Skink	*Menetia alanae*							x		NE
Shark Bay Dwarf Skink	*Menetia amaura*						x			LC
Jabiluka Dwarf Skink	*Menetia concinna*							x		DD
Common Dwarf Skink*	*Menetia greyii*	x	x	x		x	x	x		LC
Northern Dwarf Skink	*Menetia maini*	x					x	x		NE
Western Dwarf Skink	*Menetia surda*						x			NE
Saltbush Morethia Skink*	*Morethia adelaidensis*	x	x	x		x	x	x		NE
Boulenger's Snake-eyed Skink*	*Morethia boulengeri*	x	x	x		x	x	x		LC
Woodland Morethia Skink	*Morethia butleri*					x	x			NE
West Coast Morethia Skink	*Morethia lineoocellata*						x			NE
Shrubland Morethia Skink	*Morethia obscura*		x	x		x	x			NE
Lined Firetail Skink	*Morethia ruficauda*						x	x	x	NE
Storr's Snake-eyed Skink	*Morethia storri*						x	x		NE
Fire-tailed Skink*	*Morethia taeniopleura*	x	x							NE
Nangur Spiny Skink	*Nangura spinosa*	x								NE
Lined Soil-crevice Skink	*Notoscincus butleri*						x			NE
Ornate Soil-crevice Skink*	*Notoscincus ornatus*	x				x	x	x		NE
Lord Howe Island Skink	*Oligosoma lichenigera*								x	VU
Lyon's Soil-crevice Skink	*Proablepharus barrylyoni*	x								NE
Kinghorn's Snake-eyed Skink*	*Proablepharus kinghorni*	x	x			x		x		NE
Orange-tailed Soil-crevice Skink	*Proablepharus naranjicaudus*						x			NE
Spinifex Snake-eyed Skink	*Proablepharus reginae*					x	x	x		LC
Northern Soil-crevice Skink	*Proablepharus tenuis*	x					x	x		NE
Great Bight Cool-skink	*Pseudemoia baudini*					x	x			DD
Alpine Bog-skink	*Pseudemoia cryodroma*		x	x						NE
Southern Grass Skink*	*Pseudemoia entrecasteauxii*		x	x	x	x				NE
Tussock Skink*	*Pseudemoia pagenstecheri*		x	x	x	x				LC
Glossy Grass Skink*	*Pseudemoia rawlinsoni*		x	x	x	x				NE
Trunk-climbing Cool-skink*	*Pseudemoia spenceri*		x	x						NE
Fine-browed Dwarf Skink	*Pygmaeascincus koshlandae*	x								NE
Magnetic Island Dwarf Skink	*Pygmaeascincus sadlieri*								x	NE
Dwarf Litter-skink*	*Pygmaeascincus timlowi*	x	x							NE
Cooloola Snake-skink	*Saiphos cooloolensis*	x								NE
Three-toed Skink*	*Saiphos equalis*	x	x							NE
Limbless Snake-tooth Skink	*Saiphos frontalis*	x								NE
Satinay Sand Skink	*Saiphos naufragus*	x								NE
Yolk-bellied Snake-skink	*Saiphos ophioscincus*	x								NE
Three-toed Snake-tooth Skink*	*Saiphos reticulatus*	x	x							NT
Short-limbed Snake-skink	*Saiphos truncatus*	x	x							NE
Pale-lipped Shade-skink	*Saproscincus basiliscus*	x								NE
Orange-tailed Shadeskink*	*Saproscincus challengeri*	x	x							NE
Wedge-snouted Shadeskink	*Saproscincus czechurai*	x								LC
Eungella Shadeskink	*Saproscincus eungellensis*	x								NE
Hannah's Shadeskink	*Saproscincus hannahae*	x								NE
Cooktown Shadeskink	*Saproscincus lewisi*	x								NE
Weasel Skink*	*Saproscincus mustelinus*	x	x	x						NE
Heath Shadeskink	*Saproscincus oriarus*	x	x							NE
Rose's Shadeskink*	*Saproscincus rosei*	x	x							NE
Cape Melville Shade Skink	*Saproscincus saltus*	x								NE
Gully Skink*	*Saproscincus spectabilis*	x	x							NE
Four-fingered Shadeskink	*Saproscincus tetradactylus*	x								NE
Bartle Frere Cool-skink	*Techmarscincus jigurru*	x								NE
Pygmy Blue-tongue	*Tiliqua adelaidensis*					x				EN
Centralian Blue-tongue*	*Tiliqua multifasciata*	x	x			x	x	x		NE
Blotched Blue-tongue*	*Tiliqua nigrolutea*		x	x	x	x				NE
Western Blue-tongue*	*Tiliqua occipitalis*		x	x		x	x	x		NE
Shingleback Lizard*	*Tiliqua rugosa*		x	x		x	x			NE
Eastern Blue-tongue*	*Tiliqua scincoides*	x	x	x		x	x	x		NE
Orange-speckled Forest-skink	*Tumbunascincus luteilateralis*	x								LC
Varanidae (Goannas)										
Ridge-tailed Monitor*	*Varanus acanthurus*	x				x		x	x	NE
Black-spotted Spiny-tailed Monitor	*Varanus baritji*							x		NE
Short-tailed Pygmy Monitor	*Varanus brevicauda*	x				x	x	x		NE
Stripe-tailed Monitor	*Varanus caudolineatus*						x			NE
Pygmy Desert Monitor	*Varanus eremius*	x				x	x	x		NE

COMMON NAME	SCIENTIFIC NAME	Q	NS	V	T	S	W	NT	O	IUCN
Perentie*	Varanus giganteus	x					x	x	x		NE
Pygmy Mulga Monitor	Varanus gilleni	x					x	x	x		NE
Kimberley Rock Monitor	Varanus glauerti						x	x	x		LC
Black-palmed Monitor	Varanus glebopalma						x	x			NE
Gould's Goanna*	Varanus gouldii	x	x	x		x	x	x		NE
Southern Pilbara Rock Goanna	Varanus hamersleyensis						x			NE
Mangrove Monitor	Varanus indicus	x						x		LC
Canopy Goanna	Varanus keithhornei	x								NE
Long-tailed Rock Monitor	Varanus kingorum						x	x		NE
Mertens' Water Monitor*	Varanus mertensi	x					x	x		NE
Mitchell's Water Monitor	Varanus mitchelli	x					x	x		NE
Yellow-spotted Monitor*	Varanus panoptes	x					x	x		NE
Pilbara Rock Monitor	Varanus pilbarensis						x	x		NE
Emerald Monitor	Varanus prasinus	x								NE
Northern Ridge-tailed Monitor	Varanus primordius							x		LC
Heath Monitor*	Varanus rosenbergi		x	x		x	x			LC
Spotted Tree Monitor*	Varanus scalaris	x					x	x		LC
Rusty Monitor	Varanus semiremex	x								NE
Dampier Peninsula Goanna	Varanus sparnus						x			NE
Spencer's Monitor*	Varanus spenceri	x						x		NE
Storr's Monitor	Varanus storri	x					x	x		NE
Black-headed Monitor*	Varanus tristis	x	x			x	x	x		NE
Lace Monitor*	Varanus varius	x	x	x		x	x	x		NE
Acrochordidae (File Snakes)										
Arafura File Snake*	Acrochordus arafurae	x				x		x		LC
Little File Snake	Acrochordus granulatus	x					x	x		LC
Pythonidae (Pythons)										
Children's Python*	Antaresia childreni	x					x	x		NE
Spotted Python*	Antaresia maculosa	x	x							NE
Pygmy Python	Antaresia perthensis						x			NE
Stimson's Python*	Antaresia stimsoni	x	x			x	x	x		NE
Black-headed Python*	Aspidites melanocephalus	x					x	x		NE
Woma*	Aspidites ramsayi	x				x	x	x		EN
Water Python*	Liasis fuscus	x					x	x		LC
Olive Python*	Liasis olivaceus	x					x	x		NE
Centralian Python	Morelia bredli							x		NE
Rough-scaled Python	Morelia carinata						x			NE
Carpet Python*	Morelia spilota	x	x	x		x	x	x		LC
Green Python*	Morelia viridis	x								LC
Australian Scrub Python*	Simalia kinghorni	x								LC
Oenpelli Rock Python	Simalia oenpelliensis							x		NE
Colubridae (Colubrid Snakes)										
Brown Tree Snake*	Boiga irregularis	x	x				x	x		NE
Northern Tree Snake	Dendrelaphis calligastra	x								LC
Green Tree Snake*	Dendrelaphis punctulatus	x	x				x	x		LC
Wolf Snake	Lycodon capucinus								x	NE
Slaty-grey Snake*	Stegonotus cucullatus	x						x		NE
Slate-brown Snake	Stegonotus parvus	x								NE
Keelback*	Tropidonophis mairii	x	x				x	x		LC
Elapidae (Elapid Snakes)										
Common Death Adder*	Acanthophis antarcticus	x	x	x		x	x	x		NE
Kimberley Death Adder	Acanthophis cryptamydros						x			NE
Northern Death Adder	Acanthophis praelongus	x					x	x		NE
Desert Death Adder	Acanthophis pyrrhus					x	x	x		NE
Rough-scaled Death Adder	Acanthophis rugosus	x					x	x		NE
Pilbara Death Adder	Acanthophis wellsei						x			NE
Short-nosed Seasnake	Aipysurus apraefrontalis						x			CR
Reef Shallows Seasnake*	Aipysurus duboisii	x	x				x	x		LC
Spine-tailed Seasnake	Aipysurus eydouxii	x					x	x		LC
Leaf-scaled Sea Snake	Aipysurus foliosquama								x	CR
Dusky Sea Snake	Aipysurus fuscus	x					x			EN
Golden Seasnake	Aipysurus laevis	x					x			LC
Mosaic Sea Snake	Aipysurus mosaicus	x					x	x		LC
Shark Bay Sea Snake	Aipysurus pooleorum						x			NE
Brown-lined Seasnake	Aipysurus tenuis						x			NE
Robust Burrowing Snake	Antaioserpens albiceps	x								DD
North-eastern Plain-nosed Burrowing Snake	Antaioserpens warro	x								NE
Pygmy Copperhead	Austrelaps labialis					x				VU
Highland Copperhead*	Austrelaps ramsayi		x	x						NE

COMMON NAME	SCIENTIFIC NAME	Q	NS	V	T	S	W	NT	O	IUCN
Lowland Copperhead*	Australaps superbus		x	x	x	x				NE
North-western Shovel-nosed Snake	Brachyurophis approximans						x			NE
Coral Snake*	Brachyurophis australis	x	x	x		x				LC
Einasleigh Shovel-nosed Snake	Brachyurophis campbelli	x								NE
Narrow-banded Shovel-nosed Snake	Brachyurophis fasciolatus	x	x				x	x		NE
Unbanded Shovel-nosed Snake	Brachyurophis incinctus	x						x		LC
Arnhem Shovel-nosed Snake	Brachyurophis morrisi							x		NE
Northern Shovel-nosed Snake	Brachyurophis roperi						x	x		NE
Southern Shovel-nosed Snake	Brachyurophis semifasciatus	x				x	x	x		NE
Northern Dwarf Crowned Snake	Cacophis churchilli	x								NE
White-crowned Snake*	Cacophis harriettae	x	x							NE
Southern Dwarf Crowned Snake*	Cacophis krefftii	x	x							NE
Golden-crowned Snake*	Cacophis squamulosus	x	x							NE
Carpentaria Snake	Cryptophis boschmai	x								NE
Pink Snake	Cryptophis incredibilis	x								NE
Eastern Small-eyed Snake*	Cryptophis nigrescens	x	x	x						NE
Black-striped Snake*	Cryptophis nigrostriatus	x								NE
Northern Small-eyed Snake	Cryptophis pallidiceps						x	x		LC
Narrow-headed Whipsnake	Demansia angusticeps						x			NE
Black-necked Whipsnake	Demansia calodera						x			NE
Long-tailed Whipsnake	Demansia flagellatio	x						x		NE
Marble-headed Whipsnake	Demansia olivacea	x					x	x		NE
Greater Black Whipsnake*	Demansia papuensis	x					x	x		NE
Yellow-faced Whip Snake*	Demansia psammophis	x	x	x		x	x	x		NE
Sombre Whipsnake	Demansia quaesitor	x					x	x		NE
Reticulated Whipsnake	Demansia reticulata						x	x		NE
Crack-dwelling Whipsnake*	Demansia rimicola	x	x			x		x		NE
Rufous Whipsnake	Demansia rufescens						x			NE
Shine's Whipsnake	Demansia shinei							x		NE
Grey Whipsnake	Demansia simplex						x	x		NE
Collared Whipsnake*	Demansia torquata	x	x					x		DD
Black Whipsnake*	Demansia vestigiata	x					x	x		NE
De Vis' Banded Snake*	Denisonia devisi	x	x	x						NE
Ornamental Snake	Denisonia maculata	x	x							VU
White-lipped Snake*	Drysdalia coronoides		x	x	x	x				NE
Masters' Snake	Drysdalia mastersii			x		x	x			LC
Mustard-bellied Snake*	Drysdalia rhodogaster		x							LC
Bardick	Echiopsis curta		x	x		x	x			NT
Western Crowned Snake	Elapognathus coronatus						x			NE
Little Brown Snake	Elapognathus minor						x			NE
Turtle-headed Seasnake	Emydocephalus annulatus	x								LC
North-western Mangrove Seasnake	Ephalophis greyae						x			LC
Yellow-naped Snake*	Furina barnardi	x								NE
Red-naped Snake*	Furina diadema	x	x	x		x		x		NE
Moon Snake*	Furina ornata	x					x	x		NE
Dunmall's Snake*	Glyphodon dunmalli	x								VU
Brown-headed Snake	Glyphodon tristis	x								NE
Grey Snake*	Hemiaspis damelii	x	x							NE
Black-bellied Swamp Snake*	Hemiaspis signata	x	x							NE
Pale-headed Snake*	Hoplocephalus bitorquatus	x	x							NE
Broad-headed Snake*	Hoplocephalus bungaroides		x							VU
Stephens' Banded Snake*	Hoplocephalus stephensii	x	x							NT
Black-ringed Mangrove Seasnake	Hydrelaps darwiniensis	x					x	x		LC
Black-headed Seasnake	Hydrophis atriceps	x						x		LC
Dwarf Sea Snake	Hydrophis caerulescens	x						x		LC
Slender-necked Seasnake	Hydrophis coggeri	x					x	x		LC
Spine-bellied Seasnake	Hydrophis curtus	x					x	x		NE
Fine-spined Seasnake	Hydrophis czeblukovi						x			DD
Rough-scaled Seasnake	Hydrophis donaldi	x								NE
Elegant Seasnake	Hydrophis elegans	x	x				x	x		LC
Slender Seasnake	Hydrophis gracilis	x								NE
Spectacled Seasnake*	Hydrophis kingii	x	x				x	x		LC
Small-headed Seasnake	Hydrophis macdowelli	x	x				x	x		LC
Olive-headed Seasnake*	Hydrophis major	x	x				x	x		LC
Spotted Seasnake*	Hydrophis ornatus	x					x	x		LC
Ornate Reef Seasnake	Hydrophis ornatus	x	x				x	x		LC
Large-headed Seasnake	Hydrophis pacificus	x						x		NT
Horned Seasnake	Hydrophis peronii	x					x	x		LC
Yellow-bellied Seasnake	Hydrophis platurus	x	x	x	x		x	x		NE
Stokes' Seasnake*	Hydrophis stokesii	x	x				x	x		NE

COMMON NAME	SCIENTIFIC NAME	Q	NS	V	T	S	W	NT	O	IUCN
Plain-banded Seasnake	Hydrophis vorisi	x								NE
Wide-faced Sea Krait*	Laticauda colubrina								x	NE
Large-scaled Sea Krait	Laticauda laticaudata								x	NE
Tiger Snake*	Notechis scutatus	x	x	x	x	x	x			LC
Fierce Snake*	Oxyuranus microlepidotus	x				x				NE
Taipan*	Oxyuranus scutellatus	x					x	x		NE
Western Desert Taipan	Oxyuranus temporalis						x			NE
Northern Mangrove Seasnake	Parahydrophis mertoni							x		DD
Dwyer's Snake*	Parasuta dwyeri	x	x	x						NE
Little Whip Snake*	Parasuta flagellum		x	x		x				LC
Gould's Hooded Snake	Parasuta gouldii						x			NE
Monk Snake	Parasuta monachus					x	x	x		NE
Mitchell's Short-tailed Snake*	Parasuta nigriceps		x	x		x	x			LC
Mallee Black-headed Snake*	Parasuta spectabilis		x	x		x	x			NE
Lake Cronin Snake	Paroplocephalus atriceps						x			VU
King Brown Snake*	Pseudechis australis	x	x	x		x	x	x		NE
Spotted Mulga Snake	Pseudechis butleri						x			NE
Collett's Snake*	Pseudechis collettii	x								NE
Blue-bellied Black Snake*	Pseudechis guttatus	x	x							NE
Papuan Black Snake	Pseudechis papuanus	x								NE
Red-bellied Black Snake*	Pseudechis porphyriacus	x	x	x		x				NE
Dugite	Pseudonaja affinis					x	x			NE
Strap-snouted Brown Snake*	Pseudonaja aspidorhyncha	x	x	x		x		x		NE
Speckled Brown Snake*	Pseudonaja guttata	x				x		x		NE
Peninsula Brown Snake	Pseudonaja inframacula					x				NE
Ingram's Brown Snake	Pseudonaja ingrami	x						x		NE
Gwardar*	Pseudonaja mengdeni	x	x			x	x	x		NE
Ringed Brown Snake	Pseudonaja modesta	x	x			x	x	x		NE
Northern Brown Snake*	Pseudonaja nuchalis	x	x	x		x	x	x		NE
Common Brown Snake*	Pseudonaja textilis	x	x	x		x		x		NE
Müller's Snake	Rhinoplocephalus bicolor						x			LC
Desert Banded Snake	Simoselaps anomalus					x	x	x		NE
Black-naped Snake	Simoselaps bimaculatus					x	x			NE
Jan's Banded Snake	Simoselaps bertholdi					x	x	x		NE
West-coast Banded Snake	Simoselaps littoralis						x			LC
Dampierland Burrowing Snake	Simoselaps minimus						x			NE
Rosen's Snake	Suta fasciata						x			NE
Ord Snake	Suta ordensis						x	x		NE
Little Spotted Snake	Suta punctata	x					x	x		NE
Curl Snake*	Suta suta	x	x	x		x		x		NE
Rough-scaled Snake*	Tropidechis carinatus	x	x							NE
Bandy-bandy*	Vermicella annulata	x	x	x		x		x		NE
Western Black-striped Snake	Vermicella calonotus						x			NE
Wide-banded Northern Bandy-bandy	Vermicella intermedia						x	x		NE
Northern Bandy-bandy	Vermicella multifasciata						x	x		NE
Cape York Bandy-bandy	Vermicella parscaudato	x								
Pilbarra Bandy-bandy	Vermicella snelli						x			LC
Worm-like Bandy-bandy	Vermicella vermiformis							x		NE
Homolapsidaedae (Water Snakes)										
Australian Bockadam	Cerberus australis	x					x	x		LC
White-bellied Mangrove Snake	Fordonia leucobalia	x					x	x		LC
Richardson's Mangrove Snake	Myron richardsonii	x					x	x		LC
Macleay's Water Snake*	Pseudoferania polylepis	x						x		LC
Typhlopidae (Blind Snakes)										
Small-headed Blind Snake	Anilios affinis	x	x							NE
Sand-diving Blind Snake	Anilios ammodytes						x			NE
Round-tailed Blind Snake	Anilios aspina	x								NE
Southern Blind Snake	Anilios australis		x	x		x	x			NE
Shovel-snouted Blind Snake	Anilios batillus		x							NE
Dark-spined Blind Snake*	Anilios bicolor		x	x		x	x			LC
Prong-snouted Blind Snake*	Anilios bituberculatus	x	x	x		x	x	x		NE
Faint-striped Blind Snake	Anilios broomi	x								NE
Centralian Blind Snake	Anilios centralis					x		x		NE
Cape York Striped Blind Snake	Anilios chamodracaena	x								NE
Northern Blind Snake*	Anilios diversus	x					x	x		NE
Interior Blind Snake	Anilios endoterus	x	x			x	x	x		LC
Miner Blind Snake	Anilios fossor							x		NE
Gane's Blind Snake	Anilios ganei						x			NE
Beaked Blind Snake*	Anilios grypus	x					x	x		NE

COMMON NAME	SCIENTIFIC NAME	Q	NS	V	T	S	W	NT	O	IUCN
Top End Blind Snake	Anilios guentheri						x	x		NE
Pale-headed Blind Snake	Anilios hamatus						x			LC
Kimberley Deep-soil Blind Snake	Anilios howi						x			NE
Fassifern Blind Snake	Anilios insperatus	x								NE
Kimberley Shallow-soil Blind Snake	Anilios kimberleyensis						x	x		LC
Murchison Blind Snake	Anilios leptosomus						x			NE
Cape York Blind Snake	Anilios leucoproctus	x								NE
Robust Blind Snake*	Anilios ligatus	x	x				x	x		NE
Barrow Island Blind Snake	Anilios longissimus								x	NE
Buff-snouted Blind Snake	Anilios margaretae					x	x			NE
Small-eyed Blind Snake	Anilios micrommus						x			NE
Groote Dwarf Blind Snake	Anilios minimus							x		NE
Nema Blind Snake	Anilios nema							x		NE
Blackish Blind Snake*	Anilios nigrescens	x	x	x						NE
Daly River Blind Snake	Anilios nigricaudus						x			NE
Pilbara Blind Snake	Anilios pilbarensis						x			LC
Fat Blind Snake	Anilios pinguis						x			NE
Proximus Blind Snake*	Anilios proximus	x	x	x						LC
Roberts' Blind Snake	Anilios robertsi	x								NE
Cooloola Blind Snake	Anilios silvia	x								NE
Splendid Blind Snake	Anilios splendidus						x			NE
Torres Strait Blindsnake	Anilios torresianus	x								NE
Darwin Blind Snake	Anilios tovelli							x		NE
Sandamara Blind Snake	Anilios troglodytes						x			NE
Claw-snouted Blind Snake	Anilios unguirostris	x					x	x		NE
Beaked Blind Snake	Anilios waitii						x			LC
Brown-snouted Blind Snake*	Anilios wiedii	x	x							NE
Yampi Blind Snake	Anilios yampiensis						x			NE
Yirrkala	Anilios yirrikalae							x		NE
West Kimberley Blindsnake	Anilios zonula						x			NE
Flowerpot Blind Snake	Indotyphlops braminus	x					x	x		NE
Christmas Island Blind Snake	Ramphotyphlops exocoeti								x	VU
Crocodylidae (Crocodiles)										
Freshwater Crocodile*	Crocodylus johnsoni	x					x	x		LC
Saltwater Crocodile*	Crocodylus porosus	x					x	x		LC

■ FURTHER INFORMATION ■

WEBSITES

Australia's Wildlife: www.australiaswildlife.com
Australian Museum: www.australianmuseum.net.au
Australian Reptile Online Database (AROD): www.arod.com.au
Museums Victoria: www.museumvictoria.com.au
Queensland Museum: www.qm.qld.gov.au
The Reptile Database: www.reptile-database.org

REFERENCES

Atlas of Living Australia website at www.ala.org.au. Accessed 2 February 2017.

Australian Faunal Directory website www.biodiversity.org.au. Accessed 2 February 2017

Barker, D.G., Barker, T.M., Davis, M.A. and Schuett, G.W. (2015) *A review of the systematics and taxonomy of Pythonidae: an ancient serpent lineage*. Zoological Journal of the Linnean Society Volume 175 (1) 1-19.

Barrett, C. (1950) *Reptiles of Australia*. The Specialty Press Pty Ltd, Melbourne Australia

Cogger, H. (2014) *Reptiles and Amphibians of Australia* (7th edn). CSIRO Publishing.

Couper, P. J. & Hoskin, C. J. (2014) A new genus to accommodate three skinks currently assigned to Menetia (Lacertilia: Scincidae). *Zootaxa* 3884 (6): 597–599.

Department of the Environment and Water Resources. (2007) *Australia's Native Vegetation: A summary of Australia's Major Vegetation Groups, 2007*. Australian Government, Canberra, ACT.

Greer, A. E. (2006) *Encyclopedia of Australian Reptiles*. Australian Museum Online www.amonline.net.au/herpetology/research/encyclopedia.pdf Version date: 7 August 2006.

Hutchinson, M. and Williams, I. (2014) *Key to the Blind Snakes of South Australia*. Version: 12 June, 2014. South Australian Museum

IUCN 2016. *The IUCN Red List of Threatened Species. Version 2016–3.* www.iucnredlist.org. Downloaded on 18 December 2016.

Michael, D. & Lindenmayer, D. (2010) *Reptiles of the NSW Murray Catchment: A Guide to Their Identification, Ecology and Conservation*. CSIRO Publishing.

Pyron, R. A., Burbrink, F. R. & Wiens, J. J. (2013) A phylogeny and revised classification of Squamata, including 4161 species of lizards and snakes. BMC *Evolutionary Biology* 2013, 13:93.

Scarf, I., Feldman, A., Novosolov, M., Pincheira-Donoso, D., Das, I., Bohm, M., Uetz, P., Torres-Carvajal, O., Bauer, A., Roll, U. & Meiri, S. (2015) Late bloomers and baby boomers: ecological drivers of longevity in squamates and the tuatara. *Global Ecology and Biogeography* 24: 396–405.

Swanson, S. (2012) *Field Guide to Australian Reptiles* (2nd edn). Pascal Press, Glebe NSW.

Vanderduys, E. (2016) *A new species of gecko (Squamata: Diplodactylidae: Strophurus)* from north Queensland, Australia. Zootaxa 4117 (3)

Wilson, S. & Swan, G. (2013) *A Complete Guide to Reptiles of Australia* (4th edn). Reed New Holland.

ACKNOWLEDGEMENTS

The authors thank all the people who contributed their time, advice and photographic material to this book. Special thanks go to Ross Sadlier, Martin Fingland (Geckoes Wildlife), Scott Eipper (Nature 4 You), and Arne Rasmussen for reviewing the text and images and providing valuable feedback, Kate Rowland for supplying additional text (and for enduring Peter Rowland's long working days and periodic absences), and Thomas Rowland for providing the illustrations. The many photographers who have supplied us with their wonderful images most readily (Cameron Baker, Casey Clews, Chris Dryburgh, Alex Dudley, Scott Eipper, Tie Eipper, Adam Elliott, Damien Esquerre, Jules Farquhar, Bradley Foy, Ryan Francis, Nicholas Gale, Grant Husband, Brett Jarrett, Jannico Kelk, Damian Lettoof, Stephen Mahony, Angus McNab, Steve McNeil, Jordan Mulder, Ollie Neuman, Joshua Prieto, Ross Sadlier, Aniket Sardana, Doug Schurman, Shawn Scott, Peter Soltys, Ruchira Somaweera, Gary Stephenson, Geoff Swan, Gerry Swan and Valerie Taylor); we thank you for your generosity and assistance. Our family, friends and colleagues for their encouragement and unreserved support, both during the undertaking of this book and in all our times of need. This book aims to condense the published knowledge acquired by herpetologists who have studied reptiles over the years, and deliver it in a simplified format for the general natural history reader. Their dedication and patience, during countless hours of research and field study, is gratefully acknowledged and, although the nature of this work does not allow the space to list all referenced works, we thank all the authors of the material used, and assure them that their work has been treated with respect and enduring appreciation. The people who administrate and review the accuracy and legitimacy of information on the web-based databases that were consulted for taxonomic revisions, geographical mapping and links to further resources, and, of course, the people who supply their field sightings and research information to these sites. The access to this information was invaluable in many instances, and the willingness of the broad herpetology community as a whole, who unselfishly make comprehensive data available to the public, can never be overstated. Lastly, and by no means least, we thank the publishers, their wonderful staff and John Beaufoy in particular, for the opportunity to produce this book, Krystyna Mayer for her thoroughness in reviewing and editing the text and Sally Bird of Calidris Literary Agency for her professionalism and assistance.

■ INDEX ■

■ INDEX ■

▪ INDEX ▪